ALTERED
STATES OF
AMERICA

Also by Richard Stratton

Smack Goddess

Slam: The Filmmaker's Journals (with Kim Wozencraft)

ALTERED STATES OF AMERICA

OUTLAWS AND ICONS,
HITMAKERS AND HITMEN

RICHARD STRATTON

NATION BOOKS • NEW YORK

ALTERED STATES OF AMERICA
OUTLAWS AND ICONS, HITMAKERS AND HITMEN

Published by
Nation Books
An Imprint of Avalon Publishing Group
245 West 17th St., 11th Floor
New York, NY 10011

Nation Books is a co-publishing venture of the Nation Institute and Avalon Publishing
Group Incorporated.

AVALON
publishing group incorporated

Library of Congress Cataloging-in-Publication Data is available.

ISBN: 1-56025-777-6
ISBN 13: 978-1-56025-777-6

9 8 7 6 5 4 3 2 1

Book design by Jamie McNeely
Printed in the United States of America
Distributed by Publishers Group West

To Maxx, Dash, and Sasha.
For their love, belief, and support.

CONTENTS

Richard Stratton at his typewriter, Cumberland County Jail, Portland, Maine

INTRODUCTION

The Fugitive Novelist

Richard Stratton

I USED TO TELL friends I smuggled marijuana and hashish to support my writing habit. There was a kernel of truth to this; I was a writer before I became a full-time smuggler. In the heat of the outlaw life, faced with the possibility of prison or death at any given moment, I'd console myself with the thought, *This will make a great story if I live through it.*

On my last trip as a smuggler, I was in a warehouse near the docks in Beirut overseeing the loading of several containers with over a million pounds of dates I had bought in Baghdad and shipped overland to Lebanon. In Beirut, seven tons of primo blonde and red Lebanese hash from the Bekaa Valley was to be hidden in the thousands of cartons of dates and smuggled into the United States. I'd given the Lebanese specific instructions on how the hash had to be packaged in order to make it through U.S. Customs. But when I checked a couple of cartons, I saw that instead of packing the sealed metal boxes containing the hash inside the cardboard cartons with a layer of sticky, sweet-smelling dates on top and beneath the hash as instructed, the Lebanese had simply shoved the metal boxes inside the cartons with no dates for cover.

"No good," I told Mohammed, the chief of Lebanese customs, who was my partner. "You've got to unload all these containers, repack the cartons, and cover the hash in dates."

"But Mr. Richard, that will take days. We'll miss the ship. It could be weeks before we can arrange new transport."

I told him I didn't care how long it took—it had to be done right, or I would take all the cartons of hash and throw them into the Mediterranean. Mohammed refused to believe that unlike Beirut, U.S. Customs was not in my pocket. To show him I was serious, I grabbed a box of hash and heaved it into the sea. It was drama, I was playing a role, but the consequences were real. We could make millions, or people could go to jail if I didn't live up to my part.

Mohammed relented. I had to hang in war-ravaged Beirut for another six weeks before we were able to ship the repackaged load to New Jersey. Because the shipment originated in Lebanon, a drug source country, U.S. Customs flagged the containers for secondary inspection. Customs agents sealed the containers and escorted them to a bonded warehouse in Jersey City. I had distinguished the cartons containing hashish with red plastic strapping. One of the workers on the loading dock at the warehouse told me later that he had watched as an agent opened a box with red straps, dug out a handful of dates, then closed it back up, satisfied. That load grossed fifteen million dollars. My grandmother always told me, "Anything worth doing is worth doing right."

My senior year in high school I was in a near-fatal motorcycle accident while visiting my sister in Puerto Rico and spent six months recuperating. I was headed to Arizona State University to wrestle, so I took a postgraduate year at Wilbraham Academy to get back in shape both scholastically and athletically. It was my English teacher at Wilbraham, Dudley Cloud, a former editor at *The Atlantic*, who encouraged me to write. I majored in English at Arizona State, and when I told my advisor I wanted to write, he said I should leave college and go live in Paris like Ernest Hemingway.

During that freshman year at ASU, I made my first trip to Mexico. My roommate and I drove down to Nogales in his International pickup truck. On the way down, he told me that even though the town was rife with hookers, he had no intention of going with one unless she "looks like Marilyn Monroe and only wants twenty bucks." We ended up in a brothel, where he disappeared with the first non-Marilyn-Monroe-looking girl who approached him. I told the bartender I was more interested in scoring *mota* than pussy. I was only talking about a joint or two. He turned me on to his fourteen-year-old son, who took me to meet a guy with kilos for sale.

"How much?" I asked. A hundred Yankee bucks per kilo. I had three hundred on me. I did the math in my head. Sixteen ounces in a pound, 2.2 pounds in a kilo. Three kilos, 6.6 pounds, equals over a hundred ounces. In those days an ounce of commercial Mexican weed went for twenty-five dollars in Boston. For a three-hundred-dollar investment, I could make twenty-five hundred dollars, which was a lot of dough to a nineteen-year-old in 1964. So I bought three kilos, removed the door panel of my roommate's truck, and hid them in the door without telling him. I figured if I told him, he'd be too nervous driving back across the border, even though in those days there were no dope-sniffing dogs and the customs check was cursory.

As it turned out, I drove—he was too wasted from drinking tequila and fucking hookers. The next day, while he was in class, I removed the three kilos from the door and hid them in a suitcase. A week later I flew into Logan Airport in Boston with the kilos in my luggage. On my maiden smuggle, I grossed a little over two grand. I did it twice more that year, sold all the kilos to a friend's cousin, and saved up over five thousand dollars to finance a trip to Europe. While living on the Spanish island of Mallorca and writing short stories, I smuggled hash in from Morocco and hid it in false-bottom suitcases that couriers would come over and pick up. They sold the hash to dealers in Boston and brought me my share of the money.

I've always been torn between the man of action and the sedentary, solitary life of the writer. After a couple of years of traveling, I tried to settle down back at home in Massachusetts to write. Around this time I published my first short story, "The Artists of Déya," in *The Literary Review*. I got two hundred bucks for the short story. Over the next ten years, I wrote less and less as the trips got bigger and the desire for danger and excitement led me to prison.

When I finally got busted in 1982 and went on trial in federal court, first in the District of Maine, charged with conspiracy to import multi-ton loads of marijuana and hashish, my defense was that I was a writer investigating the dope trade for a book. It was immersion journalism, I claimed; I felt I had to live outside the law to know what it was really like so I could write about it from experience. That's my story and I'm sticking to it.

The early eighties were a time of innovative defense strategies in dope cases. Before I went on trial, while locked up in the Cumberland County Jail in Portland, Maine, I followed the case of a group of Vietnam vets who posed a post-traumatic stress syndrome defense, contending that the action they saw during the war turned them into degenerate danger junkies. Then there were the white Rastafarian dreadlocked brothers of the Ethiopian Zion Coptic Church. They went to trial with a First Amendment, freedom of religion defense, maintaining they were importing sacrament to be distributed among the high holy. We were all convicted, though the Vietnam vets made out the best: five years. I got the maximum sentence available at the time: fifteen years.

There was some truth to all these defenses, but what we were really doing was making a statement: the laws against marijuana are wrong and need to be challenged. We have a right as supposedly free Americans to alter our consciousness however we choose, as long as we're not hurting anyone else. The spiky green marijuana leaf was a symbol for freedom and open-mindedness. My outlaw life in the marijuana underground was always about the experience first, how living on the edge would shape my character and inform my work and my worldview. To invest in my own experience would make me a better writer, or at least give me something exciting to write about. When I was finally captured, in the lobby of the Sheraton Senator Hotel at the Los Angeles airport, my first thought was, *Okay, it's over. Now I can stop running and start writing.*

And I did. Over the next eight years, as I sojourned in the federal prison gulag, writing became my clandestine activity of choice. I wrote in longhand on yellow legal pads in the early hours of the morning when the joint was quiet. The only typewriters available were in the law library, but it was forbidden to use them for anything but legal briefs or other court-related documents. At one point all my writings were seized as contraband. It is illegal to operate a business from prison. But the authorities couldn't prove I'd actually been paid for writing, so they dropped the charges and sent the work home to my mother in Massachusetts. Over the span of years I spent in prison, I wrote a novel, *Smack Goddess*, which was published just as I got out in 1990. I wrote plays and short stories, screenplays, poems, songs, a musical, and—my blockbuster hit—legal briefs. I literally wrote my way out of prison.

After being sentenced to fifteen years in Maine, I was being transported to the federal penitentiary in Terre Haute, Indiana, when government agents pulled me off the Bureau of Prisons bus at the Metropolitan Correctional Center (MCC), the high-rise federal jail in downtown Manhattan affectionately known as the Criminal Hilton. In a meeting with representatives from DEA and the U.S. Attorney's office, I was told that unless I was ready to start cooperating with the government, they were preparing to bring a new indictment. It came as no surprise; I'd heard rumblings of a grand jury being convened in New York even as I fought the case in Maine.

First, among other targets, the feds wanted me to implicate Norman Mailer, a close friend ever since the winter of 1970 in Provincetown, Massachusetts. Hunter Thompson's name came up as well. They also wanted me to inform on prominent criminal defense lawyers from Boston and New York who were suspected of getting too close to their clients' businesses, and to rat on mafiosi from Boston, New York, and Florida who had tried to muscle in on the hippie mafia's control of the burgeoning marijuana trade.

It was an era of government star-fucking in dope cases. Just weeks after my arrest in LA, the maverick automobile designer John DeLorean was busted in a federal cocaine sting operation at the same hotel where I was brought to the ground. Mailer had long topped the feds' hit list. The prosecutor made it sound so easy: *Just give us Mailer, some of these other high-profile suspects we want, your friends and enemies, and you'll walk out of here tomorrow.* What no one could tell me was how I was supposed to live with myself for the rest of my life. Even if Mailer had been the mythical hippie godfather they imagined him to be, I couldn't see myself as the marijuana underground's Sammy "the Bull" Gravano.

With characteristic hubris, I declined their offer and told the assistant prosecutor handling my case for the office of then–U.S. Attorney Rudy Giuliani, "Bring it on. You thought my defense in Maine was wild—wait till you see what I do here."

Bring it on they did. I was charged under the Kingpin Statute with operating a "continuing criminal enterprise," known as CCE, or by the statute's number as 848, which, in the early eighties carried a minimum of ten years and up to life in prison with no possibility of parole. Had I been busted a few years later, I would have received a mandatory life sentence with no possibility of parole. Simply for smuggling pot. As I saw it, my defense strategy in New York had to be equal to the government's penchant for overkill. In keeping with the axiom *If you want a fool for a client, represent yourself,* I filed the motions, wrote the briefs, and was given permission by the court to defend myself. In legalese, I went pro se, something only crazy people do. But then again, for me, it was all about the experience: *I will write about this,* I told myself.

First, I challenged the New York indictment on double jeopardy grounds. They were using much of the same illegal activity I'd been convicted of in Maine as predicate acts to prove the New York continuing criminal enterprise charge. I had begun studying law while on trial in Maine when I came to understand that no one was going to pay as much attention to my case as I would. Criminal lawyers typically take the money and move on, stalking new clients and new fees. I had good lawyers, but none of them had the time and energy I had to devote to my defense.

As a pro se litigant, I was allowed to leave the ninth-floor unit where I was housed at MCC, break the monotony, and go down to the basement law library—maybe even see some of the women prisoners on the elevator. In the law library and attorney visiting room at MCC, I met such criminal luminaries as Edwin Wilson, the renegade CIA agent charged with selling plastic explosives to Muammar Qaddafi; the late John Gotti, who died in prison; Carmine Persico, another pro se defendant and boss of the Colombo crime family; and Frin Mullin, aka the Smack Goddess, who became the inspiration for my novel after she escaped from a maximum security women's prison. And I met political prisoners: IRA freedom fighter Joe Dougherty, former Black Panthers Sundiata Acoli and Jamal Joseph, and Weather Underground member Susan Rosenberg, whose work I went on to publish in *Prison Life* magazine.

Poring over the volumes of statutes and appellate decisions in the law library, and talking law with other jailhouse lawyers, at a certain point I realized that the law is all about language. It's like reading Shakespeare—difficult to grasp at first, but sublime and universal at its best once you get the hang of it. And, like verse, the law is subject to interpretation. What does it mean, "operating a continuing criminal enterprise"? And how is that different from "conspiracy to import and distribute" marijuana and hash, for which I'd already been convicted?

I read the latest decisions in drug cases like my own and wrote the briefs arguing that I was protected from further prosecution because of the Maine conviction. It took two years for the Second Circuit Court of Appeals in New York to rule that since I had not been charged under 848 in Maine, even though some of the substantive acts were the same, the New York indictment would stand. I went to trial in front of U.S. District Court Chief Judge Constance Baker Motley in the Southern District, Manhattan, in the Orwellian year of 1984.

The trial lasted six weeks. My strategy in defending myself was twofold. First, to prove the continuing criminal enterprise, the government would need to convince a jury that I was the boss of the operation; that I had five or more people working under me; and that I made a substantial amount of money from the enterprise. My codefendants, who supposedly worked for me, were all Jewish, while the main witnesses who took the stand against us were Arabs. I decided to stand before my mostly Jewish jury and pose the question: *Do you really believe a bunch of Arabs who claim that a WASP from Wellesley, Massachusetts, was the boss of a crew of New York Jews?* No way. Second, what this is really all about, ladies and gentlemen of the jury, is that they want an even bigger prize, Norman Mailer, and the government is prosecuting me all over again because I refuse to falsely incriminate my friend.

It sounded good in theory and was working fairly well until about midway through the trial, when Judge Motley decided she wasn't going to allow me to present my defense. She called it a "red herring" and refused to let me call several of my witnesses or inform the jury that I'd already been convicted in Maine and was serving fifteen years for much the same activity. (In New York the government alleged I had masterminded the seven-ton hashish trip—the date smuggle brought in through the docks of New Jersey—even though they had no physical evidence, only the testimony of Mohammed's son that he and his father had provided me with the hash in Lebanon. The feds knew about the date trip at the time of the Maine case, but held it in abeyance so they could prosecute me twice, which I argued was illegal.)

There I stood, stripped of my defense, but emboldened by small whiffs of 98-percent pure heroin that I was inhaling in the bullpen holding cell during breaks in the trial. Nothing like a little junk to inspire reckless abandon. I defied the judge by telling the jury flat-out that even if they acquitted me, I wasn't going to walk out of the courtroom a free man. No, I would go back to prison and finish serving the fifteen years the government had already given me in Maine. Judge Motley stopped the trial, dismissed the jury, cited me for contempt, and gave me another six months. It was worth it; what's another six months when it's all about the experience?

One night early in the trial I was asleep in my cell at MCC when the guard opened the door and deposited a new prisoner. I rolled over and went back to sleep. A few hours later, I awoke to the mournful grunts and groans of what sounded like my new cellie taking the biggest shit of his life. He was perched on the stainless steel hopper, sweating, straining to pass what turned out to be an eight-inch-long, two-inch-in-diameter cylinder of nearly pure Sicilian heroin he'd been smuggling into the country in his rectum ("keestered" or "in the suitcase" in jailhouse parlance) when he got picked up at the airport on an old warrant.

I had never done much junk before my arrest. I was a marijuana purist who refused to smuggle the white powders, believing that they brought bad karma. Mohammed's son and the Lebanese translator who testified against me at trial had been busted trying to sell ten kilos of heroin to an undercover DEA agent in New York and traded their way out by giving up names and details of the New Jersey hash smuggle. But during the trial I found that a little heroin settled my nerves and unraveled my inhibitions.

I was hardly fazed even as the jury pronounced me guilty. By that time I had already been locked up close to three years. I knew I could do time, it was just a question of how much time, so I concentrated on my allocution before the just and honorable Judge Motley at sentencing. The judge was a heavy-set black woman in her late fifties who was given to nodding off during trial. She had been a lawyer for the NAACP when President Johnson appointed her to the federal bench. I had briefly been a member of Students for a Democratic Society while a freshman at Arizona State University, before I gave up the straight life to become a full-time outlaw. So we had an element of sixties activism in common, and I felt that she had developed a grudging respect for me during the trial if for no other reason than that she learned I had moral convictions. I appealed to her sense of social well-being. She had heard the witnesses against me, junk dealers, and heard them testify that Stratton had always refused to smuggle heroin or cocaine. I was a pot smuggler during a period when, only a few years before, it looked like marijuana might become legal. At the time, two ounces or less of pot in the State of New York was considered a misdemeanor. What are tons of marijuana, I argued, but many, many ounces of marijuana?

Judge Motley did not disagree. She said she believed that pot was not as dangerous to society as heroin. Therefore, she had decided to give me the minimum ten years on the continuing criminal enterprise conviction. However, she went on, my real crime was that I refused to cooperate with the government, and because of my refusal to name names, the judge said she had determined to run the ten years on the CCE and the six months for the contempt consecutive with the fifteen years I received for the Maine conviction, giving me a total of twenty-five years and six months. Judge Motley concluded by saying that if I later had a change of heart and agreed to cooperate with the government and give up my friends and enemies, she would reduce my sentence based on the degree and value of my cooperation.

I remember being led from the courtroom, back to my cell at MCC, and thinking, *That doesn't seem right. I can get more time for refusing to rat?* But when I asked a real lawyer, he assured me that judges "do it all the time." No doubt they do, but they don't state it on the record as clearly and unequivocally as Judge Motley had done. It took me six years, during which time I appealed the conviction, appealed the contempt citation, which was tossed out, and then appealed the sentence on the grounds that it was coercive rather than punitive. Ultimately, based on the brief I wrote and the oral argument of an attorney friend, Ivan Fisher, the Second Circuit Court of Appeals agreed. They vacated my twenty-five-year sentence and remanded me for resentencing in front of a different judge.

I went back for another extended stay at my favorite jail, MCC. After more legal wrangling, I met with the prosecutor and the new judge in chambers. The prosecutor, who by this time was tired of litigating the case, said he would not oppose having the fifteen years I got in Maine and the New York ten run concurrently if I agreed to drop several other actions I had pending. At least one of those actions—that Judge Motley had unfairly stripped me of my defense mid-trial—had real merit, he said. Now I had a paroleable fifteen-year sentence running simultaneously with the non-paroleable ten. Next I took on the parole board and the Bureau of Prisons. I fought them right up until the day of my release.

. . .

Back in the winter of 1970, when I first met Norman Mailer in Provincetown, Massachusetts, I had taken a sabbatical from dope smuggling to write a novel. The previous summer I completed a writing course at Harvard, then applied for and was granted a fellowship at the Fine Arts Work Center in Provincetown, where I became editor of the center's literary journal *Shankpainter.* Living in a garret apartment on Commercial Street, writing at night and working for a builder during the day, I became friendly with a young woman who lived in the apartment below me. It turned out she was Mailer's cook and housekeeper. One night after I came in from work, the phone rang and it was Mailer. He said he'd heard a lot about me from Bobbi, my downstairs neighbor, and asked if I wanted to come over and watch the Monday night football game with him. He lived across the street, a few houses down the beach. We ended up drinking a bottle of bourbon and a bottle of cognac, talking until dawn. I had already read most of Mailer's work before I met him—I'd even seen his three films, *Wild 90, Beyond the Law,* and *Maidstone.*

Through Mailer I met Richard Goodwin, the Kennedy whiz kid and speechwriter who became a contributing editor at *Rolling Stone.* Goodwin got me the assignment to do the *Rolling Stone* interview with Mailer, and as a result of that, I got another gig to write a story on Rochdale College in Toronto. During the late sixties and early seventies, Rochdale, known as The Rock, was an experimental, open university that evolved into the soft-drug distribution center for North America, largely due to the efforts of one man, Robert "Rosie" Rowbotham. Also known as "Flower," the true hippie godfather, Rosie became the focus of my article "The Rock, the Flower, and the Man."

The piece was never published. Instead, Rosie and I became

partners. We smuggled hash into Canada then into the United States, and we smuggled marijuana into the States then into Canada. My role was as the foreign liaison. I went to the regions of product origin—Mexico, South America, the Middle East, Nepal, Thailand, wherever there was quality cannabis—and arranged to have it shipped back to North America. I loved the adventure, the challenge of going to places I'd never been, finding my way to the fields where the crops were grown, meeting and getting to know the farmers and their families, then devising and planning as tight a smuggle or "trip" as possible.

High in the Sierra Madre del Sur, the mountains of the Mexican state of Guerrero, where I had gone with a British woman in search of the famed Acapulco Gold, we were the only gringos in a small village called Xixila when a regiment of *federales* swept through the region. The village *jefe*, Adelberto, hid us in a room of his home, because the presence of gringos in the area could tip the *federales* that the villagers were putting together a load of pot and the authorities would demand their *mordida*, or bite. For two nights and three days we were sequestered in a dark, mud-floored room with no electricity. Adelberto's wife or one of his daughters would bring us food.

On the second day my lady friend asked me, "Richard, where do I go to spend a penny?" I explained there was no bathroom, what she would have to do was wait until dark, then sneak out behind the wall at the rear of the house and squat. After she had gone out to use the facilities, I heard her yelling and ran out to find that she had been knocked over and was being trampled by two huge pigs fighting over her leavings.

A week later we loaded twelve hundred pounds of loose, baled gold and lime-green buds of some of the most beautiful pot I'd ever seen into a twin-engine Aero Commander and flew it into Texas. I owned a ranch in the Texas Hill Country town of Blanco, where we'd built a three-thousand-foot airstrip. But we were concerned that the Texas Department of Public Safety and DEA had the place under surveillance, so we landed the load on the airstrip of a neighboring ranch, a huge spread that belonged to John Murchison, then-owner of the Dallas Cowboys, who had no idea we were using his place. There it was loaded into a Blue Bird motor home I'd bought from the Global Evangelism Television Network. We decided to keep the Global Evangelism logos painted on the motor home for the trip back to New York. Who would suspect a bunch of evangelists of trafficking in reefer? Our driver became known as Father Foley, and the catch phrase for the trip was *Praise the Lord and pass the costales*—the Spanish word for the big burlap sacks the pot was packed in.

Rosie and my partners in New York handled the distribution. Over the years we did it all: false-bottom suitcases loaded with slabs of primo hash; cars with hidden compartments; airplanes, sailboats, and freighters from Mexico, Colombia, and Jamaica; and finally, what became my area of expertise, the commercial container smuggle. Soon my writing habit was supplanted by a new addiction. I became like the compulsive gambler who keeps returning to the tables, upping the stakes. I was hooked on the adrenaline rush and the thrill of getting over on the narcs.

We partied like rock stars. I lived for weeks on end in a suite at the Plaza Hotel under the alias Dr. Lowell, posing as a psychiatrist as a way to explain the number of crazy people coming and going from my rooms at all hours. At the height of this insanity, I owned the six-thousand-acre ranch in Texas, a horse farm and fly-in lodge with a five-thousand-foot airstrip in Maine, and homes in New York, Toronto, and the Bahamas. Yet I lived in hotels, phone booths, and on airplanes, perpetually in transit, running from the law, running from myself, and finally, running from the empty page.

Years went by when all I wrote were to-do lists: who owed me money; who I owed money; the twenty or thirty phone calls I needed to make from different phone booths over the course of the day. I had kept a journal, writing nearly every day from my late teens, until I began to worry that if the feds ever found the volumes of my diary, any number of people might get indicted. I'd wake up in a hotel room somewhere and spend the first hour or two with a coffee and a spliff compiling my lists. Then I'd head out into the world with no clear idea of where I'd end up that night. There was method to my madness—it seemed to me that if I never made any firm plans, never had a definite schedule, and just went with the flow from phone call to phone call, it would be that much harder and more expensive for the DEA, the FBI, the IRS, and whoever else might be investigating me, to keep tabs on what I was up to and where. How could they know if I didn't?

It worked. I had a long run for a chronic smuggler, close to twenty years. I got busted in 1977 on a hash importation beef in New York but beat the case. Then one day my phone calls took me to Maine, where I was preparing to offload a freighter of thirty thousand pounds of Colombian weed—lining up fishing boats to rendezvous with the mother ship off the coast, setting up stash houses, and hiring drivers and trucks to move the load—when I broke one of my cardinal rules: never do business with someone who's strung-out on coke.

It wasn't just that cokeheads were unreliable; it was more that they seemed to attract weird, negative energy. But I had a soft spot for Fred Barnswallow, as we used to call my friend in Maine. I felt partly responsible for the latest coke binge he'd been on since he'd met my Colombian girlfriend over Halloween in Aspen, Colorado, and, unbeknownst to me at the time, she had started supplying him with kilos of blow.

I picked up Barnswallow one morning, and we drove around all day in a four-wheel-drive truck, setting up stash houses. It would be an opportunity for Fred to make a few bucks, pay off his coke debt with the Colombians, and, I urged him, to leave that shit alone and get back to what had made him one of the biggest dealers in New England—helping me move weed into Canada. It was April and the previous night a late storm had dumped half a foot of snow. I was driving Fred Barnswallow back to his palatial log home at the top of a hill when I saw a young guy in a sedan that had slid off the road and was stuck in a ditch. I pulled over, Fred and I got out, and I offered to give the guy a push with my truck. We got him out of the ditch, he thanked us, shook our hands, and, it seemed to me looking back on it later, he smiled and gazed at me curiously with his clear blue eyes.

Over the next week, I slept no more than a couple of hours a night in different hotels and motels as I oversaw the offload and inventoried and moved most of the hundreds of bales of reefer out of Maine and heading for Boston, New York, the West Coast, Toronto, and Montreal. Some friends from San Francisco gave me a brand-new Oldsmobile Toronado in exchange for the pickup I was driving. With the load almost entirely moved, I thought I'd drive farther up into the mountains of western Maine, where I had the horse farm I owned with Mailer, and chill for a few days. But as I got closer to the farm, I became increasingly paranoid, worried that someone might have spotted the Toronado with the California plates and that I might draw heat to my home. So I decided to spend the night in a motel in Farmington, the nearest town of any size to the farm, and have someone come over and pick me up in the morning.

Early the next day, after compiling my lists and smoking my morning joint, I went for coffee and to use the pay phones at a restaurant up the road from the motel. I was well known in the area, especially to local law enforcement, most of whom knew me by name. I was particularly close to the sheriff, who used to hang out at the farm from time to time and drink, play poker, and sing, *I shot the sheriff, but I didn't shoot no deputy.* One night he left his hat there and I kept it as a souvenir. The sheriff's office knew what I was up to. We had crash-landed a DC-6 on the airstrip I owned, unloaded ten tons of pot, and left the wrecked plane with its nose stuck in the woods at the end of the runway. But I spent a lot of money in the county, employed locals who couldn't get other work, and played on the Yankee hostility for outsiders and big government. When I walked into the restaurant that morning, I spotted a couple of deputies I knew having coffee and was about to go over and say hello when I picked up their vibe.

Something was definitely not right. Now all my antennae were keen. I'd sensed weirdness in the air going back to the day I'd helped that guy who was stuck by the side of the road on the hill near Barnswallow's log home. But that's the thing with paranoia—you never know how much of it is well founded, especially when you smoke a lot of herb. Still, I'd learned to pay attention to the paranoid flights, follow them to their logical—or illogical—conclusions, hunt down the fear, and ferret it out like a wild animal running loose in the attic of my mind. The deputies wanted nothing to do with me that day. They quickly looked away, glanced down at their coffee, pretended they had no idea who I was when I looked over and smiled. So I took the cue and kept walking past their booth to the men's room. I looked in the mirror and said to myself, "Stratton, you're about to get popped."

There was still snow on the ground when I walked out of the restaurant, kept walking past the Toronado with the California plates, walked along the road and past the motel where I'd crashed the night before. I walked all the way to a shopping mall and into a drugstore that had a few video games in the back. *Paranoia, paranoia, great destroyer,* I said to myself when no army of agents descended on me. Let me play a few games of Gorf, one of my favorite video games, and call the farm in an hour or so, when I'm sure I'm cool. If I'd learned nothing else over the years as a smuggler, I had learned to pay attention to my intuition.

I was into my third or fourth game of Gorf, racking up one of my all-time high scores, with a few local kids standing around watching me, when I looked up and saw them. DEA agents, maybe half a dozen of them, with their guns drawn, swarmed into the drugstore and made straight for where I stood. I took my hands from the video game controls and raised them above my head.

"Richard Stratton, you're under arrest," said one of the agents.

"Wow! Cool . . ." said a kid behind me.

One of the things you never want to get too good at is getting arrested. But it's an occupational hazard when you're an outlaw, and by this time I'd been busted maybe four or five times—in New York on the '77 hash case, in Mexico, Lebanon, previously in Maine on some non-dope-related charges—and had been detained and questioned by agents and cops at least as many times. What I noticed was that in moments of real peril, a profound calm would come over me. It was almost an out-of-body experience, as though I could step outside myself and remain disconnected from the internal emotional upheaval. I said nothing, didn't even bother to ask the agents why I was being arrested. They took me to the local lockup at the Farmington police station and left me in a tiny, dark, filthy cell. I made my one phone call, to Richard Goodwin, the former Kennedy speechwriter and sometimes-lawyer (I was his only client). Goodwin and I both assumed the bust had something to do with an IRS investigation that had been launched soon after I walked from the '77 smuggling charges. Dick said he'd call a criminal lawyer friend in Portland and see what he could find out.

Eight hours later a DEA agent by the name of Gustave Fassler came to the jail and said he was there to transport me to Portland, where I would be arraigned. Fassler reminded me of the TV detective Columbo. He had dark, wavy hair, a medium build, a New York accent, and an absentminded manner that seemed calculated to make you think he wasn't as sharp as he really was. His gun had white adhesive tape wrapped around the handle and looked like a broken toy. He made some comment about how it was against regulations for him to transport me on his own, then said, "But you won't try to escape, will you?" He apologized for having to cuff me, making me sit for the long drive on the snowy roads with my arms wrenched painfully behind my back. And he warned me that anything I might say to him in conversation on the way down could and would be used against me.

To my surprise, I liked Fassler. He was smart and had a good sense of humor. We talked all the way to Portland. I made no admissions, but told him that I believed one day people like myself would be seen as folk heroes, and guys like him would be seen as the villains in this war on plants. Fassler became the model for my DEA agent character, Bernie Wolfshein, in *Smack Goddess*. He told me that during the hours I'd spent in lockup, he and a dozen agents from Portland, Boston, even specialists from Washington, DC, had searched the horse farm and outbuildings from top to bottom and come up with only a couple of ounces of personal stash he hadn't even bothered to log as evidence.

"With you, I'm lookin' for a lot more than ounces," he said, then admitted he figured they'd been a day or two too late. "Looks like you'll walk on this one, too," he said, referring to the New York bust. But then he went on to remind me of a flight I'd once taken from Beirut to Paris when the plane had engine trouble and had to make an emergency landing in Athens. *How the hell did he know about that?* I wondered. *And how much more does he know?* I felt like Dostoevsky's Raskolnikov to his Inspector Zamyotov.

I made bail, a 250-grand surety, put up the horse farm, and was planning to stick around for the trial, until good old Fred Barn-swallow decided to flip and testify against me. Fred . . . what a beautiful loser. When they raided his place, they found several pot plants in his attic, an Uzi and a Mac-10 machine gun, a pound of cocaine, books and records of dope deals, addresses and names of people we'd installed in stash houses, bales of weed, and 60 grand in cash.

It all came together for me sometime later when I saw the clear-eyed, waylaid motorist on the witness stand and learned his name was Cunniff, a DEA agent out of Portland who had been doing intermittent drive-by surveillance on Fearless Fred's log dwelling when he slipped into the ditch. Good Samaritan Stratton appeared to him like a vision out of an intelligence file. *I know that face,* thought Cunniff. *Goddamn, it's Stratton!* I found myself playing word games in my head with his name, Cunniff. What *if* that *cunt* Cunniff hadn't slid off the road, what if I hadn't been such a nice guy. What if I had stuck to my principles: *never do business with a coke fiend.*

Ah, but it was all material, invaluable experience. Then I never would've met Fassler. When he took the stand, Gustave was truthful to a fault. Said he never found anything at my farm; in the Toronado all they got were rolls of quarters and a paperback book about Meyer Lanksy. There was nothing to connect me with any of the evidence found at Fred Barnswallow's except his testimony that I was his boss. What good did it do him? He went to prison for a couple of years, came home, and someone blew his brains out and left him in the bushes at the side of a parking lot. The feds would have liked to connect me with that unfortunate event as well, except that I was in a federal penitentiary in Virginia at the time. When questioned about Freddy's sudden death, my only comment was, "Karma has a way of catching up with you."

Mine caught up with me in Los Angeles. I had become a fugitive when I learned that Fred Barnswallow had rolled over and was going to testify against me. I said good-bye to my friends and family and fled to Beirut, where, at the time, there were no DEA or IRS agents, no real law enforcement of any kind, only CIA—both rogue and duly authorized—the Syrian army, the Phalangists, the PLO, Hezbollah, and any number of other factions and fanatics embroiled in a civil war that had been raging for over a decade. But I felt safe there, surrounded by bodyguards, holed up in the penthouse apartment of a building owned by my Lebanese connection, Mohammed, who had retired as chief of Customs and become a multimillionaire.

Mohammed never could fathom why I refused to pack a dozen or so kilos of heroin in with the tons of hashish we smuggled out of Beirut in containers loaded with dates, figs, pistachios, ceramic tiles, or whatever cover load was being used to hide the illegal goods. He was making millions from the hash, but it wasn't enough. The Bekaa Valley, once a lush swath of hash plants, had undergone a flowering of poppy and seen a number of heroin labs sprout in the villas and villages of the outlaw territory. Whenever I went to the Bekaa to visit my suppliers, I met them for coffee in a villa that doubled as a heroin lab.

"Mr. Richard," the Lebanese would implore me, "why not take a carton or two of the other, the white?" I never was able to convince them that there is a difference in trafficking in a substance that inspires creativity—makes you mellow, horny, hungry, content to eat good food and listen to music, laugh, maybe even go off on the odd paranoid flight—and a highly refined chemical that makes you crave more and more of it until you want nothing else. Karma was not a concept they were ever able to get their heads around.

"It will bring us bad luck," I would tell them. How, they wondered, could anything that brought so much money bring bad luck?

But behind my back, Mohammed had dispatched his oldest

son, Nasif, to New York with ten kilos of heroin. I had grown close to Nasif over the years, helped him and his younger brothers get enrolled in college in Florida, and partied with him in Paris, Cyprus, and the Bahamas as he began handling more and more of his father's business. They managed to get the heroin in okay— smuggling was their forté—but they had no one to sell it to. The only person they knew in New York besides me was a taxi driver named Hammoud, who came from the same village as Mohammed and acted as his translator. Hammoud was able to find a buyer, who turned out to be an undercover DEA agent. When DEA intelligence put all the pieces together and realized who Nasif's father was, they struck a deal: have your father convince Stratton to return to the United States, and when we have him in custody, we'll let you go.

In June of 1982 the Israeli army invaded Lebanon. With the war raging and foreigners being abducted on the streets of Beirut, my girlfriend and I rarely went out. One night she convinced me to take her to see an American movie, *The Shining* starring Jack Nicholson. To get from West Beirut to the theater on Hamara Street, we had to get down on the floor of the Mercedes while our driver dodged through gunfire to cross the Green Line. While we sat in the theater and watched Nicholson lose his mind, the building we lived in was hit by a rocket and the top three floors were blown off. My girlfriend left the next day. I hung around a couple more weeks, but it didn't take a lot of convincing to get me to leave Beirut. Mohammed upped the ante by telling me that a smuggler who had ripped him off for nine million dollars worth of hash was willing to pay up if I would agree to meet the smuggler in Los Angeles and assure him that the Lebanese would be satisfied with the payment and not try to kill him. I missed my family and loved ones, and I knew I would no longer be safe in Lebanon once the Israelis were in control. So I left. I traveled overland, first through the Bekaa to Damascus, Syria, then around the world and stopping in Maui to visit my girlfriend.

While in Maui, I made arrangements to meet with the son of Abu Ali, one of the Bekaa's foremost hash growers and Mohammed's partner. Abu Ali's son was at that time a Captain in the U.S. Army. The Captain decided that the best way to teach a lesson to the smuggler who ripped off his father and Mohammed was to blow up his house. "Creating a vacant lot," the Captain said, would get the guy's attention without hurting anyone. We made plans to meet in the lobby of the Sheraton Senator at LAX. The Captain would bring the plastic explosives. Once I had the money, he would blow up the smuggler's house while I had dinner with him.

I flew from Maui to LA a few days early and checked in to another hotel using phony ID. On the appointed day of our meeting, I arrived at the hotel two hours early, positioned myself on the mezzanine floor, and staked out the lobby, looking for heat. The Captain came in carrying a black bag and sat at a table in the lobby bar. For another ten or fifteen minutes I remained above, hidden behind a pillar, watching until I felt sure he had not been followed. I'd disguised my appearance by growing a beard and bleaching my hair and was wearing a hat and sunglasses, so that when I finally went up to him and said his name, at first he didn't recognize me. He stood, and we shook hands and then started through the lobby toward a rear entrance and the parking lot where I'd left my car.

As we walked through the lobby, I saw men dressed as hotel clerks and bellmen vault over the front desk and run out from behind the bellman's stand, drawing their weapons. I realized I'd been set up. I raised my hands and said, "Relax, it's cool." Some of the agents were so hyped, I was afraid they'd shoot me. I've never understood people who flee or resist arrest. It's a good way to get killed or get the shit kicked out of you. By the time the bust comes down, unless it's a fluke, you've got to assume the Man is heavily armed and you're outnumbered. For me, the fight comes later—in court. But my Lebanese American army captain was highly trained in the martial arts and not about to go without a fight. He struck a karate pose and maybe even hit a couple of the agents before they tackled him and brought him to the floor. That was the last I saw of him, rolling around on the lobby floor at the Sheraton Senator under a pile of federal agents.

We were taken, separately, to a police lockup at the airport. I was introduced to a U.S. Marshal named Sullivan from Boston. "Call me Sully," he said and told me he'd been tracking me around the world for the past couple of years. He was a nice guy, like many of the marshals I've met over the years, and a specialist at hunting down fugitives.

"Who's your friend?" Sully asked me.

"What friend?"

"That guy, thinks he's Bruce Lee . . ."

I shrugged.

"You know what he had in the bag?"

"What bag?"

"Plastic explosives," he said, ignoring my feigned ignorance. "What the hell were you going to do with plastic?"

"I don't know the guy."

"Tell it to the judge." Sully smiled. "You're facing federal explosives charges now."

Sully left me alone to ponder exactly who had set me up. If it had been the Captain, as I suspected, why would he have brought the explosives? And why would he have tried to demonstrate his skill as a martial artist? Unless it was all part of an elaborate act so I wouldn't figure him for a traitor and he could protect his identity. But, damn, he could've been killed. And now he—we—were going to pick up an explosives charge. Or so I thought. An hour or two went by, and Sully came into my holding cell for another visit.

"Now I really want to know who he is," Sully said as he sat down beside me. "C'mon, off the record. One Boston guy to another."

"What's up?"

"He's gone."

"What do you mean, gone?"

"As in . . . gone." Sully shook his head, smiled. "DOD—"

"Who?"

"Department of Defense. Some high-level brass came down here and waltzed him out. They took his little black bag of tricks, too."

I opted to make a cryptic statement. "Sometimes the left hand doesn't know what the right hand is doing."

To this day, I don't know for certain who set me up. The Captain remains the prime suspect as well as a figure of mystery in my life. The Captain spoke several languages and slept on the floor with a huge pet snake; he was trained as a pharmacist, a pilot, a weapons expert, and who knows how many other skills; and yet he was the oddest combination of discipline, paranoia, and fool-hardiness I'd ever come across in one human being. He had told me he was part of a highly trained, top-secret unit of Delta Force known as Army Support Intelligence Activity, or ASIA. He had also said he had been recruited in Lebanon, and that other men of foreign nationality—two men from various different countries— were trained at Fort Hood in Texas, then sent back out into the world to pose as civilians and provide military support for CIA covert operations.

One evening before the busts came down, I returned to the ranch in Texas and found the garage full of crates of Mac-10 machine guns destined for Beirut via Houston. The Captain and I had once met in Washington with some men who discussed trying to locate and free a Shiite Muslim cleric, Imam Moussa al-Sadr, who'd disappeared in Libya in 1978, but I was arrested in Maine before the mission got under way. He told me he had been part of Operation Eagleclaw, the ill-fated 1980 attempt to rescue the hostages in Iran. According to the Captain, the rescue mission was intentionally sabotaged to embarrass Jimmy Carter and force him from office.

Another time, he flew down to the ranch to pick me up in his twin-engine Piper Aztec. He was revving up the engines, having skipped the preflight checklist. We were getting ready to taxi out onto the airstrip to take off. I'm not one to tell another man how to fly his plane, but I noticed he'd neglected to do something important.

"Hey, don't you want to undo the tie-downs before we take off?" I asked. "You know, those ropes holding down the wings."

He grinned. "Oh, yeah. Good idea."

The foreman at the ranch in Texas told me that the Captain had moved in soon after my arrest. He shocked and disgusted the foreman, his wife, and some other guests one day when he shot one of the herd of Brahmas with a machine gun, gutted her, and ate her raw, still-twitching heart. He didn't drink or smoke but was obsessed with fucking. More than likely, he made a deal: *You can continue to operate, but Stratton has got to take the fall.*

It was late on a Friday afternoon when I was captured at the Sheraton Senator. By the time the Captain disappeared and Sully was ready to secure me in a more permanent facility, it was close to midnight. "We've got a little surprise for you," he said. He winked, wished me well, and booked me into the LA city jail for the weekend.

Known as the Glass House because the units are big, rectangular open dorms with thick Plexiglas walls that look like huge fish tanks, the city jail in downtown Los Angeles is easily the worst joint I've ever been in—and I've been in some bad ones. There were close to a hundred guys in the unit they put me in, mostly blacks and Latinos, a few Asians, and one other white guy, a drunk who slept most of the time. There were two open toilets near one wall; one of them was broken, with piss and shit backing up and pooled on the floor so that if I had to take a leak (shitting was out of the question), I had to wade through a swamp of sewage.

Most of the prisoners were crazed dust-heads coming down off angel dust runs. I was wearing a three-piece suit when I was arrested, part of my disguise—dress conservative, think radical—and a pair of handmade Lucchese cowboy boots. So my skin pigmentation wasn't the only reason I stood out. I passed myself off as a lawyer but said I wasn't taking any new cases. During one long night, a junkie in the bunk above puked all over me. Another time I caught some guy trying to steal the boots off my feet while I slept. It was so rank in the units, the cops wouldn't even venture inside. They walked around, peering in through the cloudy Plexiglas walls.

There were only a few cigarettes and no matches in the unit, so on top of the junkies, speed freaks, dust-heads, and drunks, there were at least ninety guys withdrawing from nicotine. Nerves were frazzled. The cops wouldn't let prisoners have matches, because they kept setting their mattresses on fire. When it came time to feed us, the guards herded one unit at a time down a flight of stairs to a small mess hall, where it was forbidden to speak. You had to eat the slop they fed you in silence, and you weren't allowed to give it away or take food from another prisoner. Once I saw the guards beat an obviously deranged prisoner senseless with rib-spreader nightsticks for the simple crime of muttering and laughing to himself. Recently, when the Abu Ghraib prisoner abuse came to light, I remember thinking, *What's all the fuss? This kind of stuff and worse goes on in American jails and prisons all the time.*

At one point before the end of my two-day stay in the Glass

House, we were marched from the unit and made to stand in a hallway while they hosed down our tank. Lining the tier where we waited were individual glass cubicles where they kept the known snitches, drag queens, transsexuals, hermaphrodites, and other endangered prisoners in isolation. I remember looking at them, like exotic specimens in a zoo, and feeling sad as some of the other prisoners taunted them.

Talk about loneliness, I thought. *It's bad enough to be locked up in this joint, but how much worse to be such a freak that you're not even allowed to mix with the dregs in the family of man.* To get through the two longest days of my eight-year stint, I kept telling myself, *It can only get better from here.*

The following Monday I was arraigned in federal court in Los Angeles, bail set in the millions—a sum they knew I would never make, but in those early days of the drug war, they were still required to set bail. Having been a fugitive, I was considered a flight risk. Now I was in federal custody, transported to the Bureau of Prisons correctional facility at Terminal Island in San Pedro, California. Once I waived fighting extradition, the Bureau of Prisons shipped me back to Maine using a mode of transportation known among convicts as "diesel therapy." The idea is to keep prisoners on the road so long that once you finally arrive in court, you'll beg them to let you plead guilty.

Along the way I got the Cook's tour of the expanding archipelago known as the Federal Bureau of Prisons. From Terminal Island they took me by bus to Lompoc, California, then on a Con Air flight to the penitentiary in El Reno, Oklahoma. After another short hop, I had a few days' stay at the U.S. Penitentiary in Atlanta, known as the "big house," where the Cuban Marielitos would riot over conditions a few years later. I spent a week in the hole at Talladega, Alabama, then went on an endless, grueling bus ride trussed up in shackles, a belly chain, handcuffs, and a punishing device known as the "black box," which holds your wrists together and makes it impossible to move your hands.

At last we arrived at the pen in Lewisburg, Pennsylvania. K unit, where we were housed, was one of the more interesting stops on the circuit for the sheer diversity of the convicts passing through a dark, noisy basement hallway that had been converted to a transit dorm. Mafia dons bunked with Bulgarian spies; rogue CIA agents befriended Colombian drug lords; lawyers plotted with politicians; Wall Street cowboys rubbed shoulders with Aryan Brotherhood gang members; DC blacks, hit men, armored car robbers, and bank robbers compared notes—all the while sighing, beefing, farting, yelling, playing cards, telling war stories, and laughing their way through the days until they would be transferred to a permanent prison. It was a prelude to the wild years I spent in the biggest rock 'n' roll jail of them all, the Metropolitan Correctional Center in Manhattan.

For the final leg of the journey, two U.S. Marshals from Maine picked me up at Lewisburg and took me on a circuitous ride to the Cumberland County Jail in Portland. Again, the marshals were good guys. They stopped along the way and bought me some decent food. They told me they were sorry I'd been captured, because they had been using my fugitive status as an excuse to make biweekly trips to the fly-in lodge I owned in Maine, where they'd go trout fishing while supposedly waiting to see if I'd show up. The marshals always treated me with respect. I learned later that they save their disdain for what I had chosen not to become: a snitch, a sniveling bellyacher who looks to save his own ass by implicating others.

There are some things I regret about my criminal past, but having chosen not to become a rat will never be one of them.

My reputation within the sheriff's department in Maine preceded me. After a few days in Portland, I was as comfortable as a man can hope to be while still being locked up. A girlfriend who'd been busted on my case was housed in the women's unit, and we got to visit often, until she pled guilty and was shipped out. I had a single cell in the high security section reserved for federal prisoners. There I met Thomas Reilly, aka Brother Louv, high priest of the Ethiopian Zion Coptic Church. He'd already been down for three years and was back in Portland on a new case. Each night the Coptic brothers shared their sacrament and the wisdom they'd acquired on doing time.

"There are three things to avoid in the joint," Brother Louv told me. "Homosexuals (punks), gambling, and other people's dope. Do your own time. Show respect to get respect."

Another golden rule the Coptic brothers passed on became my mantra: *Don't serve the time; let the time serve you.*

My mother was allowed to bring me a typewriter. The jail was noisy during the day, but in time I developed powers of concentration that enabled me to create my own peaceful space within the chaos around me. The Sheriff and I shared a taste for cigars and lobster. After my sentencing, I was hustled out of the jail under a cloud of suspicion on an alleged escape attempt by bribery. Supposedly I gave the Sheriff a box of Cuban *Cohibas* in exchange for his looking the other way if I decided to split, a charge to which my Maine lawyer responded: "I've heard of a man walking a mile for a Camel, but this begs credulity."

On the flight over from Hawaii, days before my arrest, I finished reading G. Gordon Liddy's autobiography, *Will.* Though Liddy is my ideological opposite, I admired him for having the strength of his convictions. He was the only one in the Watergate debacle who stood up, kept his mouth shut, and did his time. I remember reading a line in *Will* referring to Liddy's prison experience; "One of the most interesting times of my life had begun." I thought of those words often in the years to come as I took the endless, harrowing journey into my self. What's fascinating is not so much prison life; that can be as dull and deadening as the concrete walls and steel bars of the cell, or as brutal and deadly as a shank in the back. What's compelling is how you make it through the days and the long, lonely nights—how you survive.

The penitentiary is the loneliest place in the world. There's no privacy, you're never alone, constantly surrounded by other men, and yet you're always lonely. It's like living in the men's room at Pennsylvania Station. You've got nowhere to go, you possess nothing but your character. Any time they want, the guards can stop you, order you to strip, bend over, and spread the cheeks of your ass so they can peer up into that most private passageway.

I was on my way to the yard early one morning at the federal joint in Otisville, New York, when a guard came out of the mess hall and stopped me.

"Are you wearing underpants?" he asked.

I wasn't sure I heard him correctly. "What?"

"Underpants. Do you have underpants on under your shorts?"

I could see he was embarrassed, so I played with him. "Who wants to know?"

"Look, it's not me," he said. "The associate warden told me to come out here and check to see if you are wearing underwear."

"What does he want, a date?" I said and pulled down my shorts to show him I was wearing underpants. Such is the surreal indignity of everyday prison life.

The penitentiary became my monastery. Because I was always lonely, I was forced to confront myself. I would lie down alone every night and wake up alone every morning. Limited in space, serving time, there's nowhere to go but within. In a sense, prison is the ultimate freedom. No bills to pay, no appointments to keep, no responsibility to anyone but yourself. As a fugitive, running from the Man, I came to understand I was really running from myself, from the fear of failure, the fear of mediocrity and nothingness. Once I found myself in prison, there was no more running, no more hiding from the empty page. I had to write out of who I was and try to reconcile the wild, reckless, self-destructive side of my character that craved action with the contemplative, introspective side that wanted to make some sense of life and find creative fulfillment in the experience.

So many of my friends are dead, still locked up or in the wind, victims of the war on plants. I was lucky to get through it alive. At the end of June 1990, I walked out of the federal prison in Ashland, Kentucky, took a taxi to the airport, and flew to New York. I remember thinking how nice it was to see that there were still women in the world. Mailer was in Provincetown for the summer, so he let me stay at his apartment in Brooklyn Heights until I got a place of my own. Even though I had maxed out the non-paroleable sentence, I was told I would have to do three years of "special parole" and that I must report to my parole officer within seventy-two hours of my release. I went to work for Ivan Fisher, the criminal defense lawyer who had argued my appeal. For a time I contemplated going to law school, actually took the LSATs, and was about to enroll at Brooklyn Law when I realized that becoming a lawyer would be just another excuse not to write.

What impressed me through all this was the power of language to transform lives. The words of the statutes had condemned me—"conspiracy . . . operating a continuing criminal enterprise." The words of appellate case law had saved me—"Stratton's sentence is coercive rather than punitive." Because I could read and comprehend what I was reading, and because I could write clearly, argue persuasively, and tell a good story, I ended up doing less than half the time I would have done had I accepted that "they do it all the time" and submitted to my punishment, however illegal. Illiteracy, I came to believe, was the major cause of crime in our society. If talented, creative young men and, increasingly, more and more young women, can't read and write and express themselves coherently, they can always sell drugs, rob banks, and maraud on the streets until they get caught and go to prison.

One of the short stories I wrote while locked up, "A Skyline Turkey," won the PEN Prison Writing Award and was printed in *Fortune News*, published by the Fortune Society, a nonprofit prisoner advocacy group. When it dawned on me that I didn't really want to be a lawyer, I quit the law firm to become editor of *Fortune News*. That job led me to relaunch the then-defunct *Prison Life* magazine. We called *Prison Life* "The Voice of the Convict." The idea was to provide a forum for talented men and women whose lives have been short-circuited by crime and prison.

The redemptive power of language to change lives became the subject of the first feature film I worked on, *Slam*, released in 1998. Directed by Marc Levin, *Slam* won both the Grand Jury Prize at Sundance and the Camera d'Or at Cannes. The film tells the story of Ray Joshua, a young street poet and pot dealer trying to survive the ghetto of Washington, DC, and the infamous DC jail. In a climactic scene, Joshua, played by Saul Williams, saves himself from a beat-down in the prison yard by reciting a poem. The story for *Slam* grew out of work Marc Levin and I were doing on a series of documentaries produced with *Prison Life* magazine for HBO. We made *Prisoners of the War on Drugs; Execution Machine: Texas Death Row; Gladiator Days: Anatomy of a Prison Murder;* and the companion piece to *Slam, Thug Life in D.C.*, which won an Emmy in 1999. I went on to use my parole experience as the inspiration for a dramatic television series I created, *Street Time,* which aired on Showtime for thirty-three episodes from June of 2002 to October 2003.

With the production of *Street Time,* the two warring aspects of my personality made peace. As the lead writer of a TV series, at times I felt like a nineteenth-century novelist under deadline to write a serial novel, with the chapters or episodes appearing weekly; at other times I could imagine myself as the general of a small army of actors, writers, directors, and crew members all striving toward a common cause. The writer and the man of action were united, and I found I could rely on skills I'd developed over the years as a dope smuggler to be a creative producer.

As a kid growing up in the white-bread, upper-middle-class, suburban town of Wellesley, Massachusetts, I had formed the first gang that genteel bedroom community had ever known. I named us the Pink Rats after a gang of juvenile delinquents I saw on an episode of *Dragnet* and declared myself President-for-Life. I got in so much trouble by the eighth grade, my parents had to ship me off to a school for wayward boys on Thompson's Island in Boston Harbor. The one good thing all the teachers, principals, cops, and child psychologists had to say about me was that I displayed strong leadership qualities.

Those same qualities served me well as a drug kingpin. But as I walked out through the prison gates that June day, now nearly fifteen years ago, I wondered, *What could I do to satisfy my desire for action without landing me back behind bars?* Then I discovered the movie business. Or it discovered me. The Academy Award–winning documentary filmmaker Barbara Kopple hired me to write a treatment for a film about Mike Tyson. Once the project was green-lit, Barbara kept me on as a field producer. I remember running around from phone booth to phone booth (before the proliferation of cell phones), setting up interviews, coordinating camera crews, organizing transportation logistics, and thinking, *I can do this; this isn't so different from running a smuggling operation.*

Street Time brought my journey full circle. The series' main character, Kevin Hunter, played by Rob Morrow, was a pot smuggler out on parole, doing time on the street and trying, but failing, to go straight. As the creator of the show, I wrote the pilot episode and became what's known in the TV series world as the "show runner." That position is not unlike being the kingpin of a dope-smuggling enterprise with the important distinction that they can't lock you up, no matter how low the ratings might be.

The one thing nearly everyone who saw *Street Time* commented on was how realistic the show was. I mined the investment in my experience as an action junkie, dope smuggler, prisoner, and parolee to create the arc for Kevin Hunter's character. Following the writer's mandate to write what you know, I used the seven-ton hashish smuggle in the load of dates as a story-line and had my parole officer's son form a kid's gang called the Pink Rats.

On the set one day Rob Morrow and I got into a heated argument over how a scene should be played. "You're cutting my balls off!" he said when I insisted his character could not respond even when his wife accused him of being a rat.

"That's exactly how I want Kevin Hunter to feel," I told him. Being on parole is like having your balls in a vice. We got the scene on the next take.

The pieces collected in *Altered States of America* grew out of my urge to seek out men who were true to themselves and couldn't abide by anyone else's rules, for good or bad: writers, Mafia killers, Hollywood directors and actors, ex-cons, dope smugglers, CIA agents, former DEA agents—all of them men whose experience resonated with my own.

RICHARD STRATTON
NEW YORK CITY
MAY 2005

NORMAN MAILER

The Rolling Stone Interview Part I: Aquarius Hustling by Richard Stratton

No one at Harvard, his alma mater, seemed bothered in the spring of 1972 when Norman Mailer stalked onstage carrying a bottle of bourbon and a bag of ice. But early in the talk—an extemporaneous discussion of film spliced between clips from Mailer's three movies—the audience threatened to become unruly. Each paragraph of Mailer's was followed by a refrain of "Eat it!" or "Fuck you!" from a heckler who was even deeper into his bottle of booze than was the speaker.

Mailer, no stranger to public wild men, challenged the drunk. "Stand up, sir, and be recognized."

"Fuck you! Eat it!" was his echo.

Again Mailer told the man it was rude of him not to stand and state his name. When finally the heckler gave way to pressure from the audience and got to his feet, he still refused to identify himself.

"Well, let me tell you, sir," said Mailer, "there are one million, five-hundred-and-forty-eight-thousand, four-hundred-and-ninety-one people in Brooklyn who can say the word fuck better than you can."

He is our most famous writer. What other author provokes such a response from his audience? Mailer's public personality has made itself felt in so many areas of American experience—the literary world, politics, filmmaking, prize fighting and street fighting, marital infighting, drinking and partying, debating ardent female liberationists, and traveling the pervasive airs of TV talk shows—that people who do not really know his work will put into arguments for or against the man, and some experts in his work argue he is his own greatest literary creation.

Still it is Mailer's voice, the ideas he expresses in his extraordinary prose, that makes him more than a famous writer. In his 30 years of work, there is no question he has fulfilled the desire he formed at 16 to be a major writer. A reading of the important literature of this century would be incomplete without a thorough examination of Mailer's work. Books such as The Naked and the Dead, Advertisements for Myself, An American Dream, Why Are We in Vietnam?, The Armies of the Night mark Mailer among the greats.

It is spring 1974 when Norman Mailer and I met in Washington D.C. to get back inside each other's heads for a few days before we sit down to tape the interview. Mailer has come to Washington to speak at a fundraising benefit for the Fifth Estate, the citizen's counterintelligence organization whose formation was the promised "announcement of major national importance" Mailer made at his celebrated 50th birthday party in New York. (In the year since its inception, the Fifth Estate has merged with a new and similar group known as CARIC, Committee for Action/Research on the Intelligence Community.)

Once details of the evening's activities have been settled, Mailer and I leave the Fifth Estate offices and walk across Dupont Circle to the bar at Mailer's hotel. My mind is filled with ideas of how I am to approach this interview. We first met some years ago as neighbors in Provincetown, Massachusetts. It was winter, the town emptied of its summer crowds, and Mailer had returned to the place he feels he works best in to begin writing a long-projected, long-promised novel. We began as drinking and sparring partners until a torn retina forced Mailer to quit boxing.

Now, as I look across the table at him and we get into our first drink, he looks well, heavy but strong, firm through the arms and shoulders as if he's been doing a lot of push-ups lately. His color is healthy, and in the muted barroom light his curly, silver hair shines like a nebula.

After a few drinks, Mailer suddenly asks, "Listen, about the interview, I don't know if you ever read

Photograph by Annie Leibovitz

the one I did with Buzz Farber for Viva." I had—in manuscript. "Well," he says, "I think it's a pretty good interview, and certainly candid, but it did have one flaw I think we should try to avoid. Buzz is a good friend, but for the purposes of the interview he cried now and again to submerge his personality and become an anonymous interviewer, because, I suppose, that's the way most interviews are done. But I don't think it works with friends. I think it'll go farther if we forget any prepared questions—did you prepare?"

"Yes, I had, but I don't mind forgetting them."

"Well, we may be able to use some to direct the flow; if I start to stray too far from what you want to cover, you might bring me back with one of your questions. But I think we'll get better stuff if we just sit down and rap like we are now."

From Washington we travel up to Princeton, New Jersey, where Mailer talks to Larry King's journalism class, then on to New York and into a closed-circuit TV theater just in time to see George Foreman deck Ken Norton in the second round, and finally to Mailer's home in the Massachusetts Berkshires.

After a day of relaxation, we are ready to record. Mailer's library is a long rectangular room with wall-to-wall bookcases and a stereo tape recorder and record player. As a means of emptying our brains, we've just watched a Kojak episode about a hijacked morphine shipment, and are now tuning up for the interview by reading from a book of short poems. Mailer sits in a white wicker chair that creaks when he shifts position or leans forward to emphasize a point; and, poised on the edge of my seat a few feet from him, quickly forgetting the tape recorder, I will know something of what Maria Schneider must have felt when Marlon Brando succeeded in dominating every scene they did in Last Tango in Paris.

Let's talk about the reaction to 'Marilyn.' I think it's a book which finally is not going to be read by the people who respect your work.

When it came out, I said that the people who like my work most are going to like this one least. But I think they may be wrong. I think they felt, oh God, if Mailer sells out, that's one more dull piece of news for me, and they were worried. And I think they're wrong. I don't think I'm ever going to—well, I have enough respect for the powers of corruption not to say that I know I'm never going to sell out, but I don't think I'd sell out so easily, for so little. What I fear, far more than selling out, is wearing out. And I felt I was entitled, at the time I wrote Marilyn, to my way of doing things. You know, if I were an athlete and not a writer, it would be respected if I tried something that was not quite my line. I made a certain reputation by breaking rules.

> *What I fear, far more than selling out, is wearing out. And I felt I was entitled, at the time I wrote 'Marilyn,' to my way of doing things. If I were an athlete and not a writer, it would be respected if I tried something that was not quite my line. I made a certain reputation by breaking rules.*

NORMAN MAILER:
THE *ROLLING STONE* INTERVIEW

Rolling Stone, January 2, 1975 & January 16, 1975

PART I: AQUARIUS HUSTLING

No one at Harvard, his alma mater, seemed bothered in the spring of 1972 when Norman Mailer stalked onstage carrying a bottle of bourbon and a bag of ice. But early in the talk—an extemporaneous discussion of film spliced between clips from Mailer's three movies—the audience threatened to become unruly. Each paragraph of Mailer's was followed by a refrain of "Eat it!" or "Fuck you!" from a heckler who was even deeper into his bottle of booze than was the speaker.

Mailer, no stranger to public wild men, challenged the drunk. "Stand up, sir, and be recognized."

"Fuck you! Eat it!" was his echo.

Again Mailer told the man it was rude of him not to stand and state his name. When finally the heckler gave way to pressure from the audience and got to his feet, he still refused to identify himself.

"Well, let me tell you, sir," said Mailer, "there are one million, five-hundred-and-forty-eight-thousand, four-hundred-and-ninety-one people in Brooklyn who can say the word fuck better than you can."

He is our most famous writer. What other author provokes such a response from his audience? Mailer's public personality has made itself felt in so many areas of American experience—the literary world, politics, filmmaking, prize fighting and street fighting, marital infighting, drinking and partying, debating ardent female liberationists, and traveling the pervasive airs of TV talk shows—that people who do not really know his work will get into arguments for or against the man, and some experts in his work argue he is his own greatest literary creation.

Still it is Mailer's voice, the ideas he expresses in his extraordinary prose, that makes him more than a famous writer. In his 30 years of work, there is no question he has fulfilled the desire he formed at 16 to be a major writer. A reading of the important literature of this century would be incomplete without a thorough examination of Mailer's work. Books such as *The Naked and the Dead, Advertisements for Myself, An American Dream, Why Are We in Viet Nam?, The Armies of the Night* mark Mailer among the greats.

It is spring 1974 when Norman Mailer and I meet in Washington D.C. to get back inside each other's heads for a few days before we sit down to tape the interview. Mailer has come to Washington to speak at a fundraising benefit for the Fifth Estate, the citizen's counterintelligence organization whose formation was the promised "announcement of major national importance" Mailer made at his celebrated 50th birthday party in New York. (In the year since its inception, the Fifth Estate has merged with a new and similar group known as CARIC, Committee for Action/Research on the Intelligence Community.)

Once details of the evening's activities have been settled, Mailer and I leave the Fifth Estate offices and walk across Dupont Circle to the bar at Mailer's hotel. My mind is filled with ideas of how I am to approach this interview. We first met some years ago as neighbors in Provincetown, Massachusetts. It was winter, the town emptied of its summer crowds, and Mailer had returned to the place he feels he works best in to begin writing a long-projected, long-promised novel. We began as drinking and sparring partners until a torn retina forced Mailer to quit boxing.

Now, as I look across the table at him and we get into our first drink, he looks well, heavy but strong, firm through the arms and shoulders as if he's been doing a lot of push-ups lately. His color is healthy, and in the muted barroom light his curly, silvery hair shines like a nebula.

After a few drinks, Mailer suddenly asks, "Listen, about the interview, I don't know if you ever read the one I did with Buzz Farber for *Viva*." I had—in manuscript. "Well," he says, "I think it's a pretty good interview, and certainly candid, but it did have one flaw I think we should try to avoid. Buzz is a good friend, but for the purposes of the interview he tried now and again to submerge his personality and become an anonymous interviewer, because, I suppose, that's the way most interviews are done. But I don't think it works with friends. I think it'll go further if we forget about any prepared questions—did you prepare?"

"Yes, I did, but I don't mind forgetting them."

"Well, we may be able to use some to direct the flow; if I start to stray too far from what you want to cover, you might bring me back with one of your questions. But I think we'll get better stuff if we just sit down and rap like we are now."

From Washington we travel up to Princeton, New Jersey, where Mailer talks to Larry King's journalism class, then on to New York and into a closed-circuit TV theater just in time to see George Foreman deck Ken Norton in the second round, and finally to Mailer's home in the Massachusetts Berkshires.

After a day of relaxation, we are ready to record. Mailer's library is a long rectangular room with wall-to-wall bookcases and a stereo tape recorder and record player. As a means of emptying our brains, we've just watched a *Kojak* episode about a hijacked morphine shipment, and are now tuning up for the interview by reading from a book of short poems. Mailer sits in a white wicker chair that creaks when he shifts position or leans forward to emphasize a point; and, poised on the edge of my seat a few feet from him, quickly forgetting the tape recorder, I will know something of what Maria Schneider must have felt when Marlon Brando succeeded in dominating every scene they did in *Last Tango in Paris*.

Let's talk about the reaction to Marilyn. *I think it's a book which finally is not going to be read by the people who respect your work.*

When it came out, I said that the people who like my work most are going to like this one least. But I think they may be wrong. I think they felt, oh God, if Mailer sells out, that's one more dull piece of news for me, and they were worried. And I think they're wrong. I don't think I'm ever going to—well, I have enough respect for the powers of corruption not to say that I know I'm never going to sell out, but I don't think I'd sell out so easily, for so little. What I fear, far more than selling out, is wearing out. And I felt I was entitled, at the time I wrote *Marilyn*, I was entitled to my way of doing things. You know, if I were an athlete and not a writer, it would be respected if I tried something that was not quite my line. I made a certain reputation by breaking rules.

If I said at a certain point that I wanted to try and write a biography in two months—which you can't do—in other words, if I said I want to see if I can perform a piece of virtuoso, that's my right. One of the things that's interesting to people in America who are interested in what I'm doing, is to see whether I can do something or not. Usually I fail. But I wanted to try certain things that at least establish early standards in hitherto untried occupations; one of them was to try this biography.

Now you can say that it's literally impossible to do a biography of anyone that you haven't known intimately and kept detailed notes upon, can't certainly do a biography in two months. And I'd say no, no one but Marilyn.

You could spend ten years on Marilyn and might never find out what the facts were. Because every time you begin to come upon an item in Marilyn's life, everybody's arguing about it. You talk to two of her closest friends and they'll each have opposed views. Marilyn was a phenomenon. Nothing in her life demands that a fact be there on any given day. For one thing, since she grew up in an orphanage, she learned early in life that a lie was usually more effective than the truth. Certainly a lie which people wanted to hear was vastly more useful than any truth, as far as she was concerned. And she grew up among liars, people in showbiz are naturally liars. They lean to legend.

It has a lot to do with your notion of hip and existentialism, really, the way she lived.

Well, I can't, I can't say. I don't know. I mean, hip is built—at least since I wrote *The White Negro*—hip is built on the idea—and I think the idea is worth bringing back—that there are people who lead their lives in terms of their orgasm.

Men or women?

I would suspect I meant men a little more than women when I wrote it ten or 12 years ago. By now probably it's reversed and it's women who lead their lives more in terms of orgasm than men. At any rate, the first definition of the hipster is that their lives follow their orgasm: That's their morality. If the orgasm they're getting today is better than the orgasm they got yesterday, then whatever they're doing is moral for them. It's an extension of Hemingway's idea: Whatever makes you feel good is good.

Now, it's presumptuous of me to jump in and start talking about what Marilyn's orgasms were like. I don't have the remotest notion. I never did and never pretended to. It's almost impossible to tell because she was on drugs so much—not sexual drugs, but drugs which would give her tranquility. Everything we know about her drugs suggests her nerves were in such a state of lividity that orgasm was probably not her first concern. Or for that reason, was it? But again, all the evidence is so contradictory about her. Friend One says A; Friend Two says Z. You finally begin to decide that Marilyn was nothing but contradictions, which might as well be presented without too huge regard for the certified chronology of it.

So I think that the people who like my work and still are contemptuous of *Marilyn* may be contemptuous too quickly.

When I read it in galley, I thought, it's a good book. But then when I saw it with the pictures and everything, there's something that sits wrong about that book.

Well—

It's so commercial.

It is.

And that hurts, coming from you.

Well, it didn't. Of course, it came from me in the sense that I didn't withdraw my manuscript and cry out, I protest this book. You could say that if I were being true to my own standards, I should never have consented to being presented like that. But I saw it as a job I was taking on to make some money, and I may have felt *too* honorable and *too* satisfied with what I'd done. After all, I was supposed to write 25,000 words and ended up writing 90,000, and I didn't say to the publisher, give me more for this. I just said, that's their good luck, and I'm not going to carry on about it. And I was pleased with the book.

Then I had huge fights with Larry Schiller about the placement and style of the photographs. There were many photographs I wanted that weren't in the book. He finally ended up dictating where the photographs went. That was his prerogative. He'd lived with the book for several years, he had collected those photographs. I had seen the photographs when I began the book. It had not been clear to me that those were going to be the photographs and no others.

When I saw Pauline Kael's review and she said the book was a "sordid creamy object" I felt, well—

She said the book gives off "bad vibes." And in a sense it does.

Yes, I think it does. It has a mixture of incompatibles in it. Although I confess to liking the jacket, I can't say her comment is altogether unfair. I mean, I, for instance, if I had my choice, would not have picked the type the book was set in. It's a type that has almost nothing to do with my style. I didn't like the quality of the paper. However, I'm not going to sit here and bleed for the American public when the book was conceived by all in the first place as a project which would ideally make money for everyone concerned.

I do want to get to the root of one notion which I don't quite comprehend. I mean, why does a writer not have the same right to make money that a capitalist does, or an entrepreneur or a corporation? I mean, I'm worried about it because maybe a writer doesn't have the same right. But when I think of all the cheap hustlers like Mike Wallace who carried on that I was doing it for the bucks. . . .

You said, once you've decided that you are going to do a book for money, then you have to get into the existentialism of the act, which is whether you do it well or you do it badly, whether the book will finally make you deader as a writer or more alive.

If you're doing something for money, the only way you can get through it alive is to give more than was requested. The old 19th-century conception of the noble prostitute was that she fell in love with her client. And there is something to that. I mean, if you're going to be a prostitute, what chance have you got if you don't fall in love with a client? One at a time. If you sit down and you say, there is such a thing as a literary gift and God gave me one, and I'm now using it to earn a living, then the only absolution is to fall in love with the object of my fee. Which is what I'm saying I did. I don't know if you necessarily dismiss that summarily out of court.

You know when I get really discouraged? I was walking down the street the other day in New York, and saw a Marilyn Monroe date book or calendar, something like that, in a bookstore. With excerpts from Norman Mailer's text. It's beginning to get like Davy Crockett. That's not you. That's not someone who says I'm a psychic outlaw who's going to get more and more outrageous— not outrageous, but, you remember—

It was the promise I made.

I've got it written down, "The ambition of a writer like myself is to become consecutively more disruptive, more dangerous and more powerful."

Yes. Well, I wrote that in the late fifties, in *Advertisements for Myself* I assume. At that time we were moving toward the end of the Eisenhower years. To use one of Gore Vidal's few memorable labels, Eisenhower, "the great golfer," had presided over us. For eight incredibly dull and deadening years in which all of the present ills of America, the pollution, the fall of our position in the world, the oncoming nihilism, the destruction of all value, the belief that God is dead, all that began in the Eisenhower era. The profound corruption of the Nixon administration began in the Eisenhower era, although, you know, we won't pretend for a moment that the Democrats aren't almost as good at that as the Republicans. (Except they just don't have the clout of the corporations to help them in their corruption.) But, finally, you refer to a remark written by me for that period.

Now we're in a period which is the reverse of that, a period where the fundamental passion of the young is to snigger at the worn-out aspirations of the middle-aged. Snigger is the only word you can employ. You know, once we had hip, now we got hippie. Now we're in some sort of post-fascisto, apathetic hippie beatdom. Everybody feels that somehow there is shit in the nectar. So you look for some ground on which to rally. There was a time when you might say you'd blow the bugle so that the Left can find a ground on which to rally. Now it's almost as if you have to say, find a ground on which the Left can find a ground to rally, or even the Right can find a ground to rally, or there won't be any battle anywhere on earth! We'll go down the drain with the pollution.

I drove down here from Maine, where we rented a car. Every time we stopped we had to go through a frustrating ordeal to try to get the thing going again. The car wouldn't start unless we had everything fastened down and locked. Until finally I got so enraged I opened the hood of the car and aborted the whole system. When your life is being controlled at that level, you no longer even have to think about totalitarianism. Totalitarianism is here.

It's in your nervous system. Totalitarianism is the interruption of mood.

The mood is dulled to shit.

A lot of disc jockeys have their nasties, cutting off the last note of a record.

It keeps you in that frantic, anxious state until they put the next record on.

Well, it keeps you with your thumb and your forefinger on your prick. And, you know, when everybody in the world is keeping their thumb and forefinger on their prick—including the girls—then we're in that livid state known as pretotalitarianism.

Let me underline that. Totalitarianism can't succeed if a

good proportion of the population is relaxed at a given moment. It requires a state of tension where nobody's relaxed enough to recognize even simple things. At that point you need a massive shock to stimulate you. The Germans, for instance, at a certain point needed the prod that the Jews were an international conspiracy determined to take over control of Germany and absolutely demoralize their hard-earned sexual virtues. Et cetera.

But let me go back to something. The remark you quoted. I made it in '58. Now it's '74. I am no longer trying to be disturbing. I've come to a point in my life where I'm trying to put it together. If we're going to find fault with *Marilyn*, it isn't because I failed to write a book which is disturbing, but because I was trying to put a few things together—and didn't succeed. I ended with "a sordid creamy object" which cost $20, which had a huge amount of atrocious and ugly publicity, which got distorted, which alienated many of the people I wanted to read that book, which hurt my reputation, which made people doubt my right to claim or pretend anything, et cetera, et cetera.

I feel a large sense of failure about *Marilyn*, but not so much in the book itself. The book has flaws, it has faults, it has lacks. It has errors of omission. The ending is not nearly good enough. It has more faults than any book I've written. But what it also has, I think, is something that hardly anybody ever stopped to look at. It's got an interesting portrait of a woman who's almost impossible to capture.

From the time I began writing in college, I never tried to write about a difficult woman. From the beginning I always felt women were more difficult than men. They certainly are for me. This is the first time I really tried. And I think just as a piece of prose, it succeeds more than most books about women. At least, that's my claim for it.

What I'm miserable about is that after 30 years in this literary racket, I didn't have enough worldly sense to foresee some of the awful things that were going to happen. And to that extent I did let down people who have a little faith in me. I did act like a sodden besotted general. I mean, I'm trying to make a change in the way people perceive history, and I soil and besmirch my reputation this way. Shameful. Disgusting.

So I learned a lot from *Marilyn*. I entered that book with a kind of confidence I may never have again. I felt it's possible that I have as much or more to say than anybody around in American life. That was my confidence. But the painful thing I learned was that it isn't enough to be good, it isn't enough to be right, it isn't enough to have the kind of confidence other people don't have. It is absolutely not enough if you don't really have the discipline to carry your idea out to all its stages including the finished product. And know how to protect it. And I committed a small disaster for myself when the product that finally landed on every coffee table was indeed a coffee table object. And I'm going to pay for that over the years. I'm going to pay for what I should have known by the age of 50 and didn't know. And, you know, when you get to that age, you should have really made your dull mistakes earlier. I mean, once a man's 50 he's entitled only to make large and serious mistakes. In other words, he can go into something with the best will and the best intentions and a great deal of skill, and fail because he met a superior opponent. But a man at 50 shouldn't still be defeated by himself, by his own indulgence, his own vanity, his own sense of superiority, especially when it is ill founded.

So I give myself bad marks for *Marilyn* on that basis. But I think if the book ever seeps down to the point where it's some sort of poor little paperback, with no pictures, I think the book will finally have its life.

If I had the sense that God gave, you know, Truman Capote, Gore Vidal, Saul Bellow, John Updike, name them, I might have done something elegant and standoffish. To mock the bind I found myself in. Instead I plunged. I'm tired of being the most famous unpaid comic in American life.

Well, there's no reason why you shouldn't be paid.

[*Laughter*] Okay. But let's at least put down the criticism that I wasn't trying to disrupt and disturb people. By now I've come to another point of view entirely. I'm trying to put the whole thing together, at least for myself. Not for sanity but for composure. These days it's too easy to destroy, too easy, everybody's going around tearing it up. The trick now is to see if you can put it together for yourself at least.

The most interesting aspect of Marilyn *was the question of Marilyn Monroe's death. We got involved in an investigation after you had written the book. My investigation did turn up a lot of stuff.*

Stratton, I think you're giving yourself good marks. I wouldn't say a *lot* of stuff was turned up. *Some* stuff was turned up.

True, no hard evidence, of who had done what. But we did come up with certain strong indications this was no simple suicidal case, which is what everyone involved with it tried to make it out to be. For example the fact that she died with a 4.5 milligram percent level of barbiturate in her blood, and absolutely no trace of the drug in her stomach or in her duodenum and small intestines.

I thought we should talk some about exactly what was uncovered, in the investigation. What I want to do is to go over what you told the newspapers back last summer, in the press conference at the Algonquin.

Why don't we insert right here in the interview the press

release I gave out that day? I thought the reception of that press release was curious. I'll never understand the newspapers. I thought what you and I had put together was striking to say the least, yet only one paper to my knowledge printed it.

Let's insert it right here:

1. According to the lexicologist's report, August 6th, 1962 (County of Los Angeles), Marilyn Monroe died of a concentration of Nembutal of 4.5 mg. percent in her blood. It is a high concentration. Only one in eight deaths from barbiturates shows so high a level, for it is indicative of the ability to swallow huge amounts of fast-acting capsules, as many as 40 or 50 in a short period of time. (In addition, a separate coroner's report filed a week later (but dated August 6th) showed an even higher level of chloral hydrate, 8.00 mg. percent.)

2. In such cases of extreme overdose, a residue is found in the stomach. It usually consists of digested pills, pills in liquid solution, retractile crystals, half-digested barbiturate sludge, even capsules whose gelatin has not yet dissolved. Some highly visible trace of barbiturates is invariably present.

3. In Marilyn Monroe's case, nothing but 20 c.c. of brownish mucoid fluid, an amount equal to no more than a few teaspoons of liquid. "No residue of the pills is noted," states the coroner's report. Nor are any refractile crystals discovered in her stomach, and the minute liquid content of 20 c.c. is never analyzed.

4. Four prominent medical specialists (two toxicologists and two forensic pathologists) were then queried on this point. They cannot recall a case in their experience where such conditions of high milligram percentage dose in the blood and an empty belly occurred.

5. The assumption follows that a stomach pump may have

been applied in an attempt to save her life, or, conversely, a lethal overdose was injected. The coroner for Los Angeles County, Dr. Thomas Noguchi, stated for *Time* magazine that, "No stomach pump was used on Marilyn." It is, however, not easy to know whether a stomach pump was used unless damage to the stomach wall or esophagus results. There was no such damage in her report.

6. There was also, however, no evidence of refractile crystals in the stomach or the duodenum. All absence of refractile crystals in the stomach would be contributory proof toward a stomach pump (since it would suggest they were washed away by the action) but only the most sophisticated hospital equipment could produce a lavage in the duodenum. So the hypothesis of a stomach pump is twice disproved.

7. Which repeats the possibility of a lethal injection of barbiturates. Dr. Noguchi states he examined the body carefully for needle marks and found nothing.

"Very carefully?"

"Of course. It is my job."

8. How then would the doctor account for this uncommon death? His reply was that the pills could have passed quickly into the small intestine.

"What then did the examination of the small intestine show?"

"It was not examined."

Still, his own report stated, "Unembalmed blood is taken for alcohol and barbiturate examination. Liver, kidney, stomach and contents, urine and intestine are saved for further lexicological study."

9. "No other forensic pathologist or toxicologist had even suggested the attenuated possibility of all the contents of

the stomach passing so quickly to the small intestine (in whose duodenum—whole gateway to the small intestine!—no refractile crystals were found), but in any case, no test of the contents of the small intestine was made.

"Why was that not done?"

"In 1962 we didn't make tests in small intestines. The facilities were not available."

Even for a death of such unusual characteristics, and when the subject was so famous? Dr. Noguchi indicated that Department policy in 1962, 11 years ago, was that there was no need to proceed further once a high blood level indicated the cause of death.

10. In 1962, however, if facilities to examine a small intestine "saved for further toxicological study" were not available, still a psychiatrist, Dr. Litman, and a psychologist, Norman Farberow, of the Suicide Prevention Center were employed to do an in-depth "psychological autopsy" for six weeks whose results indicated that Marilyn Monroe "was a perfect suicidal case."

When asked to explain the lack of residue in the stomach, Dr. Litman announced that it was "a routine fuckup."

11. One will not cash such obvious checks as the state of hysteria, paralysis, rumor and high rumor which circulated in Los Angeles in the days after her death, or the possibility that we are dealing with one or another species of coverup. Since this inquiry, however, can hardly question people under oath, it has reached the end of its present effort.

12. The facts are moot. The explanations are without explanation. In summary, she could not have died from a simple overdose since no remains were found in her stomach, yet by the evidence no stomach pump could have been

employed, and there are by the coroner's statement no marks of a lethal injection, a set of such mutually prohibitive hypotheses that by medical logic one cannot discover how she ever died at all. There is only the premise of "a routine fuckup" which may cover a host of contradictions but fails to explain what could be routine in any atmosphere surrounding the sudden death of America's most famous movie star. So an invitation is offered to the press. Let them call for a coroner's inquest.

Some medical sources:
Dr. Cyril Wecht
Forensic Pathologist and Coroner
Pittsburgh, Pennsylvania

Dr. Michael Luongo
Chief Medical Examiner for Suffolk County
Boston, Massachusetts

John McHugh, Chief Toxicologist
Massachusetts State Police
Boston, Massachusetts

Dr. Nakamura, Chief Toxicologist
Coroner's Office
1104 North Mission Road
Los Angeles, California

—*A Statement by Norman Mailer for Release July 18th, 1973*

Since that time, I have come around again to the thesis that Marilyn was murdered. After reading Robert Slatzer's *The Life and Curious Death of Marilyn Monroe*, the greater burden of proof is now, I think, on the side of those who would call it suicide. Slatzer's evidence presents a new confusion—which is whether Marilyn was murdered at home or brought back to her house after she had died. But the case for an injection becomes more powerful either way since there is no trace of vomit anywhere in bedroom or bathroom, nor in her throat or nose (a rare, almost impossible phenomenon if one takes an overdose of pills). And of course the disappearance of her small intestine is even more crucial now since the dye in the gelatin capsule of a sleeping pill leaves its color on the walls of the intestine. Naturally, there's no report of such dye.

Moreover, Marilyn was given injections on August 1st and August 3rd by Dr. Engelberg as part of her treatment. When Noguchi stated there were no marks of a needle on her body, the assumption is that he missed these two injections, and so could have missed a third (if indeed there was no coverup).

Then again, the first policeman to arrive at the scene, Sergeant Jack Clemmons, now retired, is willing to be quoted that he thinks it was murder and is convinced her body had been moved, for she was lying in a state of composure. (Death by overdose leaves one's limbs in a contorted position.) Moreover, Clemmons's recollection is that the doctors initially told him they had been there since 12:30, or four hours before the police were called. According to the doctors, the time of their arrival was approximately 3:45 AM. A coroner's inquest might clear up this point at least.

Other leads to evidence are in profusion. A wire-tapper named Bernard Spindel, who died of a heart attack in prison, was, according to Slatzer, hired by Jimmy Hoffa's people to make tapes of Bobby Kennedy's conversations with Marilyn at a time when Hoffa may have been trying to get material on Bobby to put in the balance against the case Kennedy was building against him. Duplicates of these tapes are in Mrs.

Spindel's possession. Again, according to Slatzer, the chief of police of Los Angeles, Bill Parker, picked up all the telephone records of Marilyn's long-distance calls the last week of her life and would not make them public. It was also Parker's desire, as more than a few people in L.A. seemed to know, to be the next head of the FBI!

Finally, a most uncomfortable item—from the chief medical examiner of New York's Suffolk County, Dr. Sidney S. Weinberg: "It is extremely rare for a woman to commit suicide in the nude. . . . During the past 20 years in my own experience I have seen only one such case, and in that case it was by gunshot, not with drugs."

Of course it is also rare to find no traces of vomit and no evidence of swallowed capsules. Too many rarities may be wandering around in the same case to call it suicide.

On the other hand, one has to be an implacable opponent of the Kennedys to assume they planned a murder. Other options were open to them, including the most basic one of suffering bad publicity for a short period if Marilyn decided to attack them openly. (The temper of the press in 1962 was to suppress personal stories about prominent figures even if they were your political enemies.) The sex life of the president and by extension the sex life of his brother were still part of the American chalice. But criminal activities were not. Suppose that enemies of the Kennedys—whoever!—thought the best damage to be done to them was to murder Marilyn in such a way that it would look superficially like suicide—for the first day—and then would be later exposed as a murder. Who in America would not then believe the Kennedys were implicated? If not for Chief Parker's overweening desire to be the next head of the FBI (and his rush therefore to put a blanket over the case), America might have been living in the late summer of 1962 with a murder larger in its seeming implications than Watergate.

But indeed there is one paradoxical line of reasoning which underlines the innocence of the Kennedys. If they had done it, they would have done it better. Marilyn would have looked like a real suicide and the discovery of her body would have been better arranged. Not everyone would have been telephoning everyone else in frantic confusion at 3:00 and 4:00 AM while waiting for minutes or conceivably hours to call the police.

Let's talk about psychopathy and murder. To what degree do you think Charles Manson might be an embodiment of some of the ideas you brought up originally in The White Negro? *For some time I've been living with the unpopular thought that Manson was probably a very brave man in certain ways.*

I think there's no question he was brave. One of the more depressing manifestations of public morality is that whenever someone commits a horror or monstrosity, they have to call the criminal a coward. It's automatic. Hitler's a coward. We used to call Tito a coward. Now they call Manson a coward. Part of the pain of maturity is that you come to recognize bravery is not enough. First you break out of the barbed-wire cocoon of a middle-class life with the idea that bravery is crucial to your existence. Maybe it's because the need for bravery is the one thing the middle class has refused to teach. So there's a period in one's life where you believe that anyone who does something brave is good.

Hemingway never got over that discovery. He had a cushioned life until he broke out of it, and like all of us he never broke out of it altogether. Then, years later, you come face to face with the second recognition that people can be brave and still be no fucking good. That some brave people can be worse than cowards, and you can rue the day they discovered the grace of their own bravery, because finally they destroy even more than cowards do. Then you're face to face with the complexity of things and the difficulty of finding your way to any coherent ethics.

Manson is one of the most perfect examples of this. Because whatever else he is, you can't take away from him the fact that he's a brave man. Now, he wasn't altogether a brave man. And he wasn't a warrior. I mean, finally he was a general who sent his troops out to wreak the carnage, and he stayed behind.

But there were apparently certain aspects of his own personality which were very brave.

Well, as an intellectual he was brave.

Yes. Then there was his method of dealing with men who tried to give him trouble. He was known to offer the weapon to the person he was fighting with and say, go ahead and kill me. And if that person didn't have the nerve to kill him, which . . . they didn't . . .

Who ever has the nerve then? It's very hard to kill someone who stands before you, looks into your eyes and says, kill me.

That's bravery, and an instinctual sense of your opponent's strength, because no one ever took him up on the challenge.

Well, that's not bravery, I'd say. That's a knowledge of the con, which is something else. Manson did grow up in prisons. He certainly understood that when you get into trouble you can't handle, then you still have the option to stand there and let the other person get their executioner's desire up to the point where they're going to kill you. It's not automatic.

It's reputed that Jimmy Hoffa once said, flee a knife and charge a gun. I have no idea if he ever said it, but I think, if he didn't, somebody who knew an awful lot about the subject had to be the author. Because there is something intimate about a knife, whereas there's something closer to moral decision about a gun. If you charge the gun, the man who holds it finally has to say to himself (since it's not a physical act, but a mental act) has to say to himself that he has the right to shoot you. At that point his moral sense of himself has to be invoked. He may not feel the sanction to shoot. Whereas if you charge a man who has a knife, his physical sense of himself is invoked, it's competitive. Am I going to hold this knife while he gets it away from me and humiliates me? But if you take your own knife and hand it over to the other man, that's different from charging a man with a knife.

We go back to the original advice: Flee a knife, charge a gun. If you hand it over and say, stab me, you make the knife a gun. And Manson may have had a particularly shrewd sense that the guy he was handing the knife to was a gun man. Weapons are metaphors which fit or do not fit our lifestyle. We do not mix metaphors when it comes to execution. So what we know about Manson is that he wasn't necessarily so brave about these matters as extraordinarily intelligent.

And he had an uncanny sense of where each personality he came in contact with was coming from.

Oh, by every report he had an incredible sense of the people he was among. Obviously he had one of the more incandescent sensibilities of our time. The horror of it—not the horror so much as the pathetic aspect of it—is that once again we have a prisoner who's filled with talent, you know, the criminal who leads a prison life from beginning to end. Like Genet. Extraordinary talents. If Manson had become an intellectual, he would have been most interesting. He had bold ideas, and he carried them out—he worked for his ideas. The thing that characterizes Manson's life, whenever you look at it, is how hard that man worked for his ideas.

I like his sense of all these junior debutantes that would get into his gang. He'd have them out there, rolling in what?—not human shit, not cow shit—horse shit. Because if there's any single point of focus of social life in the upper middle class of America, it's that a young lady learns to ride a horse well and live comfortably with horse shit. Which of course is, you know, vastly more compatible than human shit or cow shit or dog shit or, perish the mark, wipe us out, cat shit. So, you know, there he has them rolling in horse shit. He knows how to get an orgy going. I mean, this man's not a small man. But the hippies sure abdicated from him. My old friend Ed Sanders, as far as I'm concerned, abdicated completely when he wrote that book about Manson. Because Sanders treated him as if he were a worm, a disgusting character. It's our terror in American life before real criminality.

Manson actually was a hippie of sorts, and Manson shocked and terrified Sanders.

Sanders is not the smallest man around. Sanders has really done a few things. He started *Fuck You,* which is one of the better early magazines, one of the magazines that created, ultimately, magazines like *Rolling Stone.* And Sanders is a funny man who writes well. He threw away his style to write *The Family.* . . . It was a phenomenon.

If I had no other way to measure the shock Manson caused in American life, I could see by the way Ed Sanders was almost lobotomized through the phenomenon of Manson.

Yes. Another way of measuring it was the day you and I went out there to see the Spahn Ranch and found it had been bulldozed into nonexistence, which seems to me strikingly American. Like our attitude toward death, cover it up, make believe it doesn't really exist.

Well, it's the American way. You know, we must destroy the past. When I was down in Dallas many years ago, a couple of years after Jack Kennedy was assassinated, naturally what's the first thing I do, I went over to see the plaza—The second thing: I went to see what happened to Jack Ruby's burlesque club. And you know, it had become a police gymnasium. They know how to do things in Dallas.

They know how to cut a connection or two.
Right on.

To what degree do you think Manson was psychopathic? He had that other side to his personality, that hustler/pimp workingman's aspect. All the time he was doing his supposedly messianic trip with these young people, he was also hustling.
Well, let's start playing with these words, set them up against each other. Not every psychopath is a hustler, not every hustler is a psychopath. Still, it's very hard to be a hustler without having some psychopath in you. It's hard to stay alive as a psychopath if you can't hustle a little. But we have to consider that at bottom the two are qualities opposed. Being a psychopath is existential. You don't know how a situation is going to turn out because you can't control it. Something inside you will not let you cut off the experience. You may be getting every warning that this experience is taking you into more and more bad places, and you can even get killed before the night's out.

Whereas the hustler tries to control the flow of the experience.
The hustler's *dignity* is that he controls the flow of the experience. He considers it obscene if he doesn't.
Of course there's no such thing as a true or pure psychopath. Nor a total hustler. The hustler has elements in himself which are unmanageable, the psychopath has veins of shrewdness, calm judgment, and a great ability to hustle. To go back to my notion of Marilyn, we usually build our personality on the inner knowledge that we have a double personality. We

assign our budding qualities to one side or the other. So there's a side of oneself that's relatively unmanageable as opposed to the side that's constructed on control. Part of the comedy in criminal affairs is to see how practical, sane, genteel, reasonable, clever, and full of the final trick the hustler is. I mean, a good hustler always has a smooth hustle. Smooth's a word that fits with hustle. A player hates it if his cool is pricked. Manson is an intense mixture of the two. He's more psychopath than just about any psychopath and more of a hustler than any average hustler that's come along. The vulgarity is to seize a personality as Dostoyevskian as Manson's and assume immediately that he has to be uniquely a hustler and everything he did was as a hustler, so don't take him seriously. Or else see him as an example of pure, evil, unrestrained psychopathy.

That's always seemed to me the problem with Truman Capote's work. I mean, even in In Cold Blood, *where he looks for those easy, quick psychological containers he can pour his characters into. I don't think he got any real insight into those two characters, the murderers in* In Cold Blood.

Well, Truman's abilities, I think, lie in another direction. Truman's always had an exquisite sense of his readership. Which I must say has changed greatly during his career. He started with a special readership. And moved out to an enormously large one. But he's always had this exceptional sense of how much they can bear. And he has always had the accompanying sense of how to vibrate their prejudices without shaking them apart.

And he knows how to end a book just beautifully, the way he ended In Cold Blood *with that young lady visiting the grave of her murdered friend.*

Truman's never without his tone. And it would be part of his virtuosity that the elegiac tone would belong naturally to him. Yes. It would be hard to think of Truman ending a book badly. The first time Truman does, I will have to sit down and read that book all over again because it's possible that Truman will have just written far and away his most adventurous book.

Because he's on to something?

The only reason Truman couldn't end a book fantastically well is because he would be on to something large. So, I agree with you about *In Cold Blood* in the sense that I don't think he got near his characters. I think that what he did do, which makes it an important book to me, is end up telling us more about the prejudices and the limited ability of the middle-class reader to encounter criminality than any book I ever read. It tells you almost nothing about the criminals, but how much it does say about that sense of everything-in-its-place that the *New Yorker* has stood for for over forty embattled years.

Perhaps Manson and people who can live with these extremities in their personalities may in fact be the survivors. And all the highly civilized people may be ending up in the worst kind of deaths to themselves. And technological destruction. If it's only in extremes that the society will save itself, then the secret fear of most people is that they're dead . . . moribund . . . and these Manson people are more alive than they are.

Yes. I think that's what they do fear. And I think the reason is we have all grown up in a society that's relatively new in its fundamental premise, a society that claims to believe in life. To coin a piece of jargon, of the worst sort, we could say that we exist in a keep-everybody-alive society. Ironically, most of the cultures to exhibit great energy in history, the societies which produced our society, were, on the contrary, built on killing. The idea common to all animals, and prehistoric and primitive man, even among civilized societies like the Greeks, the Romans, during the Middle Ages, and the Renaissance, the idea was still that if you didn't have enough right to live—in other words, if you were a drag upon the mood and the energy and the sustenance of other people— you were better off—Christ to the contrary—dead. These societies were kill societies. They got their neatness, their elegance, they got their style—out of killing.

But we are a society which says in effect, be sure you live. Life is our only gift. We're not going to get anything after this. The kill societies, to the contrary, were religious. They believed in the immanence of God, or a devil, or in demons. Primitive man spent his time placating demons in every tree. If a wind blew a sudden leaf past his face, he began to propitiate some spirit. They believed nothing was accidental. They were, in fact, more scientific than we are, for they believed that anything you can't explain is tremendously disturbing, whereas we prefer to ignore whatever we cannot dominate with our minds. We wipe out the artifacts of the past as if they have no curse.

Well, this notion, this keep-everybody-alive society—is a vulgar notion. There's nothing more livid, more cancer provoking than the face of a distorted liberal who shrieks at you, "You're talking about a human being!" They always italicize it—*hu-min. Being.* You're talking about a *life* that can be *lost*, they say. They're the same people who will turn around and absolutely insist upon destroying life, the same people who will soon leap with glee to forbid people to procreate, that is, about the time we decide there are definitely too many people on earth and we have to cut down the population or we won't survive, they will end by insisting that people be electrocuted for daring to conceive without a license.

Of course, today, they're still on the side of keep-everybody-alive. So the thought that someone might be so profoundly repulsive that everybody in their immediate neighborhood wants to let them die, is something they cannot tolerate. Nor can we for that matter. We're not as tough as we sound. We too live in this enormous supermarket of suburban guilt. Because we know we are all destroying the landscape with our homes and our highways. There's such a gassy, dead dull air over everything. Which we create. When you traveled, it used to be the only bad air you ever smelled was in a smoker on a train. Now that air is over everything.

Fresh air is the anomaly. We almost do not know what to do with it. Given this guilt we live in, we opt for keeping everybody alive because we know we're destroying everything. But that's also why we're, on the other hand, nihilistic. That's why we laugh every time a line or an idea or a disclosure cuts the feet off somebody.

If you notice, practically all the laughter that exists now, is watching somebody have their feet cut off. Nixon has created a laugh in this country which will end by wiping out just about every political institution. If the Devil wanted to destroy America he would have sent Nixon to us, because he knew Nixon's feet don't cut. Nixon would survive. Everybody would laugh themselves into a piss-out, and Nixon would still be there.

Nixon has to increase the incidence of sniggerers. But why do we have so many of them in American life? For the simplest reason: We all sit in this guilt that we don't necessarily deserve to live, and that maybe we ought to get back to the old idea of the kill society. So people like Manson just drive us up the tree. This guy's going out and doing it.

Killing people, yeah. But at the same time our whole society is very much death oriented.

Oh, we talk about keep-everybody-alive as if it really helped life, but what does it do? It insists that people die properly in a hospital. But in fact people are allowed to walk into hospitals when the beds are empty and are shoved out when the beds are filled.

Anybody who's ever been in a hospital knows that the whole game depends on whether your stay of welcome is over. It isn't what your condition is. If they're short of beds and you get on the push-out list, out you go. Then, if they have beds, they welcome you back. You can be dismissed from the hospital and called in ten days later for more tests. And why do they do these tests? Because they want to stick a finger up your ass. Why? Because they want to suffocate you. They think they're not going to be able to breathe too much longer themselves.

So the horror that Manson inspires, at bottom, I think, is that everybody's heart leaps up at the thought of him doing all that killing. You see, he is the robber bridegroom of American dream life.

It seemed to me that the Yippies were always yelling, Live, Live, Live, at the expense of everything else.

Well, for a while they were doing both. Which was, they were really—they were saying, kill a little, live a little. That's what they were really saying. They were saying, killing is not that real, and living's a little better if you play the game of killing a little. I don't think they ever went around killing people. Obviously they didn't do that. They did their best to kill institutions, kill ideas, kill things that were giving people bad life. And, you know, a great many of us, myself included, said in part, more power to them.

But they were always terrified by the idea of any actual killing.

No, I don't think they ever faced into what they were really talking about until Manson came along.

If you know the Yippies, they were really—whatever their

peccadilloes might have been—the one thing that characterized all the Yippies, they were generous people. And they did not have true violence in them.

People like Abbie Hoffman, Jerry Rubin, Ed Sanders were generous, they were generous as hell. Jerry Rubin is one of the more generous people I've known. If he has an idea, he's very happy to give it to you and let it become your idea. He really wants to give of himself and have other people accept it. As a result, he understands the fundamental principle of generosity, which is that you refresh yourself by giving. Jerry's always understood that.

What he didn't understand, from my point of view, is that if you give everything away in every direction, you're not necessarily going to get a huge return. What you may get is a total pollution of your own water. It may be that there is a form to life we all have to respect in one fashion or another, or life will not go on. I don't think Jerry Rubin necessarily ever encountered the word "entropy" at an early stage in his thinking. It may be that he's thinking about it now, I don't know.

Another aspect of Manson that upset everybody was the sex orgies carried on by the family. The real horror for the American middle class was to know Manson and his family were engaging in out-and-out sex orgies, exactly what so much of the middle class were doing themselves.

Yes, I don't think the horror was in the idea of orgy itself. After all, one of the unspoken solutions to suburban life has been the orgy. There have probably been more organized balls among respectable people in the seventh and eighth decades of American life in this 20th century than any other time, certainly in any other mass democratic society. I don't think there's been anything remotely approaching the incidence of systematized orgy we have here. People putting aside Friday night or Saturday night for their orgy, with their neighbors, their special neighbors.

But these orgies have always been, by every book report we have of them, always highly civilized, indeed the most highly civilized expression of sexual endeavor you can find. I mean, nobody at an orgy ever throws a punch. Suddenly America learns about this orgiastic life in Manson's gang that ends in mass murder. Anybody who's ever been in a civilized orgy knows that what you're left with, besides a few interesting memories to feed that part of your fantasy which still needs to be nourished, is a kind of buried bleak sense not so far from murder. I mean, I don't know that most people come out of an orgy full of love. No, a cold icelike feeling is more usually awakened. Most people sense the orgy has left them more murderous than when they started. Now, suddenly, Manson comes along with *his* orgies, and Boom, the murders do take place. Indeed, it's as if the murders were cooked to the boiling point by those orgies. Measure the shock then in the orgiastic suburbs.

Because Manson didn't come from their numbers. I mean, he had been 17 years out of 35 in prison. So he was a natural to take the orgy all the way to murder.

Well, I don't think it was that automatic. He also had something inside him he couldn't control at all. His paranoid side, where he saw the blacks taking over the country. At a certain moment he was going to rise as some sort of gray eminence for the blacks and yet at the same time do his best to wipe them out. He had those huge plans to flee to the desert when the war was coming.

In the crudest psychoanalytical terms, his real connection was to his own timetable toward disaster. It was approaching very quickly. Because he was a man of Napoleonic ambition, he took this interior sense his body and his mind were providing him—the psyche secretly saying to him, "Man, the climax is coming. You will not be able to keep your murderous impulses in hand more than another ten months, another ten days." That's why we shrink before any fanatic who comes up to us and says, the end of the world is near. What we know is, the end of *their* world is near, and we don't want the end of their world to involve the end of our world. That's no fun.

PART II: SYMPATHY FOR THE DEVIL

All right. Here are a few questions from Rolling Stone. *"Does Mailer see his socio-literary work as literature inasmuch as it is done not in response to a creative urge but in response to an assignment and to meet a deadline?"*

Literature is not a temple. Literature is an act. If you're a working literary man, it's obviously analogous to a sexual act. You're better on some days than on others. You have a relation to that act, to wit, you can have one-night stands, you can be married, have a passionate relation, a skillful relation, a depressed relation. Some of the worthiest books ever written were done in a state of constant depression. Some of the happiest pieces of literature were finished in six weeks. Stendhal was one of the world's great quick writers. Writing to a deadline is good for—very often is not only good but superior for—people who really can't write without some external sense of urgency that if they don't get the work done something awful is going to occur.

Dostoyevsky, after his first novel, never wrote a book without a deadline. In fact, it could be argued that his books got done because of the deadline.

Yeah. The answer is simple. If you're writing for deadline, the odds against doing literature increase slightly, just as if you're going to a whorehouse. If you go to a whorehouse, the odds against falling in love are slightly greater. But given the bottomless sentimentality of mankind, they're not that much greater. You can do a piece on assignment, for the bucks, and end up adoring it much more than your secret conception of what a grand piece of literature should be.

The only thing that's important about it is, there's not necessarily anything terrible about working for money. I mean, writers, God bless us, have become the saints of the 20th century. You know, we're the only people left who can't work for money. Of course, some do, you know. Vonnegut doesn't work for money; I do. Vidal doesn't work for money; I do. Updike wouldn't dream of picking up a paycheck. I'm the only one who does.

They're all making more money than you are.

I'd suspect they are. Nabokov, for example, is beyond money, but he's making more. Solzhenitsyn, God bless him! There's a man we have to respect, and he's worth six million dollars. I have to admit I'm terribly pleased with that, because what would they say about me if I were worth six million bucks?

Well, here's another Rolling Stone *question. "Does he feel any awkwardness about his flat-out lunge for money?" I think we've pretty much covered this.*

We can talk about it in a different way here. One of the reasons I'm engaged in a rolling flat-out lunge for money in stone seriousness about getting that paycheck together, is that I am one of the few wits in American life who managed to find himself in a state of marriage four and now five times. And I have come to one profound notion about women's liberation, which is this. That no one is going to take women's liberation seriously until women recognize that they will not be thought of as equals in the secret privacy of men's most private mental parts until they eschew alimony. My four ex-wives, who are all splendid, intelligent, independent women, with marvelous possibilities for their own career, who though they spoke of nothing in the years they were married to me but of damage I had done to their career, have nonetheless succeeded in the years since in living somehow without a career, but on alimony. I am still earning money for their support which is cool. After all, there are a number of people I owe money to.

But since I'm a gambling man, I'd be willing to bet that the man who composed this question about my going on a flat-out lunge after money is himself a fellow, let the witnesses around ROLLING STONE bear testimony to this, is indeed a capital fellow who has never been caught reaching for a check. If I'm wrong, please inform.

One other question from Rolling Stone. *"A specific question on his new, one-million-dollar, three-year-contract, epic novel. Does he think that so much before-the-fact pressure will tend to influence his work as opposed to* Marilyn *which grew out of a little tiny assignment?"*

A little tiny assignment! [*Laughter*] Okay. Here's the answer. Nothing can be little which is described as tiny. . . . The contract with Little, Brown is not for a book which will be written in three years, that was a piece of misreporting. I said seven years and it was reported as several. Actually the contract is for 700,000 words, 500,000 to 700,000 words over five to seven years. And the announcement of this contract will do little good to the book. The last story I ever wanted to see in the papers was any announcement of my literary plans, projects and payments.

Let's talk a bit more about the women's movement. I admit many of the women I find most exciting, most impressive, have tendencies toward women's liberation. But I don't think they understand what they call male chauvinism. I love women who have great character and spunk and are not content with being put in any simple category. But I fear the real thrust of this movement is to demean love and attraction between the sexes. A man who loves women is a pig. It's an antiromantic notion. It's sexual technology.

Hey, Stratton, this isn't the way you were talking a year ago! I mean, the women are getting to you. They're getting to me and getting to you. Let's face it, they're winning their war.

You think so. They're winning their battle, perhaps. Meanwhile we're all losing our war. What women's liberation does is diminish sexuality.

Well—I agree that the tendency is to diminish sexuality. I'm not pretending to know whether it's going to diminish sexuality for *all* time. But I think the immediate effect has been to take something out of it all. That's right in the need of the century. It's still a technological century and too much instinctive sex mucks up the machine.

There are two ways a technological society can weaken sex, through huge puritanism like the Russians, or you can do it through huge license—pornography, a sexual revolution, androgyny, gay lib, women's lib—huge license is even desirable to technology if it'll consume sexual energy and keep it at a low fucked-out level. I mean, what's the use of being able to make love to anyone, any man or any woman, if finally your incentive is taken away altogether? If the hunt is gone? The danger? The rebellion? The achievement? If you now ram it home to a woman and show her where she lives, what are you doing? Naught but revealing the secret boar in your asshole.

"My cunt is my chariot."

Well, God bless them. You know, their cunt is their chariot. No one's ever going to be able to write about the way in which my generation grew up, you know, with this secret, profoundly sentimental adoration of the subtle superiority of women to ourselves. That marvelous sense of a woman's wit, that sly sense of the point which arrived so naturally into their thought. That sense of audience a woman provides. That notion we had of ourselves as audience to a woman. That tenderness. That respect for the imminence of a mystery so intimate, so nice, so near, so funny. We were so much stronger than women, and yet not at all. They were so much more powerful than we were, and yet never at all—never in any way. We lived as such romantic and sentimental equals.

Now we've come into another world where we recognize that they lied, they cheated, they worked overtime for us as slavies, to give us this lovely sustaining notion, but all the while their egos were being rotted, their guts were filled with caustic, they were left with the dishes, they were left with the diapers. Left with the pale smell of water and grease and the slightly more unfortunate smell of formula milk and baby shit. And saw their careers going down into dull, somewhat incomprehensible dialogs with plumbers. While we came back and bayed at the moon, and said, you do not support me sufficiently, woman, to enable me to reach the moon. You know?

And then a couple of guys reach the moon, and some guys after them, and they all talk like women libertarians when they get there. In jargon. In a total, perfect, hermetic language. We'd looked upon these men in awe. These guys were cats, they were going out and doing things that really would stop up our stomach. And they had done it, they did it.

Yet they were sexless.

They weren't sexless. They were women's libbies. What no one will ever understand is, the first guys to reach the moon— they were men, you know, in terms of bravery. More man than

I for sure, maybe more than you, Stratton. They were men. But they had the minds of women's libbies. They were working for the team. They thought of only one thing, can't betray the team, cannot allow an alien idea to ever enter their eyeball, their nose, their mouth, their ear or their fingertips long enough to disrupt the ideological system.

A romantic idea is an alien idea to them.
    I don't mean a romantic idea. I mean any idea that's not in the system. You could have an anti-romantic idea, they still wouldn't let it enter. They have nothing against romance.

Women's liberation is ultimately a team effort?
    Women's liberation is an astronaut system.

[The sun is coming up when we finish taping the first session. Later the same day, we are sitting in Mailer's office, a small room off the library with desk and tables piled high—books, manuscripts, letters, magazines and papers, heaps of mail. When I ask Mailer if he wants to talk about his novel and "literary objectives, where he's at now," he groans, shifts in his seat and smiles.]
    No, you know, I don't like to talk about what I'm doing now, or what I'm planning to do. . . . But I'll tell you what we'll do, I'll tell you what's been misreported about the novel.

Fine, then I'll just splice it in somewhere.
    Whatever. . . . Well, in the first place, the book is not the story of a Jewish family taken from ancient Egyptian times through the present and on to the future. I'm hardly a family novelist. But the book will deal with time, past, present and future times.

Does it begin in ancient Egypt?
    Some early scenes in the book may take place in Egypt, yes,

but that's not to say the book begins there and inches along chronologically. No, a lot has to do with the question of time. . . . Look, just say it's an ambitious novel, as ambitious as Proust's *Remembrance of Things Past*. Now I'm not saying it will be as good as *Remembrance of Things Past*, only that it's as ambitious an undertaking. And I'm going to have to turn my habits inside out in order to write it, going to have to get rid of this speed fever and settle in for years of work on the same book.

Dick Goodwin mentioned that he thought one of the great attributes you have as a writer is your critical sense of other writers' abilities. You know we've seen it all from Advertisements for Myself, *when you wrote "Quick and Expensive Evaluations on the Talent in the Room." Then there was another very good piece in* Cannibals and Christians—"Some Children of the Goddess." *How do you feel about people who are writing now? How do you feel about Kesey, for instance?*

Well, here's where we get into trouble. I have to confess I haven't read Kesey. I haven't read a lot of people I think are probably pretty good. I read a page of Kesey's once, from *One Flew over the Cuckoo's Nest*—actually read the first two pages, and I thought, this guy's good. That didn't mean I was going to go on reading him. Maybe I'm not a lover of literature, but a practitioner of it. While nothing irritates people more than when I use an analogy from prizefighting, nonetheless, if I were a professional prizefighter, I might see a guy moving in a gym and I'd say, that guy can go. I only need that much of a look to know, that guy can go. That doesn't mean I want to rush in the ring and box him. Fuck that noise. If I go in the ring to box him, I'm using up something I want to be paid money for.

That was your feeling with Kesey? The guy can go?

My feeling is, you don't read a good writer for too little.

Never. You read him at the point in your life where there's a reason to read him. You know, people sometimes come up to me and say, "I don't know if I can talk to you because I never read a book of yours," and I can see by the way they handle themselves that they're intelligent, mannered, have one style or another and will be amusing to know. I'm usually delighted when someone hasn't read my work. That's as it should be. That doesn't mean I don't want people to read my work or that I'm not pleased with people who come up and say they've read all my work. But, there's a virtue to not reading someone's work until the time comes. It's like meeting people you really want to meet in a bar. That's the best way ever to meet anyone, by chance, and if you have a marvelous evening with them, that saves 20 social back-and-forths.

All right. You did meet Kesey in Los Angeles.

I saw him again in Oregon when I spoke out there, and spent a good hour with him. And, you know, he's a man, there's no question about that, and it's nice engaging in conversation in his house. His house has a presence. His people have presence. His friends are good. That doesn't mean I then rush back and read his book. What does it mean to say you recognize someone as a man—it doesn't mean that you recognize him as *the perfect man*.

I said to myself, Kesey's got a fine thing here, a bit of a blank there, just as he's looking at me and reading me in that fashion. Finally, we did not, you know, take a little blood off our thumbs and press them together and become brothers. That was not there between us . . . brothers. That again is as it should be, you can't have more than a few brothers in your life. The reason I'm going into this peroration about all the books I haven't read is because I obviously feel defensive, I just don't read my contemporaries.

How about Thomas Pynchon.

Well, I can't read Thomas Pynchon. I can't read him because I think, well, I think we're polar. His literary values are opposite to mine. The only book of his I ever finished was *The Crying of Lot 49*. I couldn't forgive him for the end of it. I felt he abdicated from the book. I feel that with all his talents, which are by whatever measure not negligible, I think he doesn't understand that you get killed in the name of literature in more ways than one. I think Pynchon's idea may be that you should die working at your desk; don't leave that desk for too little. I think you have to take the chance of getting killed on vacation.

Exactly the way Nathanael West got killed.

Yes, yes. I suppose the worst single thing I could say about Pynchon is that he's a capsuloid. Every time I'm reading his work I feel as if I'm surrounded by the semitransparent ribbing of an enormous plastic capsule.

Among all these people, then, is there anyone who really turns you on?

I've been a practicing literary man for many years. I've known a great many writers in one fashion or another. I do not think I can name a single novelist who is one of my close friends. I am not so certain that any other novelist—there would be ten or 20 that I would talk of as being in the league we're all in—could name another novelist as his best friend. There's something about writing novels that is not altogether different from being a Mafia don. A certain dull respect is paid across the horizon. We don't really worry about who is considered the best. We're too busy keeping our own operation going. I won't wake up in the morning and say, oh my God, is John Barth possibly a better novelist than I am? My whole feeling is that God or the Devil is finally going to bring us in for accounting, and he or she will have a clearer idea of it than John or I are going to have. In fact, when the moment comes, God may say, "Fuck that noise, have a drink."

The center of the problem, in replying to these questions, is that you have to keep shaping yourself up to the newspaper idea of you that people have formed. Which any interviewer finally feels obliged, willy-nilly, to pay attention to. It's fun to deal with. That's the way people know me. For instance, at Princeton a few days ago, I was talking at a class Larry King is giving on the Literature of Fact and a kid asked how it felt to be a commodity on a coffee table. I thought enough of the question to answer because it came out of the quintessential moronic animus of the journalistic mind. I replied that that wasn't the sort of label I stuck in my head, I didn't think of myself as a commercial object. Rather I thought of myself as an ongoing set of abilities and vices which finally looked at the mirror in this fashion: how much to discipline, how much to dissipation?

I'm interested in your reaction to the Patricia Hearst kidnapping. The Symbionese Liberation Army is the one group that's done anything really revolutionary since the Weathermen. And even the Weathermen were less radical because their program was more abstract.

We can agree that the Symbionese Liberation Army is more radical than anything since I don't know when. You might have to go back to the Bolsheviks before the first World War to find a point of comparison, back to Robin Hood to find something as extraordinary as this. Robbing from the rich to pay the poor. But I find it impossible to say more at this point, because I don't know how it's going to end. At this point, where I'm speaking, which is in late March of '74, we don't know whether Patricia Hearst was kidnapped or, as much gossip would have it, is a member of that army. Or has been converted to a member. We also don't know if it's a black army or a white army. I've heard gossip that there are two black members and any number of young white middle-class kids in that army. They may be much like the kids who, when they went to high school three and four years ago, were—according to Dotson Rader—talking about killing Lindsay because he was too good a mayor; the only way to shock people was to make them realize that no matter how good you were in this system, it wouldn't work. The better you were, the faster you were killed. The idea was to break down the system. It's possible these kids came out of that mood.

We do know there's never been a kidnapping where everybody has kept their inner discipline for so many weeks, did not kill the kidnappee, did not break apart, did not flake off to the police, but stayed together. What kind of incredible group is this? What sort of internal communion do they have? But we are at the point where the story is not resolved. When it blows up, it may prove to be the noblest or ugliest of stories. We don't know yet. So I don't see how one can begin to render judgments before one possesses some favorable proportion of the facts. My pride is that I'm not one of those people whose pride is that there's no question they can't answer in ten seconds.

We don't begin to know yet whether this is an epic, a tragedy, or if Patricia Hearst has been with them from the beginning, the highest species of family comedy the civilized world has encountered. We may have to recognize that super-realistic-Shakespearean times may soon be upon us.

I think the question is whether we still believe in the possibility for a revolution in this country.

Let's rephrase it. Do we believe in the ability to—in the possibility of irrigating the separate and total pollutions of our lives?

Revolution used to be presented to us as the cure for wickedness, greed, selfishness, stratification of the social system, the stultification of human possibility—revolution was going to overcome all this. Revolution was going to open up a future in which people could begin to learn—to use these corny, deadening phrases—to live with one another, thrive with one another, move out and create a world which was better, one for another, than any world we'd known. We've come to a point now where we can begin to recognize how many bad things happened because we did not have a revolution. Pollution is entering every last orifice of existence. So the answer to revolution now, is, you know—the terrible questions we may be coming down to—is it better to let all of us, all billions of us on earth, die slowly of various collective polluted diseases, see, but die quietly, with a little style and grace, with decorum. No one's ever come to grips with the profound human need for decorum at the end. I mean, we have to pay some respect to it. There may be a reason for it. We don't know.

Nixon has a sense about decorum.

Nixon's final plea may be, let me live and die with a little decorum. But let's not spend time there. The point I make is that there's a profound human desire to die with decorum. On the last night we have on earth, let it be a quiet night. Maybe that has something to do with the karma of the cosmos. Maybe we're supposed to die on this earth in order to create the karma of another world. It may not be that we're spineless, or that we die not with a bang but a whimper, so much as that we die making small sounds because that's as it should be. Or the exact opposite can be true—that this decorum, this apathy, is the most awful single thing ever to happen in all of every conception of Christendom and beyond. So we may die finally having a sense of absolute consternation, of horror because we didn't do enough. It may be that the last answer for revolution is to cut through the pollution. At that point, you see, nihilism begins once again to have its day. Except, one thing I know about nihilism—every nihilist I've ever known and lived with and dealt with, including myself—nihilism intensifies pollution.

The core of it is choosing one's side. Obviously I lean on the side of cutting through the pollution. But I've lived, you know—what does it mean to live to be 51 years old—it means that you no longer stand in total, hard-on, erect straight right-on possession of the answer.

At 51 you don't lean toward that, you're saying?

I lean on the side of cutting through the pollution.

You take the hard-on position then?

I take the hard-on position. I am on the side of left hard-ons and right hard-ons.

It's finally a spiritual question though. I mean, we don't know whether God or the Devil is on the side of pollution.

I tend to think that neither God nor the Devil is on the side of pollution. I know enough about the Devil to know that he has less ability to breathe than God, and so could hardly be on the side of pollution. We have to contemplate the notion that God and the Devil were in one game and got farted out by a bigger game. Technology comes out of impulses that may have very little to do with God and the Devil. Technology's almost a visitor from afar.

It's always seemed to me that technology was a perfect tool for the Devil.

Well, you're expecting technology *is* the Devil. I've come to decide that may be too simple and comfortable a notion. I mean, a devil's idea of fun is not technology. It's to have a good woman kiss his ass. That's where the Devil's living. What does he want to do with machines?

Technology may come out of another impulse altogether, out of the notion that there's no such thing as God and the Devil. Now our heads are beginning to spin before the complexities of this—but what I lean to, and argue for, is that the house-cleaning may have to begin in the highest temple of them all. Which is in the physics of energy particles. Where is the physicist who rises in this land to say that the little particles of matter and antimatter that they are dealing with are creatures rather than bits and pieces of information?

On this note, let us end our peregrinations for the night. I'd rather talk about these things tomorrow.

[It is Mailer's idea to include a discussion of rock music. I supply the records, a near-to-complete collection of Rolling Stones albums up through Goat's Head Soup, *since we decide to focus on one group to see how their music has changed in ten years.*

[Mailer's wife, Carol, is a jazz singer, so their stereo equipment is top quality. The only problem is neither Mailer nor I know for certain what all the various toggle switches and speaker controls do. Maggie, Mailer's seventh child, is asleep upstairs, and there are others in the house sleeping, so we're trying to make sure all the extension speakers are turned off. We listen to the music at a bit above medium volume.

[Sitting in his wicker chair and holding a glass of rum and tonic, Mailer listens to the music intently with his eyes closed. We've played at least two albums when Carol comes in from the movies and tells us that in all our flipping of switches we turned on the outdoor speakers and have been playing Aftermath *to the neighbors.]*

All right, let's start by talking about the music we just heard. Truman Capote was hired by Rolling Stone *to cover the Rolling Stones concert when they were here the last time to tour the States. And he finally didn't do the article because he said the Stones had no mystery for him. But there's a lot of mystery in Jagger's personality and in the personality of the group as a whole.*

There's something unsatisfying about Jagger. We must have listened to two hours of music. Jagger's always promising so much more than he delivers. You know, finally he's in a sinister bag—he is certainly of all, if we take the three, four, five, six major rock groups in the last ten years, he has been the one who was the most sinister. Yet he's finally not terrifying. Maybe that's what Capote meant, I don't know.

Jagger himself, or his music?

His music. I don't know anything about him. I think that the Beatles, you know, can hit eight bars in *Sgt. Pepper* that are more frightening, even though they're not sinister. The Beatles had more of a sense of powers they could summon by playing the wrong note at a given moment. It's as if they're more terrified by music than Jagger. Jagger's terribly spoiled. There's all that muttering in the background: "Oh, no God, you won't break this heart of stone."* What a threat. Beyond that constant dirge, beyond the throatiness which makes you think he's riding on the rims, through all that electric masturbation, you know, all that sound of distant musketry, every drumbeat, there's still a mountain of bullshit. It's not getting in and saying, I'm going to kill you, motherfucker. It's not saying, I'm here to call upon Satan. It pretends to. Some of his music I find, you know, marvelously promising. But it's irritating as hell to listen to for two hours because you keep waiting for the great payoff, and it never comes.

---

*"Heart of Stone" by Mick Jagger and Keith Richards. ©1965, Abko Music Co.

But again there's a kind of bullying that I've always distrusted in rock. Which is, it doesn't take big balls to have a big electric guitar and a huge amplifying system and 50,000 American corporations that they're all sneering at, working overtime to amplify them. You know, it's a little bit like some politician that you despise saying, I represent the people. He only represents his power in his microphone and his media, his vested electronic office.

But let's look at the Stones in context. The Stones have stayed at the top, they're still the most interesting group playing together. They're all good musicians. Even the Beatles, as musicians, with the possible exception of George Harrison, weren't very exciting. Ringo Starr could never compare with Charlie Watts for drumming ability.

Their drummer's incredibly good. In fact, I think their drummer's half of them. Because you've got all that caterwauling, you've got all those half-heard threats, that sense of sullen curses always riding in the background, you've got that sense of disarray, sense of mama with her nerves broken looking for her fix. You got all that. But what keeps it all together is you got this great big driving beat. That you can make anything you want. You can dream up a Third World coming through, Africa rising. There's a—the tension of the music is that one world's dissolving into a kind of marvelous— I mean, their comic gifts are superb. You really get this feeling of androgynous family, and androgynous family relations, like maybe it's never been done. All that's first-rate. I'm criticizing them at, you know, what I consider the highest level. But finally at the highest level, they are fucking disappointing. They depend on noise. You know, we listened to them not at top high. At middle high. And they don't make it.

If I yell my fucking head off, if I shriek in your ear, you're going to be impressed. You're going to be impressed with nothing else but that I'm breaking down. If you're weak, you'll call the cops. We're built on a culture of middle sound, so top-high sound has to make it. It's like a lot of that painting which consists of taking a billboard a hundred feet by twenty feet and putting one color on it. That's a statement. And large noise is a statement. But not all self-expression is art.

Take a song like "Sympathy for the Devil." You have to go a long way—Bob Dylan's probably the only other one, plus some songs from the Beatles—you have to go a long way before you get lines as interesting in rock music as, "Just as every cop is a criminal and all the sinners saints." [*]

What's splendid, what's new about that? Dostoyevsky used to go into an epileptic fit he grew so bored with that notion.

Well, there's nothing new about it, but compared to most rock lyrics, the Stones have at least considered Dostoyevsky.
I don't think these lyrics compare to Dylan's. I don't think they even try to—I think, in fact, I'd almost go the other way. I'd say that Jagger's lyric is interminably repetitive in order to allow for that captivating tension between the guttiness in his voice and the whine. To play that back and forth, you don't really want too good a lyric. Dylan's voice is thinner. At times I find it nasal to the point where I can do without it. There's something a little boring about a man who comes from a fine Jewish family in Minneapolis sounding like an Oklahoma Okie.

You know, Dylan is . . . not Johnny Cash. So I find that part of it a little boring. Dylan's voice is much less exciting to me than his lyrics, his lyrics are superb. Selden Rodman was the first to say this, but I think Dylan may prove to be our greatest

---

*©1968, Abko Music Inc.

lyric poet of this period. Like many another lyric poet, he can't necessarily read his own lyrics. With Dylan, what I think you feel is that it's the poetry that carries the song, not the singer.

With Jagger, it's the reverse. Jagger has got this marvelous sense of the day in which a family breaks up. The son throws acid in the mother's face, the mother stomps the son's nuts in, and then the fat cousin comes and says, what is everybody fighting for, let's have dinner. And they sit down, the son has no nuts left, the mother's face is scarred, but they go on and, you know, British family life continues. Jagger's got that like no one else's ever had it. If he'd been a writer he would have been one of the best. But that marvelous quality isn't caught in the lyrics so much as in the ensemble of everything, sound, instruments, everything.

And his voice.

His voice first.

I don't know if you can find another rock group capable of coming up with a song like "Sympathy for the Devil."

"Sympathy for the Devil," I felt, was arch, and much too self-conscious. I couldn't quite catch the words and that's one of the things about Jagger that's always suspect to me. When you play on the edge of the articulation of words it's because you're trying to do two things at once. I did hear him at one point wailing about the Russian Revolution—that the Devil was there at the planning of the Russian Revolution and, you know, that's news. No good Christian ever thought of that before. That, I thought, was finally on the edge of the revolting. You don't, you know, you don't infuse a bunch of dumb, spaced-out, highly sexed working kids with a little historical culture while you're singing. Come on! I decided Jagger must have picked up a magazine article about the Russian Revolution the day before he wrote the words. But, you know, there's more profundity in "Eleanor Rigby" than there is in "Sympathy for the Devil."

I mean, there are a lot of vulgar plays in "Sympathy for the Devil," gay-aim for game. A lot of dull choices were made. I expected to be knocked down by "Sympathy for the Devil," and I wasn't. I think maybe it's historically significant. It may be the first song that invokes the Devil in I don't know when. You might have to go back to black masses in the Middle Ages to find a lyric that invokes the Devil. But that doesn't mean it's good any more than *The Exorcist* is. Which is to say, it's phenomenal as an index of the time. What impresses us is not how good the artist is, but that he's right at the place where people are going to react. So Jagger anticipated, just as Blatty did, that there's subterranean belief in the Devil about ready to emerge. Given any kind of encouragement, it comes charging through.

Which brings us to Satanism. The Satanism of shit at the highest level. Which may introduce us to Gore Vidal. I noticed that when Gore was writing about bestsellers in the *New York Review of Books* a year ago, he started off with the following sentence: "Shit has its own integrity." Now, that was too good an idea for Vidal to claim it. He immediately passed it off on an unnamed Hollywood producer, when anyone who knows anything about writers knows it was his own idea. But he was not about to introduce it into the *New York Review of Books* as his premier presentation of an intellectual novelty. So good old Hollywood got blamed again.

"Shit has its own integrity" is the standard of Satan. It's his escutcheon. It's his flag. He appeals to people in their fashion. He says, you've been rejected, you've been wasted by the system, passed over, yet are more redolent, more interesting, more sexy, more incredible, more funky, more filled with undeliverables that have been delivered than anything they got going out there. And, for years, the Devil has fought a desperate uphill battle.

But by now, when we got those superhighways, with that gas, and the whole world's getting to look more and more like the Jersey flats, given modern life up front, the suburbs, the smell of the gas, smell of plastic in every home, carpets smell of the plastic and the kids grow up licking plastic, play with Playdough which has that smell between cheap perfume and deodorant; when you think of the prevalence not of death in every one of our phenomena but of the void—of the presence of void—in every aspect of successful life today; when you think of what it means to have arrived and to go on a grand tour of the world, which means that you travel first class on a plane which is an envelope presenting its concept of the void, you get off that airplane into an airport which in turn presents its concept of the void absolutely equal to the airplane or you go through a smog-filled superhighway to that city which looks like every other city, some of them are better than others, some are worse—Moscow, I hear, looks like Washington entering its terminal cancer . . . you then go out for your pleasures which are not as brilliant as they were in the depths of the boredom of the Victorian period; there's no such thing as a thrill for anyone alive any longer. You take all this, all this degradation of the void; because we all move around with a profound sense of degradation these days and under it there's the Devil calling, saying I'm shit, I'm the integrity of shit, I'm everything that you've wasted, I'm all that rich, crazy passionate fuck guck funky possibility, I'm that other culture. And of course there's a profound desire to move over to that.

Sooner or later we sense that either God has been aced and is off the board, or if God is still there, then he's with the astronauts and he's made a pact with technology, because God is a most ambitious general who's going to take us to other worlds and we're going to have to get leeched out in the process, maybe forever—if God's a general first and a humanitarian second. Or we're going to have to go through the dread possibility of being almost totally leeched out. That's the possibility if God is still with us. Or we have the other dire possibility that God has always been Satan and the god who pretended to be God was a visitor from some foreign place who introduced technology on this earth. We don't know, we simply don't know.

Finally, we don't begin to have enough knowledge of what primitive societies were like to guess whether the most demonic and orgiastic manifestations of their rites and celebrations were life giving, as we try to comprehend life, or Satan. The conventional notion of Satanism always has been that one surrenders one's soul to pleasure and is thereby forever destroyed. There's also a common notion, always unstated in Christianity but implicit in it, that when you give your soul to the Devil, you lose your karmic reincarnation, you're off the board.

Now, in this 20th century where our senses, our souls, are being leeched out, where we're all entering a void, the horror of modern life is that there is no horror. So we begin to wonder whether selling the soul to the Devil may not be a life-giving transaction. That's the underlying terror of modern life.

As opposed to what we've thought of as being belief in God?

Well, belief in God, by the measure of this talk, is belief in the society, that is, belief that whatever else may be finally dreadful about society, society still remains some sort of enormously imperfect vehicle of God. You know, God may be profoundly displeased with society, but society is nonetheless there to bring us along some part of that route He desires.

The Devil has always been associated with materialism. There was always, you know, the idea of the temptation of Christ with riches and the wealth of the world.

That doesn't deny what I was saying at all. The integrity of shit. What are riches but the integrity of shit?

So isn't it conceivable that what we might have done is, collectively, sold our souls to the Devil a long time ago; say in the beginning of the 19th century, before the Industrial Revolution?

If we sold our soul to the Devil centuries ago in order to prosper materially, in this 20th century we're not happy materially. That is, we're not gorging like Romans. Whatever we are, we are certainly not Romans. We are prospering electronically. And suffering materially in all the voids and stinks of plastic and pollution.

And lost our karma too, sold our karma along with our soul. We've sold our opportunity for transcendence. That's why we're terminal. You see what I mean? I think that if anything the Devil is winning. I think he's winning and I think he's gloating because he has more control at this point. I think he is the prince of this world.

That's one idea I hold. What I pose against it immediately is that the Devil is also miserable, because finally the air conditioner is not the Devil's paradise.

True. But there are those other alternatives we may get into in the next 20, 30 years, you know. That when people get sick of technology and air conditioners and all the sterile dead aspects of plastic, they're going to revert more and more to Satanism and to orgies, to bloodletting and to shit, all those things—

All right. But ask yourself: All those things you're talking about, that you just named, are they equal to technology?

Are they equal to technology?

Or are they the opposite?

The opposite.

It seems to me you ought to have your Devil, just for the sake of this little matter, one place or the other.

Yes, I said that I think technology may be a tool of the Devil, a means to an end, the end being the complete leeching out of our souls.

To drive people toward shit and blood.

Right. Right. This is Satan's cunning. In a technological and spiritually starved society, he may gain complete control.

Well, let me think about that. And have a drink.

Okay. Just to continue with this idea, it may be that technology is a transitional stage as far as the Devil is concerned. I've got to believe God is more opposed to the dead spirit of technology than the Devil would be. Because I think that the Old Testament is antitechnological. Certainly there's an awful lot of blood and horror in the Old Testament.

You just revealed yourself as a fundamentalist.

Well, maybe I am. But then it goes on to the Apocalypse, a bloody and antitechnological vision, if you will. I think that the Devil may have said to himself, well, it looks to me like the only way I'm ever going to win final control over mankind is to offer them all those things they seem to want most, material comforts, wealth, prosperity and lack of suffering, to eliminate suffering from the world. People don't want to suffer, they immediately reach for a pill, mother's little helper.

So, my notion, anyway, is that technology, science, pollution, whatever, is finally probably a tool of the Devil that is going to starve and deaden the soul to such a degree that man will reach out for the funkiness then for the horror—back to Charlie Manson.

I think you're passing over too much. To begin with, there's no reason to equate science and technology any more than we put art and bestsellerdom together. After all, there's no reason to assume a bestseller is a work of art at a lower level. That may be a legitimate way to characterize a bestseller, or the opposite may be true, that a bestseller is the precise opposite of art, and to the degree the work is a bestseller, it is meretricious.

Technology may be the opposite of science, then?

Well, I think there's much reason to believe that it is. Science, for most of its history, was essentially a poetic endeavor. Every metaphor, if you stop to think about it, is an equation. If you say, "the sparrow is on the wing," that's a scientific remark, it's a way of saying that the center of essence in the sparrow is within the wing, the sparrow is *on* the wing. It's a way of saying that the sparrow exists in two manifestations at once, body and flight, just as light consists of waves and particles. The sparrow is on the wing. As you start to bear down on the language, you begin to feel the very vibrancy of the wing. The condition of being in two states at once. The sparrow is *on* the wing. You can fix on that point endlessly because it's a metaphor, an equation, a moment of balance. Originally, science had that quality, that its fundamental recognitions were, dare I say it?—poetic.

It was an art at that point?

Absolutely an art. Technology is finally, I would suggest, a tradition, and a dull one. A statistical tradition. Technology derives from General Ulysses S. Grant, who said that if I bring enough men and enough ammunition to bear at one point on this line, and if I don't care how many troops of mine get killed, and I just keep pursuing this, if my ego is finally larger than any question that's presented to me, then I am obliged to triumph because I do not care. And he won.

Grant changed the nature of war. Before that, war always consisted of the obligation to win with a certain minimum of skill and grace. There was a code of war. Robert E. Lee subscribed to that code, he believed that you did not win battles at any price, that you didn't lose half your army to win a battle. Because at that point something dreadful would happen. Grant, having to contend with a miserable drafted army, people who did not want to fight the war—the Civil War as far as the North was concerned was not too unlike the war in Viet Nam, in the sense that the troops had absolutely no desire to fight—Grant just kept putting in more and more bodies to blast their way through the noise.

Now that's technology. Technology does not really care what happens in the aftermath, it wishes to succeed on this point. It does not even need to have theory in order to proceed, let alone art. It will push its way through. It is an ego manifestation, and—all right. There's nothing in this that says it's therefore opposed to the notion of the Devil. The Devil may indeed be ego. But we have to draw back just enough to ask ourselves one further question, and it comes up to me as follows. Where is God in all this?

Well, God may be the loss of ego.

No, no, no. Face into technology. What's God's relation to technology? Do you believe in God?

Yes.

Do you believe God is not dead at all? Is very much alive?

Yes.

God, I would take it, knowing you fairly well, is a principle of some judicious mixture of courage and love?

Right. Absolutely. And harmony, a certain kind of harmony, a physical harmony with life and one's place in life and in the cosmos that is opposed to technology.

God, as far as I'm concerned, is mystery, and anything opposed to mystery, that tries to answer out all the mystery of life, is anti-God. Technology wants to eradicate mystery. I think at this point if God exists, He exists as a revolutionary, He's got to be a violent and passionate spiritual revolutionary, because He's out of grace at this stage, very much out of grace.

Not out of grace. Out of favor.

Out of favor.

Out of favor of what? The universe . . .

No, with mankind, with technological man.

We still separate here. Because I think we have to face the possibility that technology is a third force, come to us from the cosmos. That it may have very little to do with God and the Devil.

May be separate altogether?

Virtually separate. To go back to one of my oldest and firmest ideas, what if the universe is finally a series of conceptions which are at war with one another? And what we think of as God is only one conception of this universe, out there, at war with other conceptions? What if technology is an invasion of this earth from without? Because technology gives us no evidence whatsoever of having any sympathy for the nature of our world, nothing to do with our desires for an earth on which we can dwell.

No, certainty not. Its aim would seem to be to make the planet uninhabitable in the name of making us all more comfortable. What is a higher standard of living if we are all dying?

Well, if at that point—you see—at this point we're reduced to speculation. Either the Devil invited technology here or, what I find more interesting, God entered into a dread compact. At a certain point he decided that Satan had so invaded affairs on earth that God could never begin to lead man up and outward to the stars. So some compact had to be made with technology. Technology, that spirit come to visit us from afar. If we dare to personify our divinities, there's nothing extraordinary about such speculation. Evil often triumphs, because good makes a mediocre compact out of some dire necessity. Where we're far apart is, I don't believe in an omnipotent god. I believe in a god who's like us only more so. Who has a vision of existence of which we are very much a part. Because we will either fulfill that vision of existence, or we will fail God.

No, I can't agree. God is perfection. I don't actually believe in an omnipotent god as much as in a god whose nature is finally unknowable, as is perfection.

The idea that the nature of God is unknowable, at this point, when the world's dying in the exudate of all its diseases, is a cop-out.

Not if you think of God in terms of a quality, a state of being toward which you're constantly trying to become closer, to get more in harmony with, as an ongoing struggle.

You've been saying that you want to talk about drugs a little, and I think they're related to this question in a fashion. I think drugs bear the same relation to mysticism as technology to science.

We're coming to learn that most of the world's mystics, in one way or another, have or had their drug. The mystical societies most mystics have been revering for centuries did have, in one fashion or another, their drug ritual. So, it isn't so simple a matter as saying that if you take a drug then you're a technologist and not a scientist. It does mean that there is a use of drugs among mystics and mystical societies which was reverential, ceremonial, sacramental.

The use of drugs today, if we're going to employ an analogy, is again comparable to the war in Viet Nam: If you have a great deal of money to spend and very few results to show, and if you can't find the enemy, well then, goddamnit, says Barry Goldwater, burn down the fucking foliage. Scorch those gooks, get them out of there. Denude the land and you will find what is there. That is what the allegedly best generation of our young are doing to their minds. They're saying, if I can't find the idea I was looking for yesterday, I am going to take twice as much tonight.

I'll take a thousand more mics of LSD and burn down the foliage of my mind.

Burn down the foliage of my mind to find some of those ideas I can feel running around in there. It's a military operation, it's technological.

I don't think drugs are going to find God or the Devil. I think what they're going to create is the scorched earth of consumed karma. I believe, you know, that one has to be as reverential about drugs as about sex. The mark of an utter idiot, in my mind, is to find, let's say he's a man who falls passionately in love with a woman. He finds this divine cunt and he not only fucks the hell out of her but fucks the hell out of himself until his balls are as wet as gravel. You know, he is grinding his ass up over the stones to get in one more fuck for the ego. He's gone over. He is a gassed out, farted out goose. That is our drug addict. That's what the drug addict is doing to mysticism. If God is a rabbit, the drug addict is trying to kill that rabbit with a thousand flails. All he's doing is knocking off his own toes. Not to mention the ricochet on his nuts.

In religious discussion, when we start to talk about this tripartite nature of the confusion, God, Devil, and technology, and what is with whom, it may serve us to take one little look at cosmology today. One notion that the physicists presented to us about fifty years ago was the idea of the expanding universe.

The galaxies were traveling outward. There's reason to decide that we live in a universe which expands and contracts. Curious, isn't it?

More than that, a universe in which stars expand and contract. Stars exhibit red light in their spectrum and blue-red lights as they expand, no surprise to any of us humans, and blue as they turn cold. As they contract more and more, they turn black. They become the essence of matter, become so compressed, so black, that a star which was once a million miles in diameter is now two miles in diameter, a mile in diameter. It becomes so compressed that finally it is the size of your thumbnail and weighs more than the sun. At least, that is what cosmological evidence and theory has brought certain physicists to thinking.

At that point, there's a gravitational mass so intense that it pulls in everything to it. It pulls in light. Einstein delivered the general theory of relativity, which was that light would be bent by gravity. Indeed it was, as the famous experiment in 1921 or 1922, was it 1919? showed—that light from Mercury in an eclipse was bent by the sun. Now, when we begin to consider these wholly concentrated implosions of matter which have more mass than the sun, they must pull everything into them. Everything disappears. You cannot ever see these particular stars, which are called black holes in space, because everything goes into it, and comes out where, somewhere else. Hum?

Now this is a more curious model of the universe than we're used to considering. Now physics deals with notions of matter and antimatter. Is it so outrageous then to speak of death as having a life which has as many laws as life?

Existential states of death.

Existential states of death. Exactly. We speak of the speed of light as being 186,000 miles a second and nothing can go faster than that. Except yesterday we were talking about, what if God is there to give a grace so speed can go faster? What if antimatter lives on the other side of the speed of light? We live in a universe of such peculiar immensity and intimacy.

As we see more and more into these notions, the differences between the mightiest phenomena and the tiniest seem to have almost nothing to do with space. It's as if finally space becomes no more than our metaphorical incapacity to comprehend. Throw that out. It's rather as if space becomes no more than the measure of our inability to comprehend that every process, large and small, is without meaning as a process which is large or small in itself, because everything exists in its reverberation upon everything else. One atom, one most special atom, may have more significance than a star.

So we inhabit a universe which is fell with purpose. And therefore must try to create, or at least try to exercise, our profoundest notion of champions and villains, of enemies and new gods within it. Theology will yet prove more amazing than science.

That's where I would like to let this rest. That any view we take of technology has to deal with the principle, it is either a manifest of God or the Devil or some dissertation of purpose or malignity from that universe which gives every suggestion of being a juggler's paradise. Because it can turn its pockets inside out.

[A chilly, overcast afternoon. We end our conversation on the back lawn at Mailer's home. The final taping session went till well past midnight. Then, in the kitchen for a nightcap, worked up by the intellectual blows to the head Mailer kept delivering in the last hours of the tape, we got into a long discussion of boxing, wrestling, and street fighting that resulted in an arm-wrestling contest on the kitchen table, and now a sparring session on the lawn. It's been over two years since I've boxed with this man, he's not supposed to box at all, but we've agreed to keep this cool, no trying to punch each other out.

[Mailer works in close, knees flexed, head low, that tight peek-a-boo style of his, a style similar to Joe Frazier's. It's possible to land a few punches on the top of his head, but that's like hitting a fire hydrant. "Writers," he once said after nearly knocking me out with a head butt, "have got hard heads." He's trying to move in closer to score a few quick chops to the body, his arms swinging in short arcs, his body planted on the balls of his feet, weaving, bobbing and ducking, and always managing to get his right hand up in time to block my left hook, the punch he knows I love to hit him with most. When the timing's right, the hook can come as a revelation, like an idea out of nowhere; anything can happen on the end of a good hook.

[Lubricating the joints, working the kinks out, the footing on the wet grass is poor, and we're both a little rusty, hungover, reflexes off. As I guessed, Mailer's punches are hard from the pushups he's been doing, but his condition is less than good and he's tiring quickly. But that's all right, the workout ended last night; communicating, or some of that macho bullshit done to feed the myth. And as the sweat begins to flow, the movements becoming more fluid as the blood warms the muscles, already the tension is easing out of my limbs.]

HUNTER S. THOMPSON: THE LAST OUTLAW

High Times, August 1991

In Memoriam: Dr. Hunter S. Thompson,
July 18, 1937–February 20, 2005

Art Uber Alles. *Art Above Everything. Hunter Thompson inscribed those words on a photograph he gave me of a titanium bomb he exploded in his backyard at Woody Creek. Under the picture he wrote:* It could happen to you. *But it happened to him. He self-detonated. His fascination with guns and bombs and incendiary devices peaked when he turned the weapon on himself.*

It was a time of brave writers committing the ultimate act of self-negation. Two months before Hunter shot himself, Gary Webb—author of Dark Alliance: The CIA, the Contras, and the Crack Cocaine Explosion, *who became a pariah with the establishment media for writing the truth instead of toeing the party line—killed himself with a gunshot to the head. It's as if these men of provocative words were trying to silence the insistent voices yammering in their skulls. It's a sad commentary on our times when men like Thompson and Webb chose to kill themselves rather than continue to speak and write their truth in defiance of the deluge of bullshit swamping the American consciousness.*

The first time I met Hunter he had driven up from Boston to Richard Goodwin's farm in Kingfield, Maine. It was the early seven-ties, Fear and Loathing in Las Vegas *had just been published and* Fear and Loathing on the Campaign Trail *was in the works. We shared a joint, fired a few rounds from Goodwin's Smith and Wesson .357 magnum, and became friends. I would hang out with Hunter in*

Boston, New York, Colorado, wherever we happened to be at the same time, and we faxed each other in the middle of the night when the voices demanded to be heard. It was always an adventure hanging with the good doctor. There was never a schedule, or if there was one he didn't follow it—one time we left Goodwin's home in Cambridge to get some booze and didn't make it back until the next day.

Before my arrest, the DEA attempted to entrap Hunter by having a "cooperating individual," or CI, call me and try to get me to make incriminating statements about Thompson on an obviously recorded phone conversation. After I got out of prison I was on strict supervision, called Special Parole, for three years. I was required to get permission from the Parole Board to leave the five boroughs and had to list anyone of note I came in contact with on a form submitted to my parole officer. The parole board tried to make me give up my job as a forensic specialist in the law office of solo practitioner Ivan Fisher because, they claimed, working in the office of a criminal defense lawyer I would come in contact with people involved in criminal activity. But we fought them on it and won. Michael Kennedy, the renowned defense attorney who represented High Times founder Tom Forçade (another suicide from a self-inflicted gunshot wound) shared Park Avenue office space with Ivan Fisher. Kennedy, who was the lawyer for the trust that owned High Times after Tom's death, came into my office one day, introduced himself, said he knew of my prior relationship with Forçade and invited me to write for the magazine.

For some time I wrote a column called "Crime and Punishment." High Times did an interview with me as a veteran of the Drug War. Then the editors sent me to Aspen and on to Woody Creek to interview the reclusive Dr. Thompson. Needless to say, I neglected to ask my parole officer for permission to make the trip.

The question that haunts me when someone I know and respect kills himself is, "Why?" Art Uber Alles. Tom, Hunter, Gary, these men were creative, influential artists who, it seems to me, were with us for a purpose. It's never that bad, I want to tell them. Or, if it is,

*it will get better. You think you're depressed, listen to Bob Dylan's
Time Out of Mind, and make art out of despair, as Bob does. I miss
Hunter's incendiary consciousness manifesting as a bold if slightly
addled, mumbling truth-sayer who never backed down from a verbal
rumble with the liars and scum who run this country.*

*Tom, Hunter, Gary, wherever you are—your self-murders have
wounded us all.*

HUNTER S. THOMPSON: THE LAST OUTLAW

WHEN I WAKE, THE red message knob on my phone is blinking.
"Dr. Thompson called at 6:58 AM" the man at the front desk
tells me. "He said he was just going to bed, but that he would be
available for lunch later."

Lunch, as it turns out, is at midnight. We meet at Woody Creek
Tavern, a few miles from Owl Farm, where Dr. Thompson has
been holed up these last 20-some-odd years, scene of the "lifestyle
bust" in February 1990 that led to pissant drug-possession and
sexual-assault charges leveled against America's last living high-
profile literary desperado.

With him is a gaggle of friends and admirers. They are heavily
armed when they enter the tavern: two shotguns and at least as
many pistols. Someone named Dominic is badgering Dr.
Thompson to allow him to ignite several titanium firebombs out at
the ranch. "We'll light up the whole valley," he promises. At the
next table, four ladies from France grow alarmed when they see all
the weapons. But Earl, a fugitive Native American artist, assures
them that the guns are not loaded.

Dr. Thompson is driving a mint, fire-engine-red Caprice Classic
convertible. It is snowing in the Rockies, and Hunter has the top
down. "If we drive fast enough, the snow won't settle on us," he says.

One of the ugliest decades in American history has passed since
I last spent an evening with Hunter Thompson. The eighties was

a decade of unbridled materialism and frenzied governmental incursion into the private lives of our citizenry. It was also a decade of trembling cowardice on the part of those normally willing to resist the self-righteous, hypocritical bent of our politicians—with one flagrant exception.

"We live in the Time of the Weasel, for good or ill," Thompson wrote in a recent memo to the attorneys associated with his nascent Fourth Amendment Foundation, "which puts us face-to-face with the Looking Glass and mandates Action or Death. Right. That's the only kind of language that these bastards understand. The Hog will not come out of the tunnel when seized by the snout. It must be stabbed in the ass."

Last year, the government attempted to seize Dr. Thompson by the snout and haul him off to prison. He was arrested after Gail Palmer-Slater, a 35-year-old businesswoman from Michigan, complained to police that she had been sexually assaulted by Dr. Thompson in his home, had a glass of cranberry juice thrown at her and her breast twisted when she balked at his invitation to join him in the hot tub for an interview.

The Pitkin County Sheriff's Department failed to act on the complaint. Sheriff Bob Braudis, who has known Dr. Thompson for 20 years, citing conflict of interest, turned the case over to an ambitious district attorney named Milton K. Blakey. Thompson, however, suspects less charitable motives on the part of the Sheriff's Department. He writes in a section of his latest book, *Songs of the Doomed*: "By Friday afternoon at least three sheriff's deputies had made such a Three Stooges-style mess of 'The Thompson Crime(s)' that Sheriff Braudis was frantic to get it off his hands and into the hungry maw of the DA *at all costs*."

Five days later, a team of investigators from the DA's office raided Owl Farm. After an 11-hour search, they turned up small amounts of personal stash. "Nothing but crumbs," the Doctor noted: less than a gram of coke, 39 hits of acid, some marijuana, and blasting caps and dynamite. Thompson was charged in an eight-count indictment alleging sexual assault, as well as possession of controlled substances and incendiary devices. After surviving the eighties, the outlaw journalist found himself faced with the prospect of spending the nineties in prison.

A lesser man might have copped a plea. Thompson's first attorney urged him to do just that, but he declined, opting instead to fire that lawyer and bring in the heavies—National Association of Criminal Defense Lawyers' Hal Haddon from Denver and Gerry Goldstein from San Antonio. Freed on $2,500 bond, the good Doctor was full of righteous indignation. "It got my attention," he says.

"She's in the sex business," Thompson says of the alleged victim. "She wanted me to help her start a boutique and mail-order business for marital aids and dildos—sex toys. She wanted to become the Ralph Nader of the sex business."

We are in the kitchen of his home in Woody Creek, and Thompson is recounting the events of the night which led to his latest run-in with the authorities. (Six months before the Palmer-Slater incident, the feds attempted to seize a machine gun Thompson had used to shoot at what he called a "giant killer porcupine." And before that, he was cited for pulling a shotgun from his golf bag while at the driving range of the Aspen golf course, and firing at an in-flight golf ball.)

As Dr. Thompson remembers the incident, Palmer-Slater came to Owl Farm ostensibly to interest him in her fledgling sex business. She had written him a provocative letter and sent videotapes and photos. "She was the All-American girl from Michigan State who turned into a sex queen." The margaritas flowed liberally and soon Palmer-Slater was sloppy drunk. Dr. Thompson denies Palmer-Slater's charge that he and his friends were snorting coke in her presence. "She was flaky. I didn't trust her."

"I tried to call a cab for her." Thompson demonstrates; he is sitting at the counter in his kitchen, which also serves as his writing table; he's surrounded by electronic gadgetry: a giant-screen TV set faces him; a VCR, tape deck, and fax machine at arm's reach; before him is the IBM Selectric typewriter he insists on using to compose; and next to it, the telephone. "She kept trying to grab the phone away from me. The first time she came at me, I gave her a stiff arm. But she kept coming, so I gave her one of those—" He places his hands on my chest and shoves me. "—a prefrontal lift. She was coming in hard. So she staggered back and slipped in the fuckin' cranberry juice. My hand brushed her breast as she fell and sat down heavily. That was the sexual assault."

Some theorize that the Thompson persona is theater. No one, they argue, could be this crazy and live to write about it. But what Dr. Thompson is really up to is Life as Art.

"The only thing necessary for the triumph of evil is for good men to do nothing," Thompson quotes Bobby Kennedy in *Songs of the Doomed*. He lives and writes with the sensibilities of an outlaw, a man who refuses to kowtow to unenlightened authority. He is as rigorous in the demands he places on his integrity as he is about his art. *Songs of the Doomed: More Notes on the Death of the American Dream; Gonzo Papers Vol. 3*, published soon after the Colorado sex-and-drugs case, contains some of his most vivid and visionary writing since *Fear and Loathing in Las Vegas*.

In "Let the Trials Begin," the long section that opens *Songs of the Doomed*, Thompson has written a brilliant Kafkaesque allegory about men in Trouble with The Law. The narrator, Dr. Thompson, his own greatest creation, wanders into a public library in the middle of the night. There he encounters a pathetic miscreant called Andrew.

"He was a loser. A wimp full of fear, with no pride and sure as hell no Money. . . ." After a brief struggle with the wretch, *". . . I quickly stepped over his leg and hyperextended his knee until he went rigid, then I braced him and examined the box. It was a standard-issue*

Body Beeper with a lock-on ankle bracelet—one of the New Age tools now available to law enforcement agencies everywhere, for purposes of electronic House Arrest for those who have been brought **within The System,** *but for whom there is no room in the overcrowded jails, pens, and prisons. The United States of America has more people locked up than any other country in the world, including Cuba and South Africa. Our prison system from coast to coast is bulging at the seams, and hundreds more are being crammed in every day—more and more of them saddled with the* **mandatory Sentences and No Parole** *Provisions that came in with the first Reagan Administration, which began ten years ago. . . ."*

At a time when all too many of the sixties generation have retreated into degenerate yuppism or fear-addled quietude, Thompson refuses to let the "Just Say No" dictates of the Reagan era cramp his lifestyle. Now in his fifties, he is more aware and more radical than ever. His rude awakening, begun more than 30 years ago and chronicled in *Songs of the Doomed,* climaxed when he became a defendant in THE STATE OF COLORADO vs. HUNTER S. THOMPSON.

"*This is a political trial,*" Thompson wrote at the time. "*I am a writer, a professional journalist with serious credentials in Crime, Craziness and Politics. I have mingled with dangerous criminals and attended many trials . . . from Hell's Angels, Black Panthers, and Chicago street fighters to Roxanne Pulitzer and even Richard Nixon, back in the good old days before he was run out of the White House for fraud, perjury, graft, and criminal negligence.*

"*But they have always been other people's trials. I have never been in the dock. I have never been on trial. Never accused of felonies.*

"*I am actually on trial for Sex, Drugs, and Rock and Roll. . . ."*

Ensconced at Owl Farm after the bust, Dr. Thompson mounted an aggressive defense. He immediately recognized the case for what it was, "a low-rent, back-alley cheap shot," and steadfastly refused to consider copping out to reduced charges. "This is a Fourth Amendment case," he told his "long rider" NACDL attorneys. "It is about police power." The international media, cowed though they are, loved the story. Dr. Thompson may be wild and difficult to fathom; he is often accused of mumbling, talking as though he had a mouth full of Heineken bottle caps. (Thompson apologized for mumbling "not guilty" when entering his pleas.) But everyone agrees he is honest.

This is from a man who has made his living at ". . . full-bore lying as a natural way of life." Essentially, he is a novelist. "Seems like I have a long history of constantly retreating from journalism to fiction," he wrote in *Songs of the Doomed*. *Fear and Loathing in Las Vegas*, still considered by most diehard Thompson fans to be his best book, is a novel. He got sidetracked into political journalism and now says, "Politics is a disease for dirty little animals. We were wrong from the start. . . ." He is back where he began, writing fiction. It is truth at a higher level, not literal truth so much as honest rendering of sensibility and mood that illumines Thompson's writing.

Dr. Thompson dons what looks like a fashionable squaw's apron, he has a bottle of Bombay Sapphire gin in one hand, the ever-present Dunhill cigarette and an orange in the other. Then he slams a tape into the tape deck. It's an audio version of *Songs of the Doomed*. Ralph Steadman yowls, "These long, strange nights, these long, strange nights. . . ."

"They wanted me," the Doctor says. "They wanted me *within The System*." He pulls out his "justice mallet," a curious electronic hammer that emits sounds of shattering glass when Thompson uses it to bludgeon his telephone. He's decided to change the message on the answering machine, which now goes, "There may be flies on you and me, but there are no flies on Jesus," to the crashing noise of the justice mallet.

" 'Don't worry, Andrew,' I said. 'There is damn little Justice in the world, but you are about to get your share of it.' "

It took 99 days, but Dr. Thompson got his share of justice. The government lost faith in their case.

"COMES NOW MILTON K. BLAKEY, District Attorney in and for the Ninth Judicial District of the State of Colorado, and moves this Honorable Court to dismiss this case and as grounds therefore states that:

"The People would be unable to establish guilt beyond a reasonable doubt.

"Dated this 30th day of May 1990," read the DA's Motion to Dismiss. Judge Charles Buss granted the motion and dismissed the charges with prejudice, meaning that they cannot be brought again at a later date.

"Why couldn't you have made this decision before you filed?" the judge asked Chief Deputy Attorney Chip McCrory. The DA responded that he was having witness problems and that the new findings made it clear just how difficult it would have been for the state to get a conviction.

Dr. Thompson was vindicated, but hardly pacified. "We've grown accustomed to letting anyone with a badge walk over us," he said at the time. *"Fuck that!"* he wrote in a press release issued from Owl Farm the next day. *"He denounced the Dismissal as 'pure cowardice' and said he would 'appeal at once' to the Colorado Supreme Court.*

"Thompson described the District Attorney's 'whole goddam staff' as 'thugs, liars, crooks and lazy human scum. . . . These stupid brutes tried to destroy my life,' he said, 'and now they tell me to just forget it.'

"They are guilty! They should all be hung by their heels from iron telephone poles on the road to Woody Creek!' "

Instead of hunkering down to lick his wounds, Dr. Thompson has rallied a new offensive. He has established a Fourth Amendment Foundation "to promote public awareness of the erosion of the Fourth Amendment to the United States Constitution and the consequent threat to the privacy, peace, and security of citizens in their own homes; and to provide legal assistance to citizens whose right to privacy has been infringed."

For, as he fully understands, the truly sinister aspect of the Doctor's case is that government forces, all in the name of some shadowy War on Drugs, are in fact turning this nation into a police state. In the final section of *Songs of the Doomed*, "Welcome to the NINETIES: WELCOME TO JAIL," Thompson has included a memo from his attorney, Gerry Goldstein.

"IF THEY CAN DO THIS TO THE RICH AND FAMOUS," Goldstein wrote, "If they can do this to you over spilled cranberry juice, imagine what must they be doing to the poor and ignominious every day in courtrooms across the country?" And this is exactly Thompson's point in "Let the Trials Begin."

In August of 1990, Dr. Thompson was back in court. This time he was there to file a Notice of Intent to sue the District Attorney's office, collectively and individually, with a $22 million civil law-suit for *Malicious Prosecution, gross negligence, and Criminal malfeasance with Harmful Intent.*

"The worm has turned," writes Dr. Thompson. "They are doomed. They will soon be in prison. Those bastards have no more respect for the law than any screwhead thief in Washington. They will meet the same fate as Charles Manson and Neil Bush."

Lunch has been served. It is now four o'clock in the morning. Earlier in the day—actually, the previous day—as I purchased a disposable camera, the man in the shop asked me whose picture I intended to take.

"Ah, some old freak over in Woody Creek," I told him.

"Which one?" he wanted to know. "There are a lot of them over there."

"The main one," I told him. "The last outlaw. I'm doing a story on his case for *High Times.*"

"Listen, do me a favor," the man said. "Ask him the one ques-tion that is on everyone's mind: How does he do it? How does he continue to live the way we did back then and survive?"

It is a most perplexing aspect of this baffling character. How *does* he do it? We've been drinking heavily all night. He's got a head full of THC. Every so often, like an anteater, he buries his nose and comes up gasping. The Dunhills are consumed incessantly. He keeps the hours of a vampire who's been sucking blood from speed freaks. And yet . . . yet, he makes sense. To me he makes more sense than anyone else who is writing today, because he UNDERSTANDS WHAT IS HAPPENING.

I spent the eighties in prison. When I got out it seemed to me the country had changed drastically for the worse. I worried that only those hundreds of thousands of us locked up during this despicable decade had a decent perspective on just how bad things have become. Then I read *Songs of the Doomed*.

So I asked the Doctor, "How do you do it?" We are out in his backyard, a combination one-hole golf course and target-shooting range. Dr. Thompson is demonstrating an infrared nightscope he has attached to a high-powered rifle. He even looks well. In his fringed Indian apron, and wearing some kind of wooly dive-bomber's cap, traces of chocolate cake from lunch on his lips, he looks remarkably healthy for a man who, by his own admission, has never just said no.

"I made my choice a long time ago," the Doctor says as he peers through the scope. "Some say I'm a lizard with no pulse. The truth is—Jesus, who knows? I never thought I'd make it past 27. Every day I'm just as astounded as everyone else to realize I'm still alive."

Possibly he doesn't understand, but I doubt this. I realize through the fog in my own brain that Dr. Thompson is in a kind of psychophysiological state of grace, because he has for all these years remained true to himself.

THE MARCO POLO OF POT: HOWARD MARKS

High Times, January 1992

The Return of Marco Polo

This piece at least has a happy ending. Howard Marks had his 25-year sentence reduced by a wise and compassionate judge on a Rule 35 Motion for Sentence Reduction and was released from U.S. custody in April, 1995, after serving seven years. He returned to England where he published a hilarious memoir of his dope smuggling days, Mr. Nice, *that became a best-seller in Britain and ushered in a new career for Howard as a public speaker and political candidate advocating the legalization of cannabis. Howard has a website, HowardMarksOnline, a new book,* Dope Tales, *and the BBC is adapting* Mr. Nice. *I wonder what Craig Lovato, the DEA agent who pursued Howard and manufactured a case to bring him into U.S. jurisdiction, is doing with his life.*

THE MARCO POLO OF POT: HOWARD MARKS

To live outside the law, you must be honest.

—Bob Dylan

THERE ARE CRIMINALS AND then there are outlaws. Criminals, motivated primarily by greed, prey on the weak, the naive, the desperate; yet their crimes may not always be illegal. The CEO of a corporation whose factories pollute our air and foul our waters is a criminal. Criminals harm others and imperil society for personal gain.

Outlaws are different. Outlaws make moral judgments about the outcome of their actions. They break—or ignore—specific laws, laws they find more harmful than the outlawed activity. An outlaw is a philosopher, an existentialist—a criminal is merely a parasite.

Dennis Howard Marks is an outlaw, a marijuana and hashish smuggler extraordinaire. In a career that lasted twenty years, until his arrest on the Mediterranean island of Mallorca on July 25, 1988, this peripatetic prince of pot-smuggling managed to elude authorities in a half-dozen countries, including the United States, with such style and élan that Tom Cash, the DEA's Special Agent in Charge of Miami, where Mark's wanderings were eventually brought to a halt, code-named him the "Marco Polo of Pot."

The story of Marks's life in the marijuana underground is recounted with meticulous attention to detail, if scant insight, in *Hunting Marco Polo*, by Paul Eddy and Sara Walden (Little, Brown, 1991). Our protagonist in this picaresque saga is a child of the sixties, psychological spawn of a phase in time that was not so much an era as an attitude.

The son of a sea captain, Howard was adventuresome and bright as a boy. He grew up in a working-class mining village in Wales where "smoking cigarettes and drinking pints of beer were the accepted signs of manhood among my peers. At the age of fourteen," he recalls, "I began smoking about twenty cigarettes a day and drinking a few gallons of beer a week. The interests I had were limited to sex, alcohol, and rock'n'roll."

Howard entered Oxford's Balliol College in 1964 at 19, and his personal revolution in consciousness took place during his second term there. "One day in June, 1965," he remembers, "at an informal gathering at a newly-found friend's lodging, a joint of marijuana was passed to me." As Eddy and Walden put it in their book, "From that point on, cannabis dominated his life." The physics student drifted into the dope business much as a sandlot ballplayer becomes a pro: through love of the activity, or, in Howard's case, love of the product. Patrick Lane, Marks' brother-in-law, told Eddy and Walden, "It is not love of money or love of power which drives Howard. It is love of hash." Marks expanded his passions to include sex, *drugs*, and rock'n'roll.

And what a transmutation it was. In a few heady years, Howard went from doing inebriated Elvis impersonations to importing large quantities of hashish to both Britain and the United States in the massive sound systems of illusory rock groups. While out on bond in London, after being busted in Amsterdam in 1973 on a Las Vegas hash smuggling case, Howard staged his own abduction and disappeared for seven years into the fugitive parallel universe of altered identities. He lived the outlaw life in Italy, then in New York, sliding around Manhattan in a limousine, usually in the company of beautiful women, before moving on to Miami, mecca of the dope business during the seventies and eighties. He became the Scarlet Pimpernel of Pot, making daring appearances at parties and weddings in London, only to dematerialize like some will-o'-the-wisp glimpsed in the sights of frustrated narcotics agents.

While he was on the lam, Marks and his American partners ran an air-freight scam through New York's Kennedy Airport. They brought in ton-sized loads of high-quality hashish from Afghanistan and Pakistan. Just after Christmas in 1979, Marks landed 15 tons of Colombian pot in Scotland—enough reefer, the authorities claimed, to provide every adult resident of the British Isles with a joint. They flooded the market and brought prices to record lows.

> *Agents of the law, luckless pedestrians*
> *I know you're out there somewhere with*
> *rage in your eyes and your megaphones.*
> —Steely Dan

Howard Marks was sipping a dry sherry at the bar of the Swan Hotel in Lavenham, Suffolk in May, 1980 when the heat swooped him up a second time, charging him with new counts that included the 15 tons of Colombian pot. Still facing charges from the original '73 hash-smuggling case, and with his documented penchant for failing to appear at court proceedings, this time there was no hope of bail. Howard withdrew to the confines of Brixton Prison to plot his defense. In the company of two guards, he was allowed out for one day to attend his own wedding to Judy Lane, mother of his first daughter and at the time pregnant with a second child.

It was to became the most highly-publicized marijuana trial in British history. The Marks camp presented a defense so implausible that Howard confessed he was "relieved but astonished" when the jury swallowed it and pronounced him "not guilty." In his testimony, Marks maintained that he had become involved in smuggling marijuana while actually employed as an agent gathering intelligence for MI-6, the British Secret Service. The only evidence presented to corroborate this claim was the bizarre appearance of an alleged "Mexican intelligence operative" who refused to give his name or present any credentials and insisted upon having the courtroom at the Old Bailey cleared "for security reasons" before he would testify.

"I made out that I was some kind of pot-smoking James Bond character infiltrating right-wing terrorist groups," Marks confided in a recent interview. "Nobody believed it, especially not the jury, who merely used it as an excuse to acquit me."

When Marks walked out of the courtroom a free man, the British agents who had pursued and prosecuted him with such zeal were outraged. Howard further infuriated officialdom by collaborating on a book, *High Time—The Shocking Life and Times of Howard Marks*, with David Leigh, a reporter for the *London Observer*. Published in 1984, *High Time* was mandatory reading in the British dope-police cabal.

Soon after the spectacular victory in London, Howard, and his budding family moved to the Spanish island of Mallorca. A less dedicated scammer might have retired after such a narrow escape. But Howard, like many another devotee of the cannabis plant, saw his trade as something of a mission. "I've never been able to draw the line between smoking a joint and smuggling pot," Marks told his biographers. "I smuggled for profit, of course, but only something I approved of." He elaborated in a recent interview, "My indignation at the continued illegality of hash became an obsession. I think, therefore, that my motivation was twofold: the enjoyment of solving the problems presented by laws forbidding the transport of a harmless herb, and a satisfying identification with those attempting to rectify an irrational prohibition."

In the most brilliant and audacious move of his smuggling career, Marks traveled to the Hindu Kush in Afghanistan in 1985 at the height of the Russian/Afghan war. There he sought out the legendary black Afghani "primo," the highest-quality hashish in the world, considered the smuggler's Holy Grail. Disguised as a native, he slipped across the border through the Khyber Pass near Peshawar, Pakistan, which at the time boasted the highest concentration of CIA agents in the world. Howard was escorted to a crude hash-processing plant near the town of Barak. There, provided with a hookah by his host, he selected a sample of rich hash stored in black goatskins and partook of the ritual taste test. In solidarity with the embattled *mujahedeen*, Howard's load of 24,000 slabs of primo was stamped with a logo showing a pair of Russian Kalashnikovs below which was printed: *Smoke Russia Away.*

From Afghanistan the hash was smuggled into Pakistan and loaded onto a Panamanian-registered ship, the *Axel D.* His work finished, Howard made a stop in Manila and met with a notorious expatriated British lord, "Rock'n'Roll Tony" Moynihan, to discuss pioneering a vast marijuana plantation on one of the outlying Philippine Islands. It was just one of many projects forming in Marks's fertile imagination as the *Axel D.* set sail for the New World.

Everybody's talking about crime.
Tell me, who are the criminals?

—Peter Tosh

"The champagne has arrived in Mozambique" was the coded language DEA agent Craig Lovato picked up from the tap on Howard Marks' Mallorca telephone. "Oh, fantastic," Howard replied, and went for a swim with his children. Lovato pricked up his ears. Champagne? Mozambique? He had no idea what Marks' American partner was talking about, but he knew it was not wine. Lovato dispatched a couple of agents to a hotel in Los Angeles where they poured out several bottles of expensive champagne in search of hashish—to no avail.

The DEA agent was perplexed. He had been sitting in a tiny room in Palma, Mallorca, listening to Marks' phone calls for weeks. Though he had no doubt Howard was up to something, Lovato and his colleagues around the world were unable to "catch him right," as the phrase goes, meaning they were not smart enough to nab Marks red-handed. So Lovato did what DEA agents sometimes do in such a situation: He resorted to the dubious tactic of manufacturing a case, a "no-dope historical" as such dry conspiracies are known in prosecutorial circles.

Code-named "Operation Eclectic," the pursuit, capture, and imprisonment of Howard Marks is a case study in the abuses of international law enforcement and foreign sovereignty carried out by American DEA agents in the name of the bogus, media-hyped Holy War on Drugs. Unable to decipher the jargon used by Marks and his friends, Lovato missed the load of black Afghani which had been off-loaded in Mexico and shipped north overland for distribution in California. West Coast heads rejoiced: The trip was a smashing success.

That didn't stop Lovato. He simply looked for a weak link in the Marks chain, quickly focusing on Rock'n'Roll Tony, who had absconded to Manila in the first place to avoid trouble with the law in England. Lovato and company threatened, pressured, and coerced Lord Moynihan—who was godfather to one of Howard's children—until he flipped. To save his own skin, Moynihan agreed to travel to Mallorca, wear a body recorder and tape a number of contrived conversations with Marks in which the canny smuggler would implicate himself.

Even that wasn't enough. Lovato also needed to create a crime within the jurisdiction of South Florida, where his DEA-agent wife had found an equally gung-ho assistant U.S. attorney willing to eschew the protection of due process of law in order to prosecute Howard Marks. With $50,000 provided by the DEA, Lord Moynihan moved on to Miami. There Marks hooked Moynihan up with his brother-in-law, Patrick Lane, who agreed to launder the money. Presto—instant crime.

On the day Lovato and his men, accompanied by a flock of armed Spanish police, raided the Marks' home in Mallorca, Howard was up early, as was his habit. He had cooked breakfast for his eldest daughter and was bustling about, catching that first buzz of the day, when the cops struck.

"I am the United States Government," Lovato declared proudly. "You're looking at it."

"I'm going to spend the next twenty years in jail," was the thought that jarred Howard's mind as a Spanish cop stuck a gun in his gut. Lovato had brought along a special pair of silver handcuffs belonging to a DEA colleague. As they were snapped onto Marks' wrists, Howard could hear the screams of his wife and children in the bedroom upstairs. Judy Marks, whose only "crime" was being married to Howard, was also arrested.

Howard Marks now resides at the United States Penitentiary in Terre Haute, Indiana, a brutally-overcrowded maximum security prison where he is serving a 25-year sentence for racketeering. Judy Marks pleaded to a token charge and was released with time served—more than a year, counting time spent imprisoned in Spain fighting extradition. She's back in Mallorca with her children. As her husband's convicted codefendant, she is prohibited from entering the U.S. to visit him.

At first Marks resolved to fight the Florida charges, and while awaiting trial at the Metropolitan Correctional Center in Miami, he concocted a defense certainly no more contrived than the government's case against him. However, Lovato, still posing as the United States government, had more strong-arm tactics up his sleeve.

Soon Marks's codefendants were flipping like flapjacks. As he watched his former friends line up against him, rather than risk a 40-year nonparolable sentence under the Continuing Criminal Enterprise Statute, Marks pleaded to one count of conspiracy and one count of racketeering.

He had been offered a much sweeter deal if he would agree to cooperate with Lovato in his messianic quest to become authority incarnate. But Howard has remained true to his ideals. "I was a marijuana smuggler," he would explain to his son, "and believe it is not a wrong thing to do. But the government did, and they put me in jail for it."

Questioned on his views by Eddy and Walden, Marks responded, "Of course there are some laws that should be broken. Race laws, anti-Semitic laws and other unjust laws. . . . The prohibition of soft drugs is ridiculous. I wonder what would happen if all the Americans who used marijuana simultaneously turned themselves in to the police."

Craig Lovato disagrees. While sipping a Scotch, the DEA agent told Eddy and Walden he believes it is not the government's job to dictate which substances people are allowed to ingest into their bodies. But the law is the law, says Lovato, and though he claims to have no personal animosity toward Howard Marks, he is above all else a cop and it is his job to put men and women—like

Howard Marks—who make their living in an illegal business in jail. It's the old "just doing my job" rationale, the kind of mindless cop-out that spells totalitarianism. One can imagine guards at the concentration camps closing the doors of the gas chamber with the thought, "Well, it's a dirty job, but somebody's got to do it."

"There is no such animal as a good doper," Lovato was quoted as saying by Eddy and Walden. "I can respect Marks's intelligence, but I have nothing but disdain for his character, because he has no character." A curious statement; how can one disdain something that does not exist? But then, Lovato—to whom Eddy and Walden also attribute the statement, "Intelligence is what you wipe your ass on"—is hardly a man who enjoys the life of the intellect.

"I presume he was implying that I have a bad, weak or possibly undisciplined character," Marks says of Lovato's comments. "I further presume that by 'bad character' he means possessing ethical values that are different from his. In this respect he is correct. He would not do what I did, unless it was legal, and I would not do what he did under any circumstances."

The fact that Marks continues to refuse to rat on his friends lends credence to his moral fortitude. "I do not think that I have a weak or undisciplined character—but who knows? My ethical views have been arrived at by painstaking and soul-searching exercise, and I have tried extremely hard to abide by them."

Lovato makes further attempts to justify his actions by claiming that Howard destroyed the lives of everyone he came into contact with. In reply, Marks points to yet another, more egregious example of Lovato's fabrications. "[T]his reminds me of another publicly-aired Lovato statement which upset me far more. During 1986 and 1987, I ran across a charitable organization in Thailand which devoted itself to the care and welfare of handicapped children. For entirely personal and altruistic reasons, I donated a single payment of $3,000 to this society. A few years later, my bank accounts were thoroughly scrutinized for evidence of my mythical millions, and a record of this donation was found. In a televised interview, Lovato declared that I was so bad that I even laundered my ill-gotten gains through a fraudulent Pakistani (sic) company fronting as a charity for handicapped children. I don't know whether this outrageous allegation is due to a grossly-overdeveloped personal bias or is simply an example of unprofessional, obsessive character assassination." Looking at the facts, it is closer to the truth to say that it is Lovato who has destroyed the lives of everyone Howard Marks came in contact with.

"What Lovato means, of course, is that he is mentally incapable of believing that a doper can commit a good act," Marks elaborates. "Believing is seeing, so he never sees dopers doing any good; any ostensibly good acts observed will be immediately attributed to be part of some devious Machiavellian strategy. Adopting such a blinkered attitude makes it easier to bully, persecute, incarcerate and deprive dopers of the rest of their lives' liberty and all of their assets. Blinkers have a tendency to make you blind."

It is not illegal drugs but the blind, hypocritical war against vast numbers of its own citizens by the U.S. government in the guise of men like Craig Lovato that is destroying our society. As a reviewer for London's *Time Out* magazine mused in his review of *Hunting Marco Polo*, "One thing's certain: If Howard Marks had opened a whiskey or cigarette factory instead, he'd probably have killed thousands, made millions, and be sitting in the House of Lords with all the other dopeheads right now."

Instead, Howard Marks is in a federal penitentiary doing 25 years, separated from his wife and family, limited to one overseas phone call every three months and disqualified from participating in many of the educational programs offered because he's not an American. When I asked Howard if, looking back over his outlaw career, he has any regrets, he replies, "Conspiring with Americans to do anything which led to the breaking of United States law is certainly an activity I bitterly regret having engaged in. . . . The ubiquitous nature of United States law, the ease with which one can be indicted, the near impossibility of being acquitted despite innocence or lack of evidence and the brutally inhumane sentences imposed for marijuana violations should have been enough to deter me from even smoking a joint in Katmandu in the presence of an American."

OPERATION COURIER AND THE BOMBING OF PAN AM FLIGHT 103

High Times, June 1992

The Fine Art of the Cover-Up

It's impossible for me to believe anything the U.S. government tells us. They lied about the war in Viet Nam. They lied about the Weapons of Mass Destruction. They lied and continue to lie about marijuana. I believe they lied and covered-up the truth about the Kennedy assassinations, both Jack and Bobby, and that there is ample evidence to prove they lied about who killed Dr. Martin Luther King. I would even go so far as to say I don't believe we know the whole truth about the murder of John Lennon or the mysterious death of Bob Marley.

So maybe I'm paranoid, a conspiracy theorist, and it's just an unfortunate coincidence that charismatic, iconoclastic leaders who attract large followings of young people and oppose the status quo end up dying, while the bloated scumbags who suck up the spoils from war and oppression rise to the top. I grew up in the age of Cointelpro, with FBI agents murdering and locking up dissidents, and I lived to see J. Edgar Hoover, America's preeminent lawman, exposed for using the Federal Bureau of Investigation to keep tabs on such "subversives" as Supreme Court justice William O. Douglas, Henry Miller, Albert Einstein, and Charlie Chaplin.

I also believe it is inherently American to question authority. We are a nation founded upon dissent from tyrannical regimes and religious and ideological oppression. Now we have become that which our nation's forefathers abhorred—tyrants inflicting our will on the rest of the world. Yet it is done with such finesse and subtlety and sophisticated use of propaganda that to question authority is perceived as being anti-American. Like all compulsive liars, the government will never admit to lying or making a mistake but instead makes up more lies to cover their blunders and distortions. How about this one: There were weapons of mass destruction but Saddam got rid of them just before the U.S. invaded Iraq. Now that makes sense.

On September 11, 2001, I was in Toronto scouting locations for Street Time when the planes brought down the twin towers. Our Director of Photography, Jonathan Freeman, though a Canadian, took the latest terrorist attack personally. Jonathan lost his brother on Pan Am Flight 103 and was convinced, as were many other family members of passengers on that flight, that the U.S. Government had covered-up the truth of who was behind the terrorist bombing of the Pan American jumbo jet that exploded over Lockerbie, Scotland on the night of December 21, 1988.

I was in prison when Pan Am 103 went down. Passing through K Dorm at Lewisburg on my way back to the penitentiary from MCC, New York, after my resentencing, I met a Lebanese heroin dealer from Detroit who told me that a mutual acquaintance, Khalid Jaafar, had set him up to be busted—yet Jaafar had been his supplier. What he described was a DEA operation, known as a "controlled delivery," where drugs are allowed to enter the country and be distributed. Unknowing dealers would then be targeted for arrest while the smugglers and other distributors working with DEA are allowed to continue doing business. DEA gets their arrest statistics, the cooperating smugglers and dealers get rid of competition and get paid.

The Jaafar name was well known to me, I'd visited the family villa outside Baalbek in the Bekaa Valley and met many of the family members. For years the Jaafars controlled most of the major hashish production in the Bekaa and, I'd heard, they were lately running a productive heroin lab.

"*That motherfucker got blown up on the airplane that exploded,*" *the junk dealer told me with a grin. "Fuck him. Serves him right. Rat cocksucker.*"

Khalid Jaafar a rat working for DEA? By then, nothing surprised me. Years later, after I got out of prison, I came upon Juval Aviv's Interfor Report on the Pan Am 103 bombing in an issue of Barrons, *the financial publication, that I happened to see on a newsstand. There it was, "Operation Courier," the DEA-controlled delivery scam starring Khalid Jaafar, detailed in Aviv's report as the means for how the bomb was snuck past security onto the airplane. I bought a copy of* Barrons *and did a follow-up interview with Juval Aviv. You can't make this stuff up.*

All the investigators looking into the bombing of Pan Am 103 were on the same trail, one that led to a terrorist cell in Germany, when United States government agents abruptly shifted focus and claimed they had evidence it was the Libyans under Qaddafi who had planted the bomb. Juval Aviv's report was discredited and the FBI went on a vicious smear campaign to vilify Aviv by having him charged with fraud in an unrelated case, which he beat. Qaddafi offered up a couple of hapless baggage handlers to be tried for the bombing along with $2.7 billion to settle claims by the families of Lockerbie victims in exchange for lifting crippling sanctions against Libya that were costing Qaddafi billions every year. The Libyan baggage handlers were tried in the Netherlands in a nine-month trial. There were holes in the case big enough to fly a jumbo jet through. One of the Libyans was found guilty of murder and sentenced to 20 years; the other guy was acquitted. And Pan Am, the DEA, CIA, and the government were off the hook.

OPERATION COURIER AND THE BOMBING OF PAN AM FLIGHT 103

A FIRE IN THE SKY

Four days before Christmas, on the night of December 21, 1988, the Pan American 747 jumbo jet, flight 103, departing London en route to

New York, was only two-thirds full, which was unusual in the busy trans-Atlantic corridor given the season. Many of the passengers were young American students eagerly returning home for the holidays.

At least four of the passengers—some accounts say as many as eight—were CIA or other American intelligence agency operatives, on their way back to the United States from a failed secret mission to rescue American hostages held by the radical Party of God in Beirut. Also on board was Khalid Jaafar, a chubby-faced 20-year-old Lebanese-American, scion of the family Jafaar— Lebanon's first family of narcotics.

Jaafar, who lived in Detroit, had boarded flight 103 in Frankfurt, Germany, checking a single piece of luggage. After the short hop from Frankfurt to London's Heathrow airport, passengers and baggage from Germany were transferred to a different plane, a Boeing 747 nicknamed "Maid of the Seas," for the long trip home.

The flight was less than an hour out of London, reaching an altitude of 31,000 feet over the Scottish hamlet of Lockerbie, when suddenly the night sky lit up with meteoric brilliance. The huge plane blew to pieces. Bodies of passengers and crew members fell from the sky and landed on rooftops and in fields. Hunks of the airplane demolished houses and littered the countryside over 845 square miles. A fireball of burning aviation fuel burst over Lockerbie like a giant Molotov cocktail. All 259 people aboard died in the explosion, and another 11 on the ground were killed by falling debris and flames.

Within days after the Lockerbie disaster, the largest international counterterrorism investigation ever mounted was underway. On the scene in Scotland—in addition to the local constabulary, British police and inspectors from Scotland Yard—were investigators from the FBI and a team of CIA agents. The CIA men, dressed in Pan Am uniforms, combed through wreckage looking for luggage belonging to their agents. According to one so far undisputed report, the CIA men found what they were looking for and temporarily removed at least one suitcase from the crash site.

From the outset the investigation focused on a Syrian-based organization known as the Popular Front for the Liberation of Palestine-General Command (PFLP-GC), headed by Ahmed Jibril. The PFLP-GC was suspected of undertaking the bombing for a fee—reported by ABC News to be $10 million—at the behest of Iran in retaliation for the downing of an Iranian airbus by the USS *Vincennes* over the Persian Gulf in July of 1988. All 290 civilian passengers and crew aboard the Iranian flight were killed. In the Old Testament and Islamic fundamentalist mentality prevalent in the Middle East, it was an eye for an eye.

Investigators in the Pan Am case quickly determined the bomb had been secreted in a Toshiba Bombeat cassette player wrapped in a bundle of clothing packed in a brown Samsonite suitcase. The suitcase had been loaded on at Frankfurt and stowed in forward luggage compartment 14L. The explosive device, armed with a powerful Czech-made plastique called Semtex, was ignited by a sophisticated pressure-sensitive barometer trigger set to go off at an altitude of 31,000 feet.

The next question was how: How had terrorists managed to get the bomb through Pan Am security and onto the plane? In the wake of the fear and outrage that inevitably follows the mass murder of innocent people, particularly American citizens on board commercial airliners, lawyers representing relatives of the victims surfaced to point the finger of liability and make claims for reparation. Pan Am braced itself for an onslaught of lawsuits.

AUTUMN LEAVES

Flashback to October 1988, two-and-a-half months before the bombing of Pan Am 103. In the quiet town of Neuss across the Rhine from Dusseldorf, the Bundeskriminalamt—or BKA as the West German Federal Police are known—in an operation code-named Autumn Leaves, was surveilling a flat at 16 Isarstrasse. The flat was occupid by a greengrocer of Arab descent. What interested the German police was not so much the grocer as his houseguests, among them his brother-in-law, Hafez Dalkimoni, a limping Palestinian born in Jordan in 1946.

The wooden legged Dalkimoni is legendary in terrorist circles. After his lower leg was blown off during a mission in Galilee, Dalkimoni—found by Israelis a day later still dazed and bleeding—screamed "Vengeance! Vengeance!" as he was dragged away to jail. Sentenced to life in prison, he was released in a prisoner swap orchestrated by Ahmed Jibril and soon became one of Jibril's top PFLP-GC aides. In 1985, Dalkimoni arranged for the release of 1,550 prisoners held by Israel in exchange for three Israelis.

Enter Marwan Khreeshat, one of Jibril's expert bomb makers. On October 13, 1988, Khreeshat arrived at the greengrocer's apartment in Neuss. He was carrying a brown Samsonite suitcase. West German police watched as, between rendezvous with a number of other terrorist suspects, Dalkimoni and Khreeshat went on shopping expeditions for radios, cassette players, batteries, alarm clocks, switches, glue.

The BKA stepped up the investigation. Wiretaps were installed, and soon more than 30 suspects in six West German states were linked to the Neuss cell. After a phone call to Amman, Jordan, during which Khreeshat was overheard by police to say that he "had just begun to work," and would be finished in two or three days, the BKA determined it was time for Autumn Leaves to fall.

On October 26, 1988, the police raided. Dalkimoni and Khreeshat were arrested in town where they had gone to make calls from a pay phone. Five kilos of Semtex, a detonator, both barometric and time delay fuses, six kilos of TNT, dynamite and weapons including a bazooka, a grenade launcher, and 30 hand-grenades were among the items recovered in searches. From the car Dalkimoni and Khreeshat were using when they were arrested, police seized a Toshiba Bombeat cassette player.

Three days after the raids, detectives finally got around to examining the Toshiba. What they found was a bomb made from 300 grams of Semtex explosive primed and set for detonation with a barometric triggering device. Just as a handgun with a silencer has only one explicit purpose—murdering people at close range—so a bomb equipped with a barometric pressure trigger is designed specifically to blow up aircraft.

Though Autumn Leaves was hailed by German authorities as a major setback for Middle Eastern terrorist organizations operating in Europe, of the 17 suspects apprehended all but two were soon released by West German judges citing lack of evidence. Most, including Marwan Khreeshat, quickly disappeared. By the time Pan Am flight 103 took off from London, only Dalkimoni and Abdel Fattah Ghadanfar, who occupied an apartment in Frankfurt where the bulk of the weapons were discovered, remained in prison.

For some time rumors persisted that not one, but several bombs had been built by Khreeshat in Neuss. Tragically, and for still unexplained reasons, the BKA failed to investigate further.

THE INTERFOR REPORT

Cut to New York City. Six months after the Lockerbie disaster, Pan Am was teetering on the brink of bankruptcy and faced with approximately 300 civil suits filed by relatives of the victims. The beleaguered airline's lawyers hired a Madison Avenue firm known as Interfor, Inc. to conduct their own investigation into the bombing.

Interfor is run by 45-year-old Juval Aviv, an Israeli said to be a former Mossad agent. Aviv is reportedly the model for a character known as "Avner" in the 1984 book *Vengeance,* by George Jonas. *Vengeance* is a compelling true story about a roving Mossad hit squad that assassinated a number of top Arab terrorists in retaliation for the killing of 11 Israeli athletes by Black September during the 1972 Olympic games in Munich.

The 27-page report prepared by Interfor and submitted to Pan

Am's lawyers was startling. "We focused our investigation solely on identifying, locating, and debriefing the most knowledgeable and reliable sources in intelligence, airport security and the terrorist underground to tell us who, what, when, where, how and why the bomb was placed," the report reads. Aviv goes on to detail the backgrounds of his various sources—though without naming them—before coming to the core of his complex conspiracy theory.

According to the Interfor report, Pan Am 103 was sabotaged by Ahmed Jibril's Popular Front for the Liberation of Palestine General Command, paid for by Iran, and in collusion with Libya, Syrian intelligence agents, and several other terrorist factions. The perpetrators used a Semtex bomb activated by a barometric trigger hidden in a brown Samsonite suitcase placed aboard the plane in Frankfurt. Only when it comes to the crucial question of how the bomb-laden suitcase slipped through Pan Am's security inspectors does the Interfor report reveal its shocking conclusion.

If we are to believe Juval Aviv's report, the brown Samsonite suitcase was not subjected to ordinary airport security measures because it was supposed to contain Lebanese heroin destined for the streets of the United States. The heroin was to be smuggled from the Middle East through Germany into New York, Detroit and other cities via an ingenious method—and with the full sanction of the Drug Enforcement Administration—using a Frankfurt-based CIA unit Aviv calls "CIA-1" (to distinguish them from the CIA team aboard the flight), the West German KBA, airport security, and Pan Am baggage handlers.

The report states that a Syrian named Monzer Al-Kassar met with Ahmed Jibril at Restaurant Ajami on Rue Lincoln in Paris during the autumn of 1988, around the time Dalkimoni and Khreeshat were in Neuss building bombs. Al-Kassar is married to Raghda Duba, the sister of Syrian intelligence head Ali Issa Duba. He has a mistress named Raja Al-Assad, who lives on Avenue Foch in Paris and is the niece of Syrian President Hafez Al-Assad.

Not only is Mr. Al-Kassar well connected in intelligence circles, he is also one of the most influential narcotics and arms traders operating in the European/Middle Eastern theater.

Other sources maintain Al-Kassar played a significant role in the Iran/Contra affair. He is reported to have received a payment of $1.5 million from Richard Secord and Albert Hakim to buy 100 tons of small arms and ship them to Nicaragua. Al-Kassar also facilitated early shipments of American arms to Iran which eventually resulted in the release of hostages held in Lebanon. Likewise, working for the French, he purchased and shipped weapons to Iran in exchange for the freedom of French captives held by Hizballah. The same reports claim that Al-Kassar provided drug profits to Oliver North's agents for use in arming the Nicaraguan contras.

Al-Kassar's real business, however, is heroin. At the time of the meeting with Jibril in Paris, Aviv reports Al-Kassar was using a DEA-protected route to ship suitcases full of heroin through Frankfurt to the United States. As Aviv recounts it in the Interfor report, Al-Kassar was approached by CIA agents stationed in Frankfurt who had learned of his arrangement with the DEA and knew of his well-placed contacts and past successes in hostage negotiations. The CIA offered to allow Al-Kassar continued protection for his heroin smuggling operation in exchange for information about and help in obtaining release of the American hostages in Lebanon.

Al-Kassar had previously obtained DEA connivance for his heroin-smuggling operation through the agency's relationship with young Khalid Jafaar, allegedly a DEA informant and Al-Kassar accomplice. In exchange for information about other American and European traffickers, Al-Kassar and Jafaar were allowed to import and distribute shipments of heroin in the United States.

Here's how it worked. All throughout the mid-eighties and well into 1988, couriers working for the Al-Kassar/Jafaar group (often accompanied by the family in Lebanon to watch over the couriers and make sure they didn't abscond with the goods) would board flights originating in Frankfurt. Each courier would check a suitcase packed with clothing and other innocent items.

An identical suitcase containing heroin would be switched with the checked luggage by baggage handlers after the checked bag cleared airport security inspection. The bag would then be loaded aboard an American-bound flight. Once in the United States, the couriers' bags bypassed customs because they were known to contain drugs being brought into the country as part of the DEA undercover operation.

Aviv claims Ahmed Jibril's spies monitored Al-Kassar's arms and drug smuggling activities. When Jibril and Al-Kassar met in Paris, it was to discuss Al-Kassar's role in assisting the Jibril organization to strike different Israeli and American targets in Europe. Al-Kassar, who has long been associated with Jibril, Abu Nidal, and other terrorist operatives through his close ties with Syrian intelligence, agreed to help. Aviv also reports that Jibril met with Khalid Jafaar and a Lybian bombmaker known as "The Professor" in Bonn a week before the ill-fated flight.

In the treacherous world of Middle Eastern narco-terrorism, betrayals are commonplace. The Interfor report goes on to detail an intricate last minute double-cross of the Al-Kassar/Jafaar group by Ahmed Jibril. Aviv claims Al-Kassar and Jafaar, though willing to help Jibril, did not wish to blow their lucrative setup at Pan Am in Frankfurt. Originally, an American Airlines flight was targeted. Aviv's report maintains that, just days before the bombing, Al-Kassar tipped authorities to Jibril's plans and security was tightened at all airlines except Pan Am. The BKA/CIA-1 team, because of their close contact with Al-Kassar, believed their Pan Am routes were immune to attack.

On the day of the bombing, a black Mercedes sedan was left in the Frankfurt airport parking lot. Soon a Turkish baggage handler who worked for Pan Am approached the car and removed a suitcase from the trunk. As he had done many times before, he carried the suitcase into the airport and placed it inside an employee locker in the secure area where baggage that has already been screened by security inspectors is taken from conveyors and loaded onto trucks to be stowed aboard outbound aircraft.

When the Turk saw Khalid Jafaar's suitcase trundling along the conveyor, he removed it as per the plan and took it to his locker. There, instead of switching it with the heroin-laden suitcase he had retrieved from the Mercedes, he substituted a third suitcase, "different in make, shape, material and color from that used for all previous drug shipments. This one was a brown Samsonite case" (Interfor Report, Pg. 19). Unknown to Al-Kassar, Jibril's spies had recruited the baggage handler and enlisted him in their cause.

Khalid Jafaar died thinking he was smuggling another shipment of heroin, perhaps with the understanding that at least part of the proceeds would go toward financing Jibril's organization. "Jafaar does not profile as a suicidal martyr type," reads the Interfor report. Indeed he does not. In the Syrian-controlled Bekaa Valley of Eastern Lebanon, where heroin- and hashish-dealing drug warlords reign supreme, Hizballah was founded in the village of Baalbek in 1982. The Jafaar family lives near Baalbek and has long dominated a large portion of local drug production. They deny Khalid's involvement in the bombing.

The bomb was planted aboard Pan Am flight 103 despite numerous warnings to the CIA, BKA, and American embassies in Europe. In Helsinki, Finland, a tip was called into the U.S. Embassy and posted on electronic bulletin boards. Relatives of the victims assert the plane was only two-thirds full because government employees avoided the flight.

Within hours of takeoff, according to the Interfor report, a Mossad undercover agent alerted the BKA and CIA of the planned sabotage. A vigilant BKA agent surveilling the baggage handling area grew suspicious when he noticed the different color and description of the suitcase substituted for Jafaar's bag. He called in a caution to the CIA-1 team. CIA-1 continued to ignore warnings. Aviv quotes them as responding, "Don't worry about it, don't stop it, let it go." The report asserts BKA made a videotape of the bags being switched and loaded onto the plane. A copy of the videotape was given to the CIA team controlling the operation. Even though the substituted suitcase was different from the one checked by Jafaar, they let it go because they believed the brown Samsonite contained Monzer Al-Kassar's heroin.

THE ART OF THE COVER-UP

Although at first denied by the DEA, sources within the agency later confirmed that a secret undertaking code-named Operation Courier was in place in Frankfurt sometime prior to the Pan Am bombing. "[A]s part of an ongoing investigation of heroin smuggling . . . DEA in the mid-eighties made special arrangements with West German authorities to allow its undercover operatives to carry 'controlled' shipments of drugs onto U.S.-bound flights from Frankfurt," the DEA was quoted in a *Washington Post* article in November 1990. Just when the operation was shut down is in dispute.

Official agency spokesmen insist no Operation Courier "controlled shipments" of heroin came through Frankfurt after 1987. Other agency sources maintain the operation was still in place during 1988 and that Khalid Jafaar was one such undercover operative. The agency does not deny that it had a relationship with Khalid Jafaar, though details of how Operation Courier worked and its investigative goals are still secret.

A White House commission studying aircraft terrorism concluded in May 1990 that the DEA was not connected with the bombing. Federal officials pointed out that a complete forensic examination of luggage from the flight determined no hard drugs were aboard the aircraft. Of course, if Aviv's report is accurate, the last minute suitcase switch would account for the lack of heroin recovered in the wreckage. The CIA is not talking—at least, not about the possibility its own agents were somehow responsible.

Finally, just for a moment, let us return to Autumn Leaves. It turns out that Ahmed Jibril's bombmaker, Marwan Khreeshat, may in fact have been working for Jordanian intelligence all along. In early February 1989, soon after Pan Am 103 went down, the CIA learned that Khreeshat had surfaced in Aman, Jordan. He told his Jordanian handlers he had made not one, but five, identical bombs while holed up with Dalkimoni in Neuss.

This intelligence, relayed by the CIA to German BKA agents, met with an astonishing response: the BKA already had the information and had not shared it with Lockerbie inspectors. In fact, the Germans were playing an extremely one-sided game in their handling of the Autumn Leaves fallout. The Interfor reports lead to speculation that this was because the Germans were reluctant to have their own complicity in the botched Frankfurt operation revealed.

In any case, after repeated urging, the German police returned to the greengrocer's apartment building. On the floor in the basement, just as Khreeshat had told the Jordanians, they found various electronic components. A stereo tuner being examined by experienced explosives experts blew up, killing one of the men. Two more bombs, both identical to the original bomb found in the Toshiba Bombeat cassette player, were discovered in the components. Total: four bombs. One bomb remained unaccounted for.

Imagine then, the surprise of many nongovernmental investigators when, in November of 1991, the U.S. Justice Department, with typical ballyhoo and fanfare, announced indictments in the Pan Am 103 bombing case charging two "Lybian intelligence" officers. Never mind that the concept of state-backed "Lybian intelligence" is in itself somewhat oxymoronic; the indictment and background investigation leading to the Lybian charges are fantastic. Like the "single pristine bullet" theory with which the government seeks to explain how Lee Harvey Oswald acting alone killed President Kennedy, the Lybian conspiracy theory is full of gaping holes and reeks of cover-up.

The Justice Department claims that, in mid–1990, an investigator sifting through debris collected from the Pan Am wreckage discovered a tiny piece of plastic, no bigger than a fingernail, imbedded in a shirt they say was in the suitcase of the bomb. U.S. law enforcement officials insist the fragment of plastic has been identified as a piece of circuitry from a digital electronic timer identical to timers sold to Libya in 1985 and 1986 by a Swiss manufacturer. The shirt, meanwhile, has been traced to a shop on the Mediteranean island of Malta where, according to the Justice Department, the Libyan intelligence officers named in the indictment were stationed while working for Libyan Arab Airlines.

Justice Department investigators assert the accused Libyans, Abdel Basset Ali al-Megrahi and Lamen Khalifa Fhimah, put the bomb inside a Toshiba cassette player hidden in a clothes-filled suitcase. Then, in their capacity as employees of Libyan Arab Airlines—while in reality working undercover as agents for Colonel Muammar el-Qaddafi—they obtained luggage tags and used them to put the suitcase on an Air Malta flight to Frankfurt connecting with Pan Am flight 103.

The suitcase, traveling as unaccompanied luggage from Malta on an Arab airline made it through both incoming and outgoing baggage inspections in Germany despite stepped-up security provoked by numerous warnings of a planned terrorist attack. The bomb was detonated over Lockerbie not by a pressure-sensitive device—such as the barometric trigger found in the Toshiba cassette player seized in West Germany during the Autumn Leaves debacle and as investigators had maintained all along—but by a simple electronic timer. The fact that flight 103 was delayed before takeoff in London, and that the bomb went off at exactly 31,000 feet, the same altitude at which the device found in Neuss was preset, no longer seems to be of evidentiary importance. Toshiba, coincidentally, appears to be the cassette player of choice for terrorist bombers.

The U.S. government would like to convince the world that Colonel Qaddafi's men alone, and not the Syrians nor the Iranians, were behind the Pan Am bombing. "Syria got a bum rap on this one," George Bush announced. Motive for the bombing is said to be retribution for the attack on Libya by the United States in 1986.

Furthermore, the Justice Department declared, they have a diary to prove it. Yet another diary. Just as Lee Harvey Oswald kept a diary, and Sirhan Sirhan, and the guy who shot George Wallace, so too did Libyan intelligence officer Mr. Fhimah jot notes of his terroristic errands in a journal obtained by government investigators. Prosecutors won't say how they got the diary. However, sources close to the investigation intimate it was retrieved during a clandestine CIA mission in Libya.

And what does Qaddafi have to say about all this? True to form, the Colonel asserts Pan Am Flight 103 blew up when the jet crashed into a Scottish gas station in bad weather rather than exploding in mid-air. The Libyan government issued a four-page response to the allegations, quoted by the *New York Times* as "calling for a special session of the United Nations General Assembly to define international terrorism and ban all offensive weapons in the world, including warships and warplanes, especially those that can 'refuel in the air.' It also calls for the placement of medical crews on all planes and boats as well as the prohibition of boxing and 'races exhausting to animals.' It demands the elimination of the world's locusts and 'the establishment of an international irrigation system banning the flow of rivers, rain and snow into the sea and oceans.' "

And what of the CIA team aboard Pan Am 103? Juval Aviv claims they had discovered CIA-1's arrangement with Monzer Al-Kassar and, incensed that it might have interfered with their own attempts to free American hostages, were returning to the United States with evidence to expose their fellow agency operatives. This, investigators say, may be one reason why the CIA was so anxious to get hold of the suitcase they whisked away from the Lockerbie crash site.

According to columnist Jack Anderson, President Bush (former Director of the CIA), called Prime Minister Margaret Thatcher in 1989 and agreed with her that the investigation into the Lockerbie crash had to be controlled to avoid damage to the two nations' intelligence communities. Now the Gulf War has resulted in shifting Middle-Eastern alliances with new peace talks underway, indicting the Libyans and deflecting blame from Palestinians, Syria and Iran not only is politically expedient but it also puts a lid on possible CIA/DEA complicity in the disaster.

Many family members of flight 103 victims remain unconvinced. In an April 1990 letter to Bush and Thatcher, signed by Paul Hudson and Jim Swire, cochairs of "UK Families-Flight 103," the two leaders were called to task for "entirely believable published accounts [that] . . . both of you have decided to downplay the evidence and string out the investigation until the case can be dismissed as ancient history." Hudson, a lawyer from Albany, is also the president of "Families of Pan Am 103/Lockerbie." His 16-year-old daughter, Melina, was returning home from school in England when she died in the crash.

"Anything that will prevent a cover-up . . . that will keep others from experiencing what we have, is important," Paul Hudson's wife, Eleanor, was quoted as saying. "It appears that the government either has the facts and is covering this up," Paul Hudson added, "or doesn't know all the facts and doesn't want to."

At a meeting with the families of the victims soon after the indictments were announced, Lawrence S. Eagleburger, the Deputy Secretary of State, angrily defended the Bush Administration's stated position that investigators had found no evidence linking

Syria or Iran to the bombing. "He got very irate," said one of the victims' relatives. "He wasn't happy with people calling himself, the President, the State Department and the FBI liars."

Now that the War on Drugs has usurped the Cold War as the moral and political justification for American meddling in the affairs of other nations, the Drug Enforcement Administration, with agents operating in over 40 countries, has been wedded to the CIA. As Noriega's case—the most elaborate drug bust in history—and the Pan Am 103 case both demonstrate, it is a marriage made in hell.

Photo credit: Victor Fisher

ALTERED STATES OF AMERICA:
THE CIA'S COVERT LSD EXPERIMENTS

Spin, March 1994

Permanently Altered States of Mind

In the winter of 1992 I was having a drink in a midtown bar after attending a Town Hall meeting where Oliver Stone discussed using real events—the JFK assassination—as the basis for a fictional film. On my way out of the bar I ran into Danny Schecter "the News Dissector," a progressive journalist and media critic I'd met while working on the Barbara Kopple film about Mike Tyson. Danny called me over and introduced me to a documentary filmmaker who shared my interest in the connection between the intelligence community and international arms and drug trafficking. I started telling them about a movie I'd seen only a few days before, a wild underground feature about drugs and rogue government agents called Blowback. *The filmmaker turned to me and said, "You saw* Blowback? *I made that movie."*

That was how I met Marc Levin. After I'd seen Blowback, *as I walked out of the movie theater, I said to the person with me, "I want to meet the guy who made that movie." Sometimes you get what you want.*

Marc and I traded phone numbers. He called a few days later, invited me over to his studio and showed me clips from a documentary he was working on, Mob Stories, *for Sheila Nevins at HBO. At one point, after I told him a little of my history, Marc asked if I still smoked pot. I was on parole, subject to random urine tests, but I'd seen my parole officer just a few days earlier and wasn't expecting to see him again for a few weeks. It was a good time to light up.*

"Yeah," I said. "In fact I just happen to have a joint right here." We got high, Marc turned me on to a book called Acid Dreams: The Complete Social History of LSD: The CIA, The Sixties, and Beyond by Martin A. Lee, and said he wanted to make a feature film based on the life of one of the main characters in Acid Dreams, a larger-than-life undercover narcotics cop named George Hunter White, who was hired by the CIA to test LSD on unwitting subjects back in the fifties. I read the book and after more meetings, Marc hired me to write the screenplay. So began a rich collaboration that is still going strong some 13 years later.

While doing research at the National Archives in Washington, D.C. for Acid Test, the screenplay I wrote about George Hunter White, I looked through the papers of another author, John Marks, who wrote The Search for the Manchurian Candidate: The CIA and Mind Control, and I stumbled onto a trove of declassified documents. In those papers I found a Long Island address for Ira "Ike" Feldman, one of George White's top operatives in the LSD testing program after White left New York and set up shop in San Francisco. Like White, Feldman was a former drug agent with the Federal Bureau of Narcotics under Harry Anslinger. In "Altered States" I tell the story of my debriefing of Ike Feldman.

Acid Test made the rounds in Hollywood. Most of the executives who read it were at first disbelieving that anything this bizarre could have happened in the good old U.S. of A. in the fifties and, further, were disinclined to make a movie that showed the CIA in such a psychedelic light. Another comment was that White was unsympathetic, a bad dude; he busted Billy Holliday, among others. But he was fascinating, the incarnation of the madness that is the War on Drugs. A friend who read the screenplay told an editor at Spin magazine about it and I got an assignment to write what became Altered States of America.

Every so often a writer has the great good fortune to publish work that has a real impact on other peoples' lives. A few weeks after Altered States of America came out in Spin, I was contacted by Eric

Olson, the son of Frank Olson, who died when he plunged to the pavement from a tenth-story hotel room window in New York City. A friend of Eric Olson's was seated next to a passenger on an airplane who was reading the Spin *piece. The friend contacted Eric and told him he should take a look at the article, there was something in there about his father. Eric, who was an eight-year-old boy when his father died, had long been obsessed with his father's death and determined to find out what really happened in the hotel room that night in November of 1953. At the time, the government lied to the Olson family about Frank's death, saying he had fallen or jumped from the hotel window, neglecting to add that he'd been given a massive dose of LSD a week before and that he was voicing serious doubts about secret biological and chemical warfare experiments he'd been doing for the CIA.*

I put Eric in touch with Ike Feldman, who, when I first interviewed him, said he didn't know if Olson jumped or was pushed. Later, at a news conference, Ike admitted that the word in the intelligence community at the time was that Olson had been terminated by the CIA because he was seen as a security risk. In 1994, Eric Olson had his father's remains exhumed and a forensic examination performed by James E. Starrs, Professor of Law and Forensic Science at the George Washington University Law Center. Professor Starrs concluded that the "overwhelming probability" was that Frank Olson's death was not a suicide but a murder. In 1996, the Olson family presented their findings to the New York District Attorney's office and a formal homicide investigation was opened.

In the years since this piece was published, I've been deposed in a number of civil cases brought by people who are suing the government for having been dosed with LSD back in the fifties by George White or Ike Feldman, or Sidney Gottlieb, the Dr. Strangelove of the CIA's romance with acid, who in March of 1999 went to the grave with his dark secrets.

For updated developments in this ongoing investigation into the lies our government tells visit Eric Olson's website, frankolsonpro-ject.org. It'll blow your mind as much as a hit of Sandoz' finest.

ALTERED STATES OF AMERICA:
THE CIA'S COVERT LSD EXPERIMENTS

"I was a very minor missionary, actually a heretic, but I toiled wholeheartedly in the vineyards because it was fun, fun, fun. Where else could a red-blooded American boy lie, kill, cheat, steal, rape, and pillage with the sanction and blessing of the All-Highest?"
—George Hunter White

THE MEETING WAS SET for noon at a suitably anonymous bastion of corporate America, a sprawling Marriott Hotel and convention center on Long Island. Driving out of the city, I was tense and paranoid. For one thing, I was leaving Manhattan without permission from my parole officer. What was I going to tell him? "I want to travel to Long Island to interview a former narcotics agent who worked undercover for the CIA dosing people with LSD." My parole officer would have ordered a urine test on the spot.

Then there was the fact that previous run-ins with drug cops had usually resulted in criminal prosecutions. I spent most of the eighties in prison for smuggling marijuana. How would this ex-agent of the Federal Bureau of Narcotics (FBN), forerunner of the Drug Enforcement Administration (DEA), take to a retired outlaw writing a story about MK-ULTRA, the CIA's highly secretive mind-control and drug-testing program?

Ira "Ike" Feldman is the only person still alive who worked directly under the legendary George Hunter White in MK-ULTRA. The program began in 1953 amid growing fear of the Soviet Union's potential for developing alternative weaponry. The atomic bomb was a sinister threat, but more terrifying still were possible Soviet assaults on the mind and body from within—through drugs and disease. In an attempt to preempt foreign attacks and even wage its own assaults, the CIA funded a group of renegade agents to experiment with ways to derail a human being.

For years, Feldman had ducked reporters. He agreed to meet with me only after a private detective, a former New York cop who also did time for drugs, put in a good word. There was no guarantee Feldman would talk.

I recognized Feldman immediately when he waddled into the lobby of the Marriott. I had heard he was short, five three, and I'd read how George White used to dress him in a pinstriped zoot suit, blue suede shoes, a Borsalino hat with a turned-up brim, and a phony diamond ring, then send him onto the streets of San Francisco to pose as an East Coast heroin dealer. Now in his seventies, Feldman still looks and talks like Edward G. Robinson playing gangster Johnny Rocco in *Key Largo*.

Feldman leveled a cold, lizard-like gaze on me when we sat down for lunch. He wielded a fat unlit cigar like a baton, pulled out a wad of bills that could have gagged a drug dealer, slipped a 20 to the waitress and told her to take good care of us.

"What's this about?" Feldman demanded. "Who the fuck are you?"

I explained I was a writer researching George White. White, a world-class drinker known to polish off a bottle of gin at a sitting and get up and walk away, died of liver disease in 1975, two years before MK-ULTRA was first made public.

"Why do you want to write about White? I suppose it's this LSD shit."

No, I said, not just the LSD. George White deserved to have his story told.

"White was a son of a bitch," Feldman said "But he was a great cop. He made that fruitcake Hoover look like Nancy Drew."

Again he gazed stonily at me. "Lots of writers asked me to tell my story. Why should I talk to you?"

I decided to come clean. "I used to be part of your world," I answered. "I did eight years for the feds because I refused to rat when I got busted for pot."

Feldman stared at me for a long time. "I know," he said. "I checked you out. That's why I'm here. Now get out your pencil." He waved for the waitress and palmed her a 50 to cover the tab.

"The LSD," Feldman began, "that was just the tip of the iceberg. Write this down. Espionage. Assassinations. Dirty tricks. Drug experiments. Sexual encounters and the study of prostitutes for clandestine use. That's what I was doing when I worked for George White and the CIA."

For my next interview with Feldman, I rented a day room at the Marriott and brought along a tape recorder. Feldman tottered in, pulled a small football-shaped clear plastic ampule out of his pocket and plunked it on the table. It was filled with pure Sandoz LSD-25. He also showed me a gun disguised as a fountain pen which could shoot a cartridge of nerve gas. "Some of the stuff George White and I tested," he explained.

"It all began because the CIA knew the Russians had this LSD shit and they were afraid the KGB was using it to brainwash agents," Feldman told me. "They were worried they might dump it in the water supply and drive everybody wacky. They wanted us to find out if we could actually use it as a truth serum."

Actually, it all began with a mistake. In 1951, Allen Dulles, later appointed director of Central Intelligence, received a report from military sources that the Russians had bought 50 million doses of a new drug from Sandoz Pharmaceuticals in Basel, Switzerland. A follow-up memo stated that Sandoz had an additional ten kilos— about 100 million doses—of the drug, lysergic acid diethylamide (LSD-25), available for sale on the open market.

Dulles was alarmed. From the beginning, LSD was lauded by military and intelligence scientists working on chemical warfare compounds and mind-control experiments as the most potent mind-altering substance known to man. "Infinitesimally small amounts of LSD can completely destroy the sanity of a human being for considerable periods of time (or possibly permanently)," stated an October 1953 CIA memo. In the wrong hands, 100 million doses would be enough to sabotage a whole nation's mental equilibrium.

Dulles convened a high-level committee of CIA and Pentagon officials who agreed the agency should buy the entire Sandoz LSD supply lest the KGB acquire it first. Two agents were dispatched to Switzerland with a black bag containing $240,000.

In fact, Sandoz had produced only about 40 grams of LSD in the ten years since its psychoactive features were first discovered by Albert Hofmann. According to a 1975 CIA document, the U.S. Military attaché in Switzerland had miscalculated by a factor of one million in his CIA reports because he did not know the difference between a milligram (1/1,000 of a gram) and a kilogram (1,000 grams).

Nevertheless, a deal was struck. The CIA would purchase all of Sandoz's potential output of LSD. (Later, when the Eli Lilly Company of Indianapolis perfected a process to synthesize LSD, agency officials insisted on a similar agreement.) An internal CIA memo to Dulles declared the agency would have access to "tonnage quantities." All that remained was for agency heads to figure out what to do with it.

"The objectives were behavior control, behavior anomaly–production, and countermeasures for opposition application of similar substances," states a heavily redacted CIA document on MK-ULTRA released under a 1977 Freedom of Information Act request. The chill winds of the Cold War were howling across the land. Dulles was convinced that, as he told Princeton University's National Alumni Conference, Russian and Chinese Communists had secretly developed "brain perversion techniques . . .

so subtle and so abhorrent to our way of life that we have recoiled from facing up to them."

Pentagon strategists began to envision a day when battles would be fought on psychic terrain in wars without conventional weaponry. The terrifying specter of a secret army of "Manchurian Candidates," outwardly normal operatives programmed to carry out political assassinations, was paraded before a gullible and easily manipulated public.

Ike Feldman remembers that time well. A Brooklyn boy, he was drafted into the Army in 1941. Army tests showed he had an unusual facility for language, so he was enrolled in a special school in Germany where he learned fluent Russian. By the end of the war, Feldman was a lieutenant colonel with a background in Military Intelligence. The Army sent him to another language school, this time in Monterey, California, where he added Mandarin Chinese to his repertoire.

While with Military Intelligence in Europe, Feldman first heard of George White. "White was with the OSS [Office of Strategic Services, forerunner of the CIA]. I heard stories about him. Donovan [William "Wild Bill" Donovan, founder of the OSS] loved White. White supposedly killed some Japanese spy with his bare hands while he was on assignment in Calcutta. He used to keep a picture of the bloody corpse on the wall in his office."

In the early fifties, after a stint in Korea working for the CIA under Army auspices, Feldman decided he'd had enough of military life. He settled in California. "I always wanted chickens," Feldman recalled, "so I bought a chicken ranch. In the meantime, there wasn't a hell of a lot to do with chickens.

"Before long, I got a call—this time from White," Feldman continued. " 'We understand you're back in the States,' he says. 'I want you to come in to the Bureau of Narcotics.' This was '54 to '55. White was District Supervisor [of the Federal Bureau of Narcotics] in San Francisco. I went in. I go to room 144 of the Federal

Building, and this is the first time I met George White. He was a big, powerful man with a completely bald head. Not tall, but big. Fat. He shaved his head and had the most beautiful blue eyes you've ever seen. 'Ike,' he says, 'we want you as an agent. We know you've been a hell of an agent with Intelligence. The CIA knows it. You speak all these languages. We want you to work as an undercover agent in San Francisco.' "

What Feldman didn't know at the time was that George White was still working for the CIA. White's particular area of expertise was the testing of drugs on unwitting human guinea pigs. During the war, one of White's projects for the OSS was the quest for a "truth drug," a serum that could be administered to prisoners of war or captured spies during interrogations. After trying and rejecting several substances, the OSS scientists settled on a highly concentrated liquid extract of *cannabis indica*, a particularly potent strain of marijuana. Never one to shrink from the call of duty, White first tried the drug on himself. He downed a full vial of the clear, viscous liquid and soon passed out without revealing any secrets.

Meanwhile, at the CIA's Technical Services Staff (TSS), the department specializing in unconventional weaponry such as poisons, biological warfare, psychoactive substances, and mind control, Dr. Sidney Gottlieb was searching for a candidate to head MK-ULTRA. Gottlieb, a club-footed scientist who overcame a pronounced stutter in his rise to head the TSS, had discovered White's name while perusing old OSS files on the Truth Drug Experiments. White's credentials were impeccable: A former crime reporter on the West Coast before he joined the narcotics bureau, White had soon become one of the top international undercover agents under Harry Anslinger, the grandfather of America's war on drugs.

After meeting with Gottlieb, White noted his initiation into the world of psychedelics in his diary: "Gottlieb proposes I be CIA consultant and I agree."

Moonlighting for the CIA, with funds disbursed by Gottlieb,

White rented two adjoining apartment safe houses at 81 Bedford Street in Greenwich Village. Using the alias Morgan Hall, he constructed an elaborate alter-identity as a seaman and artist in the Jack London mode. By night, CIA spy Morgan Hall metamorphosed into a drug-eating denizen of the bohemian coffeehouse scene. With a head full of acid and gin, White prowled downtown clubs and bars. He struck up conversations with strangers, then lured them back to the pad where he served drinks spiked with Sandoz's finest.

"Gloria gets the horrors . . . Janet sky high," White dutifully recorded in his diary. In another entry, he proudly noted, "Lashbrook at 81 Bedford Street—Owen Winkle and the LSD surprise—can wash." In recognition of the often bizarre behavior brought on by the drug, White assigned LSD the code-name "Stormy."

According to an agency memo, the CIA feared KGB agents might employ psychedelics "to produce anxiety or terror in medically unsophisticated subjects unable to distinguish drug-induced psychosis from actual insanity." In an effort to school "enlightened operatives" for that eventuality, Dulles and Gottlieb instructed high-ranking agency personnel, including Gottlieb's entire staff at TSS, to take LSD themselves and administer it to their colleagues.

"There was an extensive amount of self-experimentation for the reason that we felt that a firsthand knowledge of the subjective effects of these drugs [was] important to those of us who were involved in the program," Gottlieb explained at a Senate Subcommittee hearing years later. In truth, CIA spooks and scientists alike were tripping their brains out. "I didn't want to leave it," one CIA agent said of his first LSD trip. "I felt I would be going back to a place where I wouldn't be able to hold on to this kind of beauty."

But as covert LSD experiments proliferated, things down at CIA headquarters began to get out of hand. "LSD favors the prepared mind," wrote Dr. Oscar Janiger, a Los Angeles psychiatrist and early LSD devotee. Non-drug factors such as set and setting—a person's mental state going into the experience and the surroundings in which the drug is taken—can make all the difference in reactions to a dose of LSD.

Frank Olson was a civilian biochemist working for the Army Chemical Corps' Special Operations Division (SOD) at Fort Detrick in Frederick, Maryland. In another sub-project of MK-ULTRA code-named MK-NAOMI, the CIA had bankrolled SOD to produce and maintain vicious mutant germ strains capable of killing or incapacitating would-be victims. Olson's specialty at Fort Detrick was delivering deadly diseases in sprays and aerosol emulsions.

Just before Thanksgiving in 1953, at a CIA retreat for a conference on biological warfare, Gottlieb slipped Olson a huge dose of LSD in an after-dinner liqueur. When Gottlieb revealed to the uproarious group that he'd laced the Cointreau, Olson suffered a psychotic snap. "You're all a bunch of thespians!" Olson shouted at his fellow acid trippers, then spent a long night wandering around babbling to himself. Back at Fort Detrick, Olson lapsed in and out of depression, began to have grave misgivings about his work, and believed the agency was out to get him. Ten days later, he crashed through the tenth-floor window of the Statler Hotel in New York and plummeted to his death on the sidewalk below.

"White had been testing the stuff in New York when that guy Olson went out the window and died," Feldman said. "I don't know if he jumped or he was pushed. They say he jumped. Anyway, that's when they shut down the New York operation and moved it to San Francisco." The Olson affair was successfully covered up by the CIA for over 20 years. White, who had been instrumental in the cover-up, was promoted to district supervisor.

Unfazed by the suicide of their colleague, the CIA's acid enthusiasts were, in fact, more convinced of the value of their experiments.

They would now focus on LSD as a potent new agent for offensive unconventional warfare. The drug-testing program resumed in the Bay Area under the cryptonym Operation Midnight Climax. It was then that White hired Feldman.

Posing as Joe Capone, junk dealer and pimp, Feldman infiltrated the seamy North Beach criminal demimonde. "I always wanted to be a gangster," Feldman told me. "So I was good at it. Before long, I had half a dozen girls working for me. One day, White calls me into his office. 'Ike,' he says, 'you've been doing one hell of a job as an undercover man. Now I'm gonna give you another assignment. We want you to test these mind-bending drugs.' I said, 'Why the hell do you want to test mind-bending drugs?' He said, 'Have you ever heard of *The Manchurian Candidate*?' I know about *The Manchurian Candidate*. In fact, I read the book. 'Well,' White said, 'that's why we have to test these drugs, to find out if they can be used to brainwash people.' He says, 'If we can find out just how good this stuff works, you'll be doing a great deal for your country.'"

These days, Feldman takes offense at how his work has been characterized by former cops who knew him. "I was no pimp," Feldman insisted. Yet he freely admitted that his role in Midnight Climax was to supply whores. "These cunts all thought I was a racketeer," Feldman explained. He paid girls $50 to $100 a night to lure johns to a safe house apartment that White had set up on Telegraph Hill with funds provided by the CIA. Unsuspecting clients were served cocktails laced with powerful doses of LSD and other concoctions the CIA sent out to be tested.

"As George White once told me, 'Ike, your best information outside comes from the whores and the junkies. If you treat a whore nice, she'll treat you nice. If you treat a junkie nice, he'll treat you nice.' But sometimes, when people had information, there was only one way you could get it. If it was a girl, you put her tits in a drawer and slammed the drawer. If it was a guy, you took his cock and you hit it with a hammer. And they would talk to you. Now, with these drugs, you could get information without having to abuse people."

The "pad," as White called the CIA safe house, resembled a playboy's lair, circa 1955. The walls were covered with Toulouse-Lautrec posters of French cancan dancers. In the cabinets were sex toys and photos of manacled women in black fishnet stockings and studded leather halters. White outfitted the place with elaborate bugging equipment, including four microphones disguised as electrical outlets that were connected to tape recorders hidden behind a false wall. While Feldman's hookers served mind-altering cocktails and frolicked with the johns, White sat on a portable toilet behind the two-way mirror, sipping martinis, watching the experiments, and scribbling notes for his reports to the CIA.

"We tested this stuff they call the Sextender," Feldman went on. "There was this Russian ship in the harbor. I had a couple of my girls pick up these Russian sailors and bring 'em back to the pad. White wanted to know all kinds of crap, but they weren't talking. So we had the girls slip 'em this sex drug. It gets your dick up like a rat. Stays up for two hours. These guys went crazy. They fucked these poor girls until they couldn't walk straight. The girls were complaining they couldn't take any more screwing. But White found out what he wanted to know. Now this drug, what they call the Sextender, I understand it's being sold to guys who can't get a hard-on."

One such drug, called papavarine, is injected directly into the penis with a half-inch needle containing about two raindrops' worth of the medicine. "I tell [the men] to thrust it in like a bull-fighter finishing off the bull," said a San Antonio urologist in a recent report on the new therapies used to treat male impotence. "Dangers include injecting too much drug, so that an erection can last dangerously long and kill penile tissue." The potions are not administered orally, as they were by the CIA, because the drug must affect only the penis and not the rest of the body. Drug companies are now working on a cream that can be rubbed directly onto the penis before intercourse. Feldman claims we have the CIA to thank for these medical breakthroughs.

"White always wanted to try everything himself," Feldman remembered. "Whatever drugs they sent out, it didn't matter, he wanted to see how they worked on him before he tried them on anyone else. He always said he never felt a goddamn thing. He thought it was all bullshit. White drank so much booze, he couldn't feel his fucking cock.

"This thing"—Feldman held up the fountain pen gas gun— "the boys in Washington sent it out and told us to test the gas. White says to me, 'C'mon, Ike. Let's go outside. I'll shoot you with it, then you shoot me.' 'Fuck that,' I said. 'You ain't gonna shoot me with that crap.' So we went outside and I shot George White with the gas. He coughed, his face turned red, his eyes started watering. He was choking. Turned out, that stuff was the prototype for Mace."

I asked Feldman if he'd ever met Sidney Gottlieb, the elusive scientist who was the brains behind MK-ULTRA. "Several times Sidney Gottlieb came out," Feldman assured me. "I met Gottlieb at the pad, and at White's office. White used to send me to the airport to pick up Sidney and this other wacko, John Gittinger, the psychologist. Sidney was a nice guy. He was a fuckin' nut. They were all nuts. I says, 'You're a good Jewish boy from Brooklyn, like me. What are you doing with these crazy cocksuckers?' He had this black bag with him. He says, 'This is my bag of dirty tricks.' He had all kinds of crap in that bag. We took a drive over to Muir Woods out by Stinson Beach. Sidney says, 'Stop the car.' He pulls out a dart gun and shoots this big eucalyptus tree with a dart. Then he tells me, 'Come back in two days and check this tree.' So we go back in two days, the tree was completely dead. Not a leaf left on it. Now that was the forerunner of Agent Orange.

"I went back and I saw White, and he says to me, 'What do you think of Sidney?' I said, 'I think he's a fuckin' nut.' White says, 'Well, he may be a nut, but this is the program. This is what we do.' White thought they were all assholes. He said, 'These guys are running our Intelligence?' But they sent George $2,000 a month for the pad, and as long as they paid the bills, we went along with the program." Gottlieb, who now lives in Virginia, refused to be interviewed for this article.

"Another time, I come back to the pad and the whole joint is littered with these pipe cleaners," Feldman went on. "I said, 'Who's smokin' a pipe?' Gittinger, one of those CIA nuts, was there with two of my girls. He had 'em explaining all these different sex acts, the different positions they knew for humping. Now he has them making these little figurines out of the pipe cleaners—men and women screwing in all these different positions. He was taking pictures of the figurines and writing a history of each one. These pipe cleaner histories were sent back to Washington."

A stated goal of Project MK-ULTRA was to determine "if an individual can be trained to perform an act of attempted assassination involuntarily" while under the influence of various mind-control techniques, and then have no memory of the event later. Feldman told me that in the early sixties, after the MK-ULTRA program had been around for over a decade, he was summoned to George White's office. White and CIA director Allen Dulles were there.

"They wanted George to arrange to hit Fidel Castro," Feldman said. "They were gonna soak his cigars with LSD and drive him crazy. George called me in because I had this whore, one of my whores was this Cuban girl and we were gonna send her down to see Castro with a box of LSD-soaked cigars."

Dick Russell, author of a recent book on the Kennedy assassination titled *The Man Who Knew Too Much*, uncovered new evidence to support the theory that Lee Harvey Oswald was a product of MK-ULTRA. One of the CIA's overseas locations for

LSD and mind-control experiments was Atsugi Naval Air base in Japan where Oswald served as a Marine radar technician. Russell says that after his book was published, a former CIA counter-intelligence expert called him and said Oswald had been "viewed by the CIA as fitting the psychological profile of someone they were looking for in their MK-ULTRA program," and that he had been mind-conditioned to defect to the USSR.

Robert Kennedy's assassin, Sirhan Sirhan, while working as a horse trainer at the Santa Anita race track near Los Angeles, was introduced to hypnosis and the occult by a fellow groom with shadowy connections. Sirhan has always maintained he has no memory of the night he shot Kennedy.

One of the CIA's mob contacts long suspected of involvement in John Kennedy's assassination was the Las Vegas *capo mafioso* John Roselli. Roselli had risen to prominence in the Mob by taking over the Annenberg-Ragen wire service at Santa Anita, where Oswald's killer, Jack Ruby, sold a handicapper's tip sheet. Ike Feldman told me Roselli was one of White's many informants.

"On more than one occasion, White sent me to the airport to pick up John Roselli and bring him to the office," said Feldman. Roselli was originally from Chicago, where White had served as District Supervisor of the Federal Bureau of Narcotics from 1945 through 1947. Following a big opium smuggling bust in 1947, Jack Ruby was picked up and hauled in for interrogation, then later let off the hook by none other than White. Federal Bureau of Narcotics files indicate Jack Ruby was yet another of White's legion stool pigeons.

The connections between MK-ULTRA mind-control experiments, the proliferation of the drug culture, Mob/CIA assassination plots, and the emergence of new, lethal viruses go on and on. Fort Detrick in Maryland, where Frank Olson worked experimenting with viral strains (such as the deadly microbes Sidney Gottlieb personally carried to Africa in an aborted attempt to assassinate Patrice Lumumba), was recently the locale of a near disaster involving an outbreak of a newly emerged virus. The event was chronicled in a lengthy article published in the *New Yorker*. Though the *New Yorker* writer did not make the connection between Fort Detrick, SOD, Frank Olson, and MK-NAOMI, he told of a number of monkeys who all died of a highly infectious virus known as Ebola that first appeared in 55 African villages in 1976, killing nine out of ten of its victims. Some epidemiologists believe AIDS originated in Africa. Feldman claimed the CIA used Africa as a staging ground to test germ warfare because "no one gave a goddamn about any of this crap over there."

The MK-ULTRA program, the largest domestic operation ever mounted by the CIA, continued well into the seventies. According to Feldman and other CIA experts, it is still continuing today under an alphabet soup of different cryptonyms. Indeed, one ex-agent told me it would be foolish to think that a program as fruitful as MK-ULTRA would be discontinued. When the agency comes under scrutiny, it simply changes the name of the program and continues unabated.

The public first learned of MK-ULTRA in 1977, with the disclosure of thousands of classified documents and CIA testimony before a Senate Subcommittee on Health and Scientific Research chaired by Senator Edward Kennedy. Ike Feldman was subpoenaed and appeared on a panel of witnesses, but the senators failed to ask him a single question. Sidney Gottlieb, complaining of a heart condition, testified at a special semi-public session. He delivered a prepared statement and admitted to having destroyed perhaps one set of files. Another set was turned over to Senate investigators. The full extent of the CIA's activities under the rubric of MK-ULTRA may never be known.

George White retired from the Narcotics Bureau in 1965. The last ten years of his life, he lived in Stinson Beach, California, where, known as Colonel White, he went on the wagon for a few years and became chief of the volunteer fire department. Local residents remember him once turning in four kids for smoking pot, and in another incident, spraying a preacher and his congregation with water at a beach picnic. He was also known to terrorize his wealthier neighbors by driving his jeep across their lawns. After White's death, his widow donated his papers, including diaries, to an electronic surveillance museum. As information on MK-ULTRA entered the public domain, people who had known White only in his official FBN capacity were stunned to learn of his undercover role as Morgan Hall.

Ike Feldman, kept alive by a pacemaker, lives with his wife in a quiet suburban Long Island community where he tends his garden and oversees a number of business interests. According to George Belk, a former head of the Drug Enforcement Agency in New York, Feldman quit the drug agency following a probe by the internal security division. "Feldman was the sort of guy who didn't have too many scruples," said Dan Casey, a retired FBN agent who worked with Feldman in San Francisco. "For him, the ends justified the means." A DEA flack confirmed Feldman "resigned under a cloud" at a time when a number of agents came under suspicion for a variety of offenses, none having to do with secret drug-testing programs. Feldman asserts he still works for the CIA on a contract basis, mostly in the Far East and Korea.

On the day of our last interview, over lunch at a restaurant in Little Italy, Feldman told me the CIA had contacted him and asked him why he was talking to me.

"Fuck them," Feldman said. "I do what I want. I never signed any goddamn secrecy agreement."

I asked him why he decided to talk with me. "There's too much bullshit in the world," Feldman said. "The world runs on bullshit."

"To make a long story short," he said, using one of his favorite verbal segues, "I want the truth of this to be known so that people understand that what we did was good for the country."

We ambled down the street to a Chinese grocer, where

Feldman carried on a lengthy conversation with the owner in Chinese. A couple of young girls, tourists, wanted to have their picture taken with Feldman. "Are you a gangster?" they asked.

"No," Feldman replied with a wave of his cigar, "I'm a goddamn CIA agent."

As we walked on, I asked Feldman to explain how his work had been helpful to the country.

"I learned that most of this stuff was necessary for the United States," he said, "and even though it may have hurt somebody in the beginning, in the long run it was important. As long as it did good for the country."

I pressed him. "How so?"

"Well, look," Feldman gestured with his cigar, "We're goddamn free, aren't we?"

THE METAMORPHOSIS OF MICHAEL LEVINE

From Gung-Ho Narc
to Drug War Dissident

Prison Life, October 1994

From *Prison Life* to Expert Witness

Prison Life *magazine, my ill-fated foray into the world of periodical publishing, began with a phone call from a guy named Joe Strahl who had worked as a civilian in charge of running a prison commissary. I was editing the not-for-profit* Fortune News *at the time and reading a lot of good writing coming out of our prisons. Strahl originally envisioned* Prison Life *as an advertising vehicle for companies selling products to the "captured market" of prisoners, either through the institution's commissary or by mail-order. The magazine was being written mostly by writers who had never set foot in a prison. I saw* Prison Life *as a potential glossy, national outlet for the writing and art being created in our prisons, and as an opposing voice to the shrill chorus of propagandists hyping the war on crime and perpetuating the worst stereotypes about prisoners.*

When Strahl and I met for lunch a few weeks later, Prison Life *had ceased publication. The problem neither of us were willing to confront at the time is that prisoners don't have a lot of money to spend, what they can buy is heavily regulated, and they'll wait for a magazine to be passed around to 20 or 30 other readers before they'll cough up the dough for a subscription. Strahl had hooked-up with some bottom-feeders in the magazine publishing world who pulled the plug on his financing after putting out three issues. In the weeks and months that followed, I acquired the name* Prison Life *from Strahl and re-launched the magazine with a new editorial mission as the Voice of the Convict. The idea was to put out a hard-hitting and* entertaining magazine produced by convicts and ex-cons but aimed at a larger, free-world audience interested in first-hand stories about crime and the criminal justice system.

Our first issue came out in March of 1994. To set the tone, we put a legendary convict, Herbie Sperling, on the cover. Sperling is doing life with no parole for drugs. In October of '94 we followed with ex-DEA agent Mike Levine's interview debunking the Drug War. In the three years that followed we published 11 more issues, attracted a huge amount of positive national press, TV and radio coverage, and won an Utne Reader Alternative Magazine award. Even though the magazine often sold out on the handful of newsstands we convinced to carry it, because we could never attract sufficient advertising dollars, we ended up losing a lot of money before we were finally forced to cease publication in 1997. Looking back, I realize I should have published Prison Life as a non-profit and gone for grant money to finance it. Nevertheless, like prison itself, editing Prison Life was an invaluable experience that led to much of what I've done since and am still doing in the world of crime and punishment.

During the late-eighties and early-nineties America's prison population doubled and then tripled. The politically motivated lock-'em-up-and-throw-away-the-key, three-strikes-you're-in-for-life, mandatory-minimum sentences crusade brought about the biggest prison-building boom in history and established America as the world leader in its incarceration rate, length of sentences, number of executions, and instances of prisoner abuse. The get-tough-on-prisoners policies of the same period brought about the elimination of the one initiative proven to help criminals rehabilitate themselves and become law-abiding citizens: education programs. There was so much tax money being squeezed out of civilians to fund this misguided, phony war on crime and drugs that private corporations and publicly traded companies like Wackenhut and Corrections Corporation of America got in on the game by building private prisons for profit. We chronicled it all in the pages of Prison Life.

Marc Levin showed Prison Life *to Sheila Nevins at HBO. Sheila told Marc she wanted to meet me and when I walked into her office a few days later, she presented me with a pair of shackles and said she was chaining me to the leg of the sofa until we agreed on a deal. Before we left Sheila's office that day we had formulated a plan to produce a series of documentaries on prison-related issues for her America Undercover series.*

"What's the first subject you want to take on?" Sheila asked us. Marc and I already had our answer: the War on Drugs, the engine powering the thriving prison-industrial complex. Former DEA agent Michael Levine was on the cover of the then-current issue of Prison Life *denouncing the "phony" drug war. And so in January of 1996 we published the companion issue of* Prison Life *along with our first documentary for HBO,* Prisoners of the War on Drugs, *that aired on January 8th.*

My work with Sheila Nevins brought me into the world of dramatic series television when HBO hired me to work as the technical consultant on the prison series Oz, *which I left over creative differences after the first season. Marc and I went on to make* Slam, Whiteboyz, *and* Street Time, *the Showtime series. Based on my writing and film work on prisons, I have been qualified in state and federal court as an expert witness on prison culture and prison violence. One of the cases I worked on as an expert witness we developed as the documentary,* Gladiator Days: Anatomy of a Prison Murder.

Mike Levine is one of the nation's foremost expert witnesses for defendants who are victims of over-zealous law enforcement. He's a trial consultant and lecturer on human intelligence, covert operations, narcotics trafficking, police procedure, RICO and conspiracy investigations, and the use of excessive force. He has testified as an expert in over 500 civil and criminal trials internationally and domestically. He hosts a radio show, Expert Witness, *with Kristina Borjesson, author of* Into the Buzzsaw, *on WBAI in New York. The show is devoted to debunking the lies told by our government. To find out more about Mike's work, log on to expertwitnessradio.org.*

Talk about coming full circle—in the final episode of my Show-time TV show Street Time, *I cast Mike Levine as Luc Rivard, an international dope smuggler caught in a DEA sting. I even used the set-up from my bust in the lobby at the Sheraton Senator at LAX as an early scenario in the show. I had Levine, as Rivard, position himself on the mezzanine of a hotel and watch his contact enter to make sure they weren't under surveillance. It was art imitating life. Levine says he gets more flack from his former law enforcement colleagues for his portrayal of a dope dealer in* Street Time *than he does for his controversial books.*

THE METAMORPHOSIS OF MICHAEL LEVINE

I READ FORMER UNDERCOVER DEA agent Michael Levine's first book, Deep Cover *(Delacorte, New York, 1990) while in prison serving a 25-year sentence for smuggling marijuana and hash. In those days I felt about DEA agents about the same way I imagine they felt about me: a mixture of loathing and fascination that is the nexus of the outlaw/lawman symbiosis and has more to do, I sus-pect, with how alike cops and criminals are than how different they might be.*

A few years later, I was standing in a book store in Los Angeles when my wife, Kim, who is a former undercover narcotics agent and writer, handed me Levine's latest book, The Big White Lie *(Thunder's Mouth, New York, 1993). I bought the book and added it to the stack on my desk—"required reading" on America's holy war on drugs. Like most ex-POWs, I am obsessed with trying to understand the events that resulted in my being locked in prison.*

Some months passed and I still hadn't got around to reading the book. We were in the process of buying a home in upstate New York, and the real estate agent, after hearing we were writers, asked if we had ever heard of Michael Levine. He said his sister had sold Levine and his wife a home not far from where we were thinking of buying.

This inspired me to pull The Big White Lie out of my "must read" stack and dig into it. Two days later I closed the book and knew I had to meet this guy. The next day Kim and I drove to town to drop off some packages at Federal Express. As we were pulling away from the drive-through, I happened to look over at the driver in the opposite lane.

"That's Mike Levine," I said to Kim. I thought I recognized him from his picture on the book jacket; something just told me to look up and there was Levine.

Kim, who had been on "Larry King Live" with Levine when her book, Rush, was first published, thought I was hallucinating. "You just want to meet the guy so badly you see him everywhere."

"No, that's him." I was sure of it. Kim got out of the car and, showing both her hands so Levine could see that she wasn't armed, walked toward the car.

"Mike?" she asked warily. Levine looked back at her. "Kim Wozencraft. We were on—"

"Oh yeah. Hey Kim. How ya' doin'?" It was Levine all right. The force was with me that day, and the force wanted me to meet Mike Levine.

Why did I want to meet this agent, this man who a decade or so ago was my sworn enemy and would have done everything within his large powers to lock my ass in a "cage," as Levine is fond of calling prison? This former comrade-in-arms of the men who in fact did put my ass in stir for the better part of the eighties? Because Mike Levine, with considerable help from his wife, Laura Kavanau-Levine, wrote a book that is called The Big White Lie, a book that is essential reading for every Joe citizen dumb enough to believe the politicians and swallow whole government propaganda on this insane, bullshit war on drugs that is destroying our nation.

When former drug smugglers, who may know what they are

talking about, come out and say that the biggest international dope dealers are either CIA assets or enjoy CIA protection, the statement is seen as self-serving. It helps the cause of truth considerably when scholars like Alfred McCoy write and publish well researched, documented studies on the relationship between CIA and some of the world's dope producers. (The Politics of Heroin: CIA Complicity in the Global Drug Trade, *Lawrence Hill Books, New York, 1991.*) *But when a man with Levine's hard-earned credentials, a man who believed in the drug war and fought bravely and honestly for his government to the highest and most perilous levels, only to discover the shocking truth that he had been sold out by the very people he was working for, when such an insider comes forward and writes a book telling the truth, it is of monumental importance. Levine's writing* The Big White Lie *is the equivalent of General Norman Schwarzkopf writing a book proving the Army is the full of shit and debunking the Gulf War as a bad joke all about big money.*

So I met Mike Levine. It was eerie sitting across the table from him, breaking bread with him, talking about the drug war. Levine was a special brand of DEA agent. Levine worked undercover; he spent most of his 25-year career pretending to be a drug dealer. I spent a good part of my career pretending I was not a drug dealer. I wondered if I would have known the guy was an agent had someone introduced us back in the old days. I'm sure Levine would have made me.

Levine is big: over six feet, over two hundred pounds. He's dark; they used to call him "El Judio Triqueño," the Dark Jew. He is strong and moves like an athlete poised on the balls of his feet. He's a martial arts expert, a tough, likable man with a roughhouse boyish quality, who, I have no doubt, could snap and instantly become deadly at the drop of a dime bag.

But why put the guy on the cover of Prison Life *magazine? This guy put people in prison, over three thousand by his own count. He was a fuckin' cop! We decided to put Michael Levine on the cover because we believe what he has to say is vital to the American prison population. Most of the people reading this magazine are in prison on drug charges or for drug-related crimes. Many of the 1.5 million Americans behind bars wouldn't be there if more people listened to what Mike Levine had to say about the drug war and withdrew their support for politicians who promote this sham. The war on drugs is a major part of what we know as the bloated and corrupt criminal justice system that costs taxpayers billions and is in fact a scam perpetrated on middle-class taxpayers and a form of genocide inflicted on the poor.*

I got to know Mike Levine over the course of a long winter and had a number of in-depth discussions with him about the drug war. I may not agree with his ideas on how to solve the drug problem, but I trust Levine's information just as I have come to trust him as a man. Knowing Mike Levine has brought me the hard realization that all cops are not necessarily bad people; some are just misguided.

From my own experience in the international drug trade I know what Levine has to say is true. When I was smuggling hash out of the Middle East during the long and bloody civil war in Lebanon, (a war that had more to do with fighting for control of the multibillion-dollar drug trade than it did with religion) I met and worked with intelligence operatives and major criminals who openly traded in arms and drugs with CIA connivance and protection. In fact, you couldn't operate for long in the Middle East, or anywhere else for that matter, without CIA connections. Ostensibly, our government aids drug trafficking for political reasons like supposedly fighting communism. But people in the business know that this rationale, if true at all, is clearly secondary to the profit motive.

Levine and I got together to record a distillation of our ongoing dialogue, a kind of précis of Levine's career, and the subject of his books. But it is to those books, and particularly to The Big White Lie, *that I invite the reader. Read them if you care at all about why you are in prison.*

• • •

I grew up on Tremont Avenue and Southern Boulevard in the Bronx, 48th Precinct. I was a bad kid, really bad, arrested twice before I was 16. I was lucky enough to join the military before I got into serious trouble. I was a violent kid and looking back on it I was really afraid, scared to death. The neighborhood was changing from Italian, Jewish and Irish to Puerto Rican and Black. On the streets I used to lie and say that I was half Puerto Rican. You might say I was already undercover. I have a talent for picking up languages. My first girlfriend was Puerto Rican and I picked up street Spanish very quickly with a good accent. Later on, as an undercover narcotic agent in Bangkok, Thailand, within two months I had picked up enough Thai from bar girls to get around pretty good.

But what really started me toward my career in undercover was fate. I believe in fate, in destiny. In 1959 I was a military policeman assigned to Plattsburg Air Force Base. I had joined the boxing team, I was 19 years old, over 6 feet and 227 pounds, and like all 19-year-olds, I couldn't conceive of my own death. That's why 19-year-olds make such wonderful soldiers. I got into a fight with a guy named Heywood over a three-dollar hat. We were both military policemen. He pulled his gun, stuck it in my stomach and pulled the trigger. It misfired. There were a bunch of witnesses and he was later arrested. Later, when they test fired the gun, it fired every time.

What that incident taught me was the truth of an old Arab saying: "Any day is a good day to die." The saying became my mantra. From that moment on I had only one fear in life, that I would reach a final moment on earth and say the words: "I wish I had . . ." I was in a rush to live out every fantasy that I could imagine; visit every country I was ever curious about; taste it, feel it, eat it, try everything my imagination could conjure before that final moment came. And what better way to live out a fantasy than to become an international undercover agent for the government? And that's exactly what I did, and I got quite good at it. The better I got the easier it was for me to create any fantasy I wanted and the government would fund it, as long as the bottom line was that someone went to jail.

I played every role you could imagine to bust dope dealers. I played a priest, an Arab sheik, a Cuban terrorist. I was an undercover member of both the American Nazi Party and the Marxist Leninist branch of the Communist party at the same time. I even passed myself off as a Mafia don to two corrupt DEA agents who sold me the names of informers out of the DEA computer.

Around the same time the kicks started to wear off, I found out that my brother was a heroin addict. I started listening to all the rhetoric of the politicians about the holy war on drugs, and about the evil, dark enemy that was destroying my baby brother. I developed a foaming at the mouth hatred for drug dealers. I blamed them for destroying kids like my brother, destroying our country and all that shit, and I was on a fucking mission from god to destroy them, and I didn't care if I died doing it. We're all going to die. If you could choose the way you go, what would it be? Well, I chose undercover. That's how spaced-out I was, until reality set in.

My first glimpse of reality was in 1971 when I went deep cover in Bangkok, Thailand. I spent about a month hanging with Chinese heroin dealers. We're talking about the time in history when the biggest heroin seizure was still the French Connection, less than 70 pounds. These guys were producing hundreds of pounds of heroin a week. They thought I was a representative of the Mafia and wanted to impress me; they were trying to talk me into buying heavy weight. So they invited me to visit what they called "the factory" up in Chiang Mai, the center of their heroin production. But in the middle of the night I was brought into the embassy and told

I would not be allowed to go to the heroin factory. The factory was part of the anti-communist support system and was protected by CIA. As long as they did the CIA's bidding, the guys who owned the factory had a license to support themselves by selling American kids drugs, and not only kids on the streets of the U.S., but GI's on the battlefield as well. It was the first time in my life that I was stopped by my own government.

I didn't know what was going on back then. I was a good soldier, I wouldn't have believed it if anyone told me the truth. I was simply told that our government has other priorities and that the case had no end with the guys I was dealing with. They wound up delivering one kilo of heroin to me and were busted in front of the Siam Intercontinental Hotel along with some guys making false-bottom suitcases. These guys were expendable, but the factory owners had CIA sanction to produce tons of dope, and all of it was going into the veins of Americans, including my brother.

The case ended up getting a lot of publicity. It was the first time one undercover agent arrested the smuggler and financier of a heroin-dealing organization in America, and then went overseas to bust their source. I was given a special Treasury Act award, and let myself get carried away with my own press clippings. They made me feel like I had already won the drug war single-handedly. I shoved the reality of what I had just lived through, along with my brother's slow death, into the corner of my mind where it couldn't hurt me. Later I would learn that this heroin exporting organization used the dead bodies of our GIs killed in Viet Nam to smuggle their junk. The stuff was hidden in the body cavities and the body bags.

I returned to the U.S. and to my job as a Special Agent in the Hard Narcotics Smuggling Group of Customs. There was a brutal turf war going on between Customs and then the Bureau of Narcotics and Dangerous Drugs. One of Nixon's last acts as President was to create the Drug Enforcement Administration to end the jurisdictional war. On the morning of July 1, 1973, I woke up as a DEA agent.

For a long time while I did nothing but undercover work; hundreds of cases, back to back, cocaine and heroin, seven days a week, never going home. I blocked out the whole Bangkok experience and was back fighting my holy war with drug dealers. Black, white, yellow, Jew, Italian, it made no difference to me. If you sold dope you were my enemy, and I would do anything to destroy you.

My wake-up call seemed to begin with my brother's death in February 1977. I was teaching a class on Narcotics Undercover Tactics to the Brooklyn district attorney's investigators when I was told that my brother had committed suicide. He left a note that read: "To my family and friends, I can't stand the drugs anymore." And, again, if you believe in fate as I do, almost immediately I received word that I was to be transferred to Buenos Aires, Argentina as the DEA attaché.

During those years the demand for cocaine, and later crack, had begun to explode. The South American producers couldn't even come close to meeting it. The biggest drug dealer alive was a man unknown to anyone in America, a Bolivian named Roberto Suarez. I was recently shown a transcript of secret testimony before a closed senate committee chaired by Senator John Kerry. A man named Ramon Milian Rodriguez, who was the main money launderer for the Medellin Cartel, told the Senators that Roberto Suarez is the biggest drug dealer who ever lived. Suarez was the Medellin Cartel's main supplier of cocaine base, and, according to Rodriguez, most of the coke that entered the U.S. that wasn't supplied directly by the Colombians came from the Suarez organization.

People think that cocaine is synonymous with Colombia, but that's not true. In the seventies and eighties especially, Bolivia was producing 90 to 95 percent of the cocaine base in the world. You shut down Bolivia in the late seventies and you shut down the world's cocaine supply. You win the drug war. The whole thing was under the control of one man, Roberto Suarez. When I got down to South America in 1978, Suarez's organization, then called La Mafia Cruzeña, The Santa Cruz Mafia, which later became *La Corporacion,* or The Corporation, couldn't fill 10 percent of the American demand. They needed to take control of the Bolivian government, which was then anti-drugs, so that cocaine production wouldn't be bothered by law enforcement. They needed to eliminate all the smaller dealers and improve production methods. To catch up with the $100-billion American demand, they had to create what became the General Motors of cocaine. That's what they started to do. They brought in neo-Nazis from Europe, all working for an escaped Nazi war criminal, a man named Klaus Barbie, known as "The Butcher of Leon," to handle their security. They began killing the competition, improving production and buying off key government officials. My job was to penetrate this organization.

To do this, I created a fictitious Mafia family. We had a team of some 30 undercover agents posing as pilots, chauffeurs, bodyguards, and collectors. A beautiful Puerto Rican agent was flow in from Los Angeles to pose as my wife. We had to rely on the Bolivian government to work with us secretly; they were the last vestiges of anti-drug feeling in South America, and they never betrayed us. They recognized the burgeoning power of drug trafficking and realized they could lose their country to drug dealers unless something was done.

When it began to look as if our sting operation was going to be wildly successful, our whole government turned on us. Our fake Mafia family was given a low-rent, three-room bungalow to use as a Mafia mansion; we were given one beat-up old green Lincoln that had been seized and didn't have proper registration as our whole Mafia fleet; our undercover pilots were given a plane so inadequate that Suarez's people were taking bets that it would never get off the ground with a load of drugs. I could go on for an hour with all the shit that was pulled to screw us up. It's all in the book, and the government has not denied a thing. They can't. They just pretend that I never wrote it.

So, along with this group of undercover agents, I decide to make this case in spite of the DEA suits. In fact, that became our rallying cry: "Let's make this case in spite of DEA." And we did. While my undercover pilots picked up the biggest load of drugs in history, about 900 pounds of cocaine, directly from Suarez in the Bolivian jungle, I paid nine million dollars in cash to two of the biggest drug dealers who ever lived, José Gasser and Alfredo "Cutuchi" Gutierrez. They were arrested leaving a Miami bank with the money. This was a first not only for the DEA but for all law enforcement. Had we been allowed to let the buy go through, we would've been part of the Corporation. We could've just gobbled them up, the whole war on cocaine would've been over before it began. Instead, what happened was the government cut the whole operation short, and made us do a buy-bust instead of a buy. I still felt that we had done well. There was enough evidence to indict half the Suarez organization and half the Bolivian government that he'd bought off. The whole drug world was watching this case. DEA had given the U.S. war on drugs a respectability it would never again achieve. The arrest made worldwide news. It was called the greatest sting operation in law enforcement history. They based a lot of the Al Pacino movie *Scarface* on this case. Once again, I got swept away with my own press clippings. While the undercover team was basking in the limelight, the case was quietly being destroyed by our government.

José Gasser, one of the wealthiest men in Bolivia, whose family ran the government from behind the scenes for decades, was allowed to go free by the Assistant United States Attorney Michael Sullivan, the man who, ironically, would later prosecute that other CIA asset, Manuel Noriega. Sullivan is still the chief of the criminal division of the Miami U.S. Attorney's office. All the charges against Gasser were dropped. I couldn't believe it. The guy is busted walking out of a bank with nine million dollars in drug money and the chief assistant U.S. Attorney drops all the charges! His codefendant when he was arrested, Gutierrez, said he was willing to make a full statement and testify against Gasser, and the United States Attorney didn't even put the case before the Grand Jury. Mysteriously, no one ever took the statement from Gutierrez. None of this was reported by the press.

Three months later, Judge Alcee Hasting's lowered Gutierrez's bail to one million dollars. Gutierrez put the money up in cash and walked out of jail. I was making frantic phone calls from Buenos Aires and I couldn't even get DEA in Miami to follow him. Within hours, Gutierrez got on a private plane and left the country. It was the biggest cocaine seizure in U.S. history and no one was left in jail and no one in the media covered the story. Actually, the only member of the media who wrote that something strange was going on was *High Times* magazine. In any case, the first thing that Gasser did when he got back to Bolivia was publish a full-page replica of his unconditional release from U.S. custody. DEA and the U.S. war on drugs became the laughing stock of the South American drug world. It has never recovered.

I started to complain with cables and phones calls to DEA, to the Department of Justice, to State. I was outraged. At the same time, I learned that the very people I had arrested were planning to overthrow the Bolivian government, which had been helpful to the DEA. I was informed by the Argentinean secret police, who were nothing but mass murderers on the payroll of both DEA and CIA, that they had people in Bolivia aiding the drug dealers and their neo-Nazi security force in fomenting the revolution, and that they were all working for the CIA. The CIA was helping the biggest drug dealers in the world take over Bolivia. How could this be? I investigated the Gasser family and learned that they were tied to the World Anti-Communist League since the early sixties and were well-established CIA assets. I thought I was losing my mind.

To keep myself from going crazy I began keeping notes that would eventually become the book, *The Big White Lie*. The evidence was indisputable. Yet, back then, living through it, I couldn't believe what was happening, it was like I was living out "Seven Days of the Condor" or something. Then the revolution actually happened. I warned DEA about it but no one gave a shit. Once the revolution took place, the very people in the Bolivian government who helped us were tortured, killed and exiled from their own country. It was the bloodiest revolution in Bolivia's history. To this day they call it the "Cocaine Coup." It was the first time in history that a government was taken over by drug traffickers, only what the press wasn't telling the world was that the traffickers had been released from a U.S. jail by the CIA. It was the beginning of what became the Corporation. Within months Bolivia would be exceeding the world's demand for cocaine. It was the beginning of the cocaine and later the crack epidemic. It was the end of the U.S. war on drugs.

I continued complaining to anyone who would listen, only no one wanted to hear what I had to say. I toyed with the idea of becoming a whistle blower, but I'd already had some experience with the phonies a lot of our political leaders are. When they use the word loyalty, they are not talking about loyalty to the American people. They mean loyalty to a political party. The American people, in the can or out, are the last thing in the world these guys care about.

Around this time, *Newsweek* published an article about the Cocaine Coup and the cocaine-dealing government of Bolivia, which had by now broken down into separate branches of government. The whole Bolivian government was now in the cocaine business, thanks to the CIA. In the article they name as the heads of the Bolivian drug-dealing factions José Gasser and Alfredo Gutierrez, the same guys I paid nine million bucks to, and a woman, who became an important part of my book, Sonia Atala, known as the Queen of Cocaine. I didn't know it then, but I would end up living with Sonia in a deep cover assignment called Operation Hun. Sonia, by the way, was Pablo Escobar's first source of cocaine base. If you read *The Big White Lie* you realize that Sonia and other key members of the drug-dealing Bolivian government were CIA assets, which makes the prime source of Escobar's cocaine the CIA. The CIA is therefore America's primary supplier of cocaine. You can imagine that for me, as an undercover DEA agent putting my life on the line to fight the drug war, the realization came as a terrible blow.

Why do they do it? Why does the CIA aid and abet certain international drug kingpins while men like you are sent out at considerable personal risk and huge expense to U.S. taxpayers to fight a war that in fact our government does not want to win?

If they were forced to answer that question they would probably say something like, "to defeat Communism." But the truth is they've never even been forced, publicly, to admit what they are doing. In my opinion, and the opinion of a lot of other people in law enforcement, a good many of these guys are just cashing in, like the one guy recently caught, Aldrich Aimes, the guy who was spying for the Russians. They documented only a half million bucks paid to Aimes from the Russians, yet they found that he had spent around two-and-a-half million. Where do you think the rest of the money came from? The man was also the head of CIA narcotics unit. Believe me, the government does not want to talk about that because it would be like lifting up a rock and exposing a whole slew of worms like Aldrich. The point is, our intelligence agencies don't answer to anyone, and when they're caught they hide behind National Security, or they just flat out lie. They lie to Congress, they lie in court, and they even lie on *Larry King Live*.

When *The Big White Lie* was published in October of 1993, I was on *Good Morning America*, and I leveled all my charges. *Good Morning America* was the only national television show that would put me on the air with *The Big White Lie*. A day later, Admiral Stansfield Turner, who was head of CIA during the Bolivian cocaine revolution, appeared on *Good Morning America*, which was very unlike the CIA. He said he was there to "put the lie to the book." Almost every conversation in the book was tape recorded, so there is no way he could contradict a word of what I wrote. He in fact admitted that he had never read the book. He said that when he was head of Central Intelligence, he couldn't even get them to be interested in working drug investigations, which is a perfect example of how incredibly inept and naïve both he and President Carter were in their handling and understanding of CIA. Of course he couldn't get them interested in working drug cases—they'd have to investigate themselves. They were supporting the biggest dealers on the face of the earth, from the Mujihedeen in Afghanistan and the Contras and the drug-dealing Bolivian government to the drug-dealing tribes of South East Asia. None of these CIA people will sit face to face with me on one of these open talk shows; no one will attack my books on a factual basis. They'll never say Levine said this and it's not true. They'll just give this blanket statement that it never happened and the media accepts it without question. Every show that I've ever appeared on has offered the government an opportunity to appear with me—I encourage it—but they refuse because they have too much to hide, and I'm one of those who knows where all the bodies are buried.

Three weeks after Stansfield Turner made his statement, the CIA was caught smuggling a ton of cocaine into the U.S. from Caracas, Venezuela. The story was on *60 Minutes* and on the front page of *The New York Times*, and if you blinked you missed it because the media dropped it like a hot potato. I was doing a radio show in California at the time, the *Michael Jackson Show*, and I said, "What do you say now, Admiral Turner? Let's talk about this." Michael Jackson, to his credit, tried to get Turner on the air, he of course refused.

The next thing that happened, James Woolsey, the new head of Central Intelligence, who is nothing more than a defense attorney for the CIA, went on damage control media appearances around the country. Of course, every national show gave him an open mike with no hard questions, the kind of questions a disillusioned DEA agent could ask, and there are many of us. He appeared on *Larry King Live,* looked into the camera and lied to several million Americans. He said that the cocaine—and there was over a ton—never hit the street. He said it was an intelligence-gathering operation gone awry. Total, absolute lies. I checked with my own sources, and found that not only did CIA help run a ton of coke into the U.S., but there may have been much more than that one ton smuggled into our country by the CIA.

The transcripts mentioned, which record the secret testimony of Ramon Milian Rodriguez before a closed session of Senator John Kerry's Senate Subcommittee on Terrorism and Narcotics, make it clear that a good many public officials know the truth of the drug war yet they continue to lie to the American public, both for political reasons and because of the huge amounts of money involved in the international narcotics trade.

Of course they know. How else do you explain how a United States Senator, John Kerry, could say things like, "Our covert agencies have converted themselves to channels for drugs," and "They have perverted our system of justice," which is what Kerry said after hearing witnesses like Milian Rodriguez lay out the evidence of CIA complicity in the illegal drug business. Yet none of these CIA-sanctioned drug dealers go to jail. Isn't what Kerry's describing treason? How can he make a statement like that and not indict anyone?

You mean like Oliver North?
Look, in the Iran-Contra report of an investigation, paid for by

tens of millions of dollars of taxpayer money, our congress wrote: "All those who sought leniency for General Bueso-Rosa, a drug-smuggling murderer, and all those who looked the other way at Manual Noriega's drug dealing are responsible for what is happening on the streets of America today." If you read the report you would know that they are referring to none other than Ollie North, Presidents Bush and Reagan and the CIA, yet they wouldn't name them, nor would they move to indict a single government official for conspiracy to put drugs on our streets.

Conspiracy is an easy charge to prove. I've done it hundreds of times. And I'll bet there are a lot of other people reading this magazine who know from first-hand experience just how easy it is to get convicted of drug conspiracy. All you've got to prove is knowledge, an agreement and an overt act. Unfortunately, our elected officials don't have the courage to protect us. This current crop of leaders will go down in history as the epitome of criminality and cowardice in government.

It's been proven: North had an interest in a Swiss bank account that was worth several million dollars. He bought a car with $15,000 cash that he told Congress was part of a slush fund he had hidden in his closet, accumulated from throwing change in there, along with an old accident settlement. Since when are accident settlements paid in cash? Ask any of your readers behind bars what would have happened if they tried to tell DEA that bullshit. But North got away with it. He had 543 pages in his personal diaries with notations in his own handwriting about drugs, including statements like, "Aircraft needed to pick up 1500 kilos." On one page he had the notation: "$14 million to finance came from drugs." And that was after he had blacked out most of the statements he thought were incriminating. He refused to tell Congress what was on the pages that he had blacked out; he took the Fifth. North was banned from Costa Rica by Oscar Arias, the Nobel Prize-winning President, for gun-running and smuggling.

My friend, another DEA agent named Cele Castillio, the agent who was in charge of El Salvador when North's Contras were running cocaine by the ton up to the U.S. has come out with a new book and told the truth: the DEA and the whole American embassy knew that North's people were running dope up to the U.S. Cele was told to keep out of it by the U.S. Ambassador himself, Edwin Corr. He told Cele, "It's a White House operation."

North may well be elected Senator, some say that he'll run for President. All Senator Kerry's rhetoric not withstanding, no government official will ever stand trial for the tons and tons of drugs they helped flood this country. Why? Because Americans don't know how to fight back, and they are content to swallow any shit the politicians throw at them.

The transcripts of the Rodriguez testimony account for only two of the twelve executive sessions that were full of evidence of government cover-up of drug trafficking, all kept secret from the American people. Jack Blum, who was chief investigator for Senator Kerry, resigned from the committee and said, "I am sick to death about the truths I cannot tell." *The Big White Lie* is one of those truths. The transcripts tell an overpowering, nauseating truth.

In 1980, Ramon Milian Rodriguez, a man who is sitting in the Federal can right now for laundering over 200 million dollars a month in drug money, was so overcome by the amount of power that he had—he said that he could virtually buy anyone, any country that he wanted—that he went to the CIA and told them what he was doing and the CIA told him to keep doing it. He named the CIA agents he spoke to. They later asked him for favors and money in return, including the $10 million he paid to Felix Rodriguez, the CIA guy who worked directly for North. Milian Rodriguez testified that he made money-laundering deals with the heads of every major U.S. bank in Panama, and that they all knew it was drug money and none of them was indicted—not a banker, not a CIA agent, no one.

You and I both know, we've been there. This so-called drug war is all about money, big money. It's about money and power and political corruption and political cowardice. It's easy to get a street dope pusher and put his face on television, then put him away for 30 years. But if you have political power, if you are protected by the CIA or if you are the CIA or the head of a major U.S. bank, you've got a get-out-of-jail-free card.

I'll give you an example of how this bogus war is being waged, an example from my own career as a narcotics agent. It is the story of John Clemens. John Clemens is a good example of what happens if you're just a walking around American with no power, and how easy it is to get an indictment and conviction for conspiracy.

On July 4, 1971 I arrested a guy named John Davidson smuggling three kilos of heroin at JFK airport. He flipped and gave up the financier, a guy named Alan Trupkin, who was waiting for him and the dope in Gainesville, Florida. We were on a plane that night to deliver the heroin. We substituted powder for most of the smack, leaving about a gram of real stuff in the false-bottom suitcase. We ended up in a trailer in the middle of a swamp outside of Gainesville. Davidson called Trupkin to tell him that he just got in. This, by the way, was his seventh trip that year. When he called Trupkin, I was taping the phone call. John Clemens, a 22-year-old unemployed musician got on the phone during the conversation because Trupkin couldn't remember how to get to the trailer. Clemens got on the phone and said, "I know the way. I can show him." The statement was recorded. It was the only statement the kid ever made that could be used against him. So this kid who made absolutely nothing from the deal—they used to toss him a bag of heroin from time to time for favors—showed Trupkin the way to the trailer. He was in technical violation of the conspiracy law and in possession of about a gram of heroin. He was there. He aided the guy. So he was indicted, convicted at trial and sentenced to 30 years in prison. The smuggler, Davidson, flipped and worked for the government. He got five years. The financier of the operation, Trupkin, got 15 years because he pled guilty in the middle of the trial and made a deal.

Now compare that to North, who's got 543 references to drugs in his personal hand-written notes, including statements like, "Aircraft needed for 1500 kilos," and "financed by drugs," as well as compelling evidence that he had profited from his activities. None of this was investigated by the professional narcotics investigators, none of it was put before a grand jury. North should be indicted, and some people are talking about him becoming the next President. Meanwhile, John Clemens, as far as I know, is still doing hard time.

You've worked with a lot of the informants over the years as a DEA agent. Do you find them reliable? (I thought back to when I was on trial first in the District of Maine, then in the southern District of New York. In both cases there was no physical evidence connecting me to the marijuana conspiracy, just the testimonies of some lying sacks of shit, yet I got convicted and sentenced to 25 years.)

I never met an informant who didn't lie. An informant will do anything to save his ass. Unfortunately, many informants are a lot slicker than some of the agents. And there are agents who just want to make cases and don't have much of a conscience. That happens all the time. I was hired as a consultant for the defense on one case where the informant was wanted in different countries and so he made a deal with government agents. He was supposed to deliver one Class One dope dealer in exchange for our government protecting and paying him. So the guy went out and found an ignorant illegal alien who was working his butt off 70 hours a week as a parking lot attendant. The informant told the parking lot attendant that he had a bunch of dumb gringos who were willing to give him money for cocaine and that all he had to do was tell them he'd bring the dope later and these gringos would front him about $300,000.

So the parking lot attendant had a couple of meetings with undercover agents and he played the role the informant gave him. The undercover agent asked for a sample, but the parking lot attendant couldn't even come up with a line of coke to give him. Next we cut to a hotel room where a hidden video camera caught the undercover agent sitting on one side of the table and the parking lot attendant on the other side. Between them was a briefcase containing $300,000. They let the guy count the money. In Gomer Pyle Spanish the undercover agent then asked the guy if he would promise to deliver drugs for the money. The guy was nodding his head up and down, his eyes were bugged out. You can see him thinking: Can the gringos really be this stupid? The guy was busted and charged with conspiracy to deliver an enormous load of cocaine. The informant already got paid something like $17,000 for the case.

Part of the testimony for the defense was that all of that government time and effort and money should be spent on the streets of America getting violent criminals and hard-core addicts off the streets—not illegal alien parking lot attendants. That's one of the big reasons we have 25,000 homicides a year in this country, why whole segments of our country are war zones. We're spending billions to fight a war that doesn't exist. In the last decade we spent more than $100 billion on this bullshit war and got absolutely nothing for our money. If we had aimed that money at violent criminals and the treatment of hard-core drug addicts instead of things like the half billion dollars we spent on military radar last year, which didn't even catch a single drug smuggler, and the thousands of bullshit drug seizures and arrests paraded as drug war "victories," millions of lives and billions of dollars would have been saved—including the life of my son who was a New York City police officer killed by a crack addict, and my brother who was a life-long heroin addict. Yet this year our latest "leader," President Clinton, has budgeted more money than ever before, $13.5 billion, for more of the same crap.

In The Big White Lie *you recount how you became a total paranoid. You were investigated by your own agency; you began to wonder what side you were on; you came to fear for your life after you wrote a letter to* Newsweek *exposing the CIA's role in the Bolivian cocaine coup.*

I think I'm still alive because I was so paranoid. I didn't tell people I was leaving Argentina because I no longer trusted anyone. While I was cooling my heels in Puerto Rico, the Argentine secret police, the same killers who worked for the CIA and who were also working for DEA, broke into my house, only, surprise, I was not there. So they sat around all night waiting for me to come home, drinking booze just like they did when they had visited me. The gardener showed up the next morning and they split, leaving the bottle of Scotch and the glasses on the floor, just the way they usually did. That's the kind of arrogance these guys have—they literally had a license to kill. Paranoia for a DEA agent working in South America is a healthy emotion.

I wrote a letter on U.S. Embassy stationery to *Newsweek*, return-receipt requested, telling them that they had missed the real story. I told them that the real story was the CIA's secret support of this drug-running government in Bolivia and escaped Nazi war criminals. But more than that, I told them the real story was the ultimate betrayal of the American people. Weeks went by and I received the postcard indicating that *Newsweek* had received the letter. Then nothing. A month later, within a 24-hour period, first the Argentines tried to kill me, and when that failed I was placed under investigation by DEA's Internal Security Division. I was falsely accused of everything from black marketing and stealing government funds, to having sex with my undercover partner, a married DEA agent assigned to play my wife. They even wrote me up for playing rock music on my radio and disturbing other people at the embassy.

Then they force-transferred me to Washington, D.C., where I

was kept under investigation, followed, my phones tapped, you name it. As a government agent you have no rights, you are literally at the mercy of these people. I was holding on for dear life. In the middle of this madness, I was asked to go undercover to pose as the lover and business partner of Sonia Atala, the woman known as the Queen of Cocaine. When *The Washington Post* reviewed *The Big White Lie*, they called it an "edge-of-the-seat thriller," but questioned how the government could have me under investigation and at the same time send me undercover on their most sensitive case. I have the proof backing up every single event that I wrote about. The question should not be posed to me; it should be posed to the people who sent me out on the assignment.

Sonia Atala was one of the people running the Bolivian government, and she was one of my targets. In Bolivia she had a Nazi paramilitary unit under her command, her house was the main government torture chamber, and suddenly she turns up in the U.S. working for DEA. As it turned out, she was also a CIA asset, protected by them. And while she was working as an informant, she never stopped selling dope. She in fact was arrested for selling cocaine to DEA undercover agents while working for DEA and CIA. Of course she was never tried for the arrest because she had carte blanche to sell Americans dope.

I am probably one of the most investigated men in the agency because I was one of the most outspoken, and because I represent a threat. I represent a threat to giant bureaucracies making a big buck off this drug war. I don't remember who said it but the quote goes, "If you create a bureaucracy, the bureaucracy's first enemy are the people who created it." That's the nature of the bureaucracy. In the drug war, these bureaucracies are created to try and solve the problem, but that would put them out of a job. Now if you think they are going to put themselves out of a job, I've got a Class One cocaine dealer posing as a parking lot attendant I want you to meet.

We've gone from two federal drug agencies and a $20 million

budget in 1965, when I started in the business, to an $11.5 billion budget and 54 federal and military agencies screaming for more money when I retired in 1989. The American people have gotten absolutely nothing for their money, but the bureaucracies have profited handsomely; they gobble up the gush of taxpayer funds like hungry animals. Who's paying for it? All of us. And it's not the police agencies, it is a lot of so-called "good guys," the treatment-on-demand programs that have absolutely no effect on hard-core drug addicts but which make a hell of a lot of money. According to the *Village Voice*, the guy who heads up Phoenix House makes a $600,000 a year salary. The Partnership For a Drug Free America and other federally-funded programs that churn out television ads and informational booklets and hold rallies and marches and fund drives really don't want this phony war to go away. There are a lot of people who make a lot of money, which can only be justified as long as we have a drug problem. I'm a threat to all of these so-called good guys. I can very well understand why they would come after me.

EVERYBODY MUST GET STONED

Oliver Stone Goes to Prison

Prison Life, March 1995

EVERYBODY MUST GET STONED

Oliver Stone Goes to Prison

Prison Life, March 1995

Prison Life Goes to Hollywood

It's a testament to Oliver Stone's generosity as an artist that he was willing to sit for an interview to be published in a convict magazine that at its peak only had a circulation of a mere thirty thousand. I read that Stone had been locked up for marijuana, so I knew we had at least that much in common. Stone got turned on in Viet Nam during the war and came home with a new worldview. He hadn't been back on this continent a week when he was busted with Vietnamese pot at the border and locked up facing federal drug smuggling charges.

My meeting with Stone was set up through an agent at Creative Artists Agency (CAA). An article about Prison Life *had appeared on the front page of the business section of the* New York Times, *and in a single afternoon I got calls from all three major talent agencies in Hollywood wanting to represent me and* Prison Life. *Three years later* Slam *won Sundance, and the agents circled again. When I met with CAA that time, I told them, "But you already represent me."*

Hollywood has long been mining the prison drama. At a certain point, mid-life in publishing the magazine, I noticed there were over 20 L.A. production companies subscribing to Prison Life. *Ex-con turned actor Danny Trejo, featured on the cover of the March 1996 issue, told me he got the part in* Con Air *because a casting director had seen his mug on the cover of* Prison Life. *We did a whole issue on prison movies and actors who'd done time: Trejo, Charles Dutton, the poet and playwright Miguel Piñero, and we outed Tim Allen as a snitch. We did an interview with Susan Sarandon on* Dead Man Walking *and with Taylor Hackford on his epic prison drama,* Blood In, Blood Out, *which was shot in San Quentin and written by the National Book Award-winning ex-con poet, Jimmy Santiago Baca, who we also featured in the magazine. Taylor Hackford told me Jimmy Baca was so freaked out being back in the joint while they were shooting* Blood In, Blood Out, *he hunkered down in an empty cell with his typewriter and wouldn't come out. I remember a moment of surreal role reversal while shooting* Slam *in the D.C. Jail. I had a walkie-talkie, I was running back and forth from the tier where we were shooting to the guard's control center, telling them to open this cell door, close that one. I had become a surrogate hack. I had to stop myself and do a reality check.*

Stone's films never provoke bland responses; people either love Oliver Stone movies or they hate them so much they think he should be locked up. I was doing a segment of the TV interview show Politically Incorrect *on the day I met Oliver (who was also on the show) for the interview. I went on first, with the author Fran Lebowitz, who called Stone a phony bag of wind and said he should do us all a favor and stop making movies. Her anger was vitriolic. He should continue making movies if for no other reason than to keep pissing people like her off.*

Oliver wrote me a note after the article appeared saying he enjoyed meeting me and wanted to get together again. I met with him in L.A. and New York, wrote a screenplay for him with Daniel Voll, based on an article Daniel had published in Esquire *about neo-Nazis in the American military. Oliver wanted me to introduce him to the cult hero, ex-con writer Eddie Bunker. The night I brought them together at a Santa Monica restaurant, Oliver came in, got down on his knees, took Eddie's head in his hands and said, "What a great face! I've got to put you in one of my movies." Eddie and I wrote a treatment for Stone for another prison movie based on a documentary I did with Marc Levin,* Gladiator Days:

Anatomy of a Prison Murder, *and an article I wrote for* Esquire, *"The Making of Bone Crusher," reprinted in this book.*

Stone is our Orson Welles. His movies are big, bold, original; some would say over-the-top. But when your creative consciousness is forged in the jungles of Viet Nam hunting Viet Cong high on acid and Cannabis Indica, only to come home and go directly to jail . . . from then on, nothing is over the top.

EVERYBODY MUST GET STONED

INT. PRISON CELL—DAY
MOVE IN ON: Billy and Eric do yoga exercises. As they
stretch in ritual movement, bodies glistening
with sweat, they repeat a mantra-like phrase.
BILLY/ERIC
Prison-monastery. Cloister-cave.

THE SCENE IS FROM *Midnight Express,* the classic dope smuggler's prison horror movie written by Oliver Stone and directed by Alan Parker. The words, prison-monastery, cloister-cave, the concept conveyed by juxtaposing those words, and the mantra-like repetition, sustained me through more than one long lonely day in a prison cell. A prison is a monastery, a cell, a cloister—a cave at the center of the universe. It is all in the mind, all in how you look at it: your vision.

I went to see *Midnight Express* when it first came out in 1978. At the time, that was what I did: I smuggled hash out of countries like Lebanon and Turkey. Watching the film, I felt my guts tighten with fear: the same fear I felt every time I was approached by a cop or a customs officer, the fear I was addicted to. I thought, *This is too real. Get me out of here.*

Oliver Stone's films do that to me. They make me feel as though I should get up and run before I get caught in the obsession he's trying to exorcise. But it is too late, I am riveted to the seat, glued to the screen, already held in thrall by the same obsessions.

During the eighties, when movies written and directed by Stone started coming out, I was in custody, held in maximum security federal pens. Late at night, in a smoky, crowded cellblock TV room, I watched *Scarface* (1983, written by Stone and directed by Brian De Palma) with a tough audience, men who knew bullshit when they saw it, men who lived the coke-and-power-crazed criminal life depicted by Stone's main character, Tony Montana. The convicts were mesmerized; there was none of the usual jeering and hooting provoked by most Hollywood renditions of their experience.

But it was *Salvador* (1986), then *Platoon* (1986), that really got to me. After watching both films, I went back to my cell and hit the bunk nearly wrung out from the emotions I'd felt. I was enraged, confused, inspired. Most of all, I wanted out—out of fucking prison so I could join the fight. I saw myself as a prisoner of war, a dedicated writer searching for truth, a revolutionary burning with hatred for the sanctimonious arrogance and hypocrisy of a government that could wage war in Viet Nam to defend freedom and lock me up for 25 years for smuggling pot. It was all related: pot, Viet Nam, freedom, our lying government. And Oliver Stone was on to it. I went to sleep wondering, *Who is this guy? How does he know about this shit?*

One of the first things I did after I got out was to rent *Born On the Fourth of July* (1989). A week later, *Wall Street* (1987). Same thing. I was blown away. Watching Tom Cruise as paraplegic Ron Kovic, I barely moved. It is the incredible intensity Stone manages to get actors to bring to the tormented, compelling characters he creates that make his films so enthralling. Tom Cruise has never been as tightly wound since, Michael Douglas never so despicable. In *Talk Radio* (1989), which I also saw on video, Stone began to reveal his hand as a cinematic virtuoso. Even as I watched the movie on a TV screen, I had a disorienting sense of having been granted omniscient point of view, as though I were seeing each frame from somewhere in the middle of the action.

The Doors, released in 1991, was the first Stone-*auteured* film I saw on the big screen. It is the only way to experience that movie. Big. Loud. Overpowering. Relentless and dangerous. Excessive. Like a rock concert, like a Doors concert, like a Doors concert on acid, and like the times: the sixties. That's what I like about Stone's films—the danger. He has a dangerous vision, a vision of character forged through life-and-death risk-taking, excess, despair, and courage.

Stone has such courage, as an artist and as a man. An only child, son of a well-off Jewish businessman and a loving, Roman Catholic, French mother, Stone was a Park Avenue kid and a Yalie. At twenty-one, he quit it all and went off to war. After a bitter fight with his parents, he dropped out of college, joined the army and shipped out to Viet Nam as an infantryman.

I understand the impulse. I'm sure it came more from needing to discover himself than from wanting to kill communists. I've often wondered how I would have handled combat. I would have gone to Viet Nam had I not been turned on to pot and radicalized at early age. Yet the question remains: Would I have had the courage to fight and kill? Stone volunteered for combat, he was wounded twice and awarded the Bronze Star for bravery. He smoked Vietnamese pot every day for months, ate acid, listened to the Doors and went out hunting Vietcong. How's that for pushing the surreal envelope? No wonder the man is so far out there—far enough, indeed, to discover it was all a horrible mistake. As a film-maker, Stone has been creating powerful testaments to an apocalyptic vision of America that was galvanized fighting guerrilla war high on psychedelics in the jungles of Viet Nam.

And then came *JFK* (1991). Never has a film excited such inflamed, polar controversy. Never has a big budget Hollywood movie had such an impact on our national psyche. Only Oliver Stone has the guts to make such a movie. Only Oliver Stone has the power and integrity as an artist to get such a film made. At a time when most of our esteemed artists have chosen the easy way out, cowering before the keepers of the bottom line, Stone remains true to his heart, true to his instincts, true to his creative vision.

Well before the movie was shot, a pirated version of the script was making the rounds and the vicious guard dogs of our national mendacity were excoriating Stone for supposedly taking liberties with historical fact. *So what?* I thought. Every great artist interprets so-called reality. What matters is the truth of the artist's vision.

JFK, all three-plus hours, passed quickly before my eyes and resonated in my mind and solar plexus like a pot-induced paranoid fantasy. So many of us who grew up during the sixties are victims of the same obsessions. *It's all a fucking conspiracy!* Hadn't I always known that? True, the cocksuckers who are conspiring to manipulate history don't know what the fuck they are doing. But that only makes it worse.

From the time 30-odd years ago (30 very odd years ago) when I took that first hit and journeyed forever one toke over the line, I knew why the stuff was illegal. You get high and you begin to question reality. That is what happened to Oliver Stone. He got stoned and he's never been the same since. None of us will ever be the same. Not Newt Gingrich, nor Hunter Thompson. Not John Lennon, God rest his soul. Not Ken Kesey, nor Robert Stone. (Another stoned Stone.) Not Bob Dylan. Everybody must get stoned. Only Bill Clinton is exempt, still steeped in bullshit because he didn't have the guts to inhale. Sure, Bill.

The afternoon I went to see *Natural Born Killers*, I thought it might be interesting to smoke a little Ulster County weed to get in the proper frame of mind. It should come as no surprise that some of the best pot in the world comes from the hills around Woodstock,

New York. I got out of the cab, lit up a joint, took a couple of hits, then strolled around the corner and into the movie theater.

Moments into the opening sequence I was gripping both arm-rests and holding on for dear sanity. *Holy shit,* I thought, *this is madness. I'm losing it. I'm too high.* The vertiginous cinematography, the balletic violence, the hallucinatory colors and images dazzled me, scared me. Again I thought I should flee the theater before I saw what Stone wanted to show me about violence in America.

I met Oliver Stone a couple of weeks later in a large, plush TV studio conference room on W. 57th Street in Manhattan. We were both there as guests on different segments of *Politically Incorrect,* a cable TV show on Comedy Central. Stone had agreed to meet after I sent him a few copies of *Prison Life* with a note saying I wanted to talk with him about his prison experiences.

I had been warned that Stone liked to insult people when he first met them as a way of throwing them off guard. I wasn't worried about that. One thing nearly a decade of prison will do for you is teach you how to handle charged meetings with men who like to come on as heavies. Stone wasn't at all pompous or insulting. He was intense, dressed in black, wired, lean and restless as an outlaw in a holding cell. But he was essentially cool, sincere, it seemed to me. I had the feeling that he is still out there roaming around in some hairy state of consciousness seeking self-discovery at all costs.

We began by talking about *Midnight Express.* The script won Stone an Oscar and jump-started his career.

"*Midnight Express* was a hell of a story. The movie was done on a very low budget. Not much was expected from it at that time. It was a big surprise, you know, a sleeper hit. It cost about three or four million dollars to make and must have grossed one hundred million dollars internationally. It put me on the board, as well as Alan Parker.

"I wish they had shot the ending that was scripted, the original ending which was his escape through Greece. Billy actually got out without killing anybody. There was a change, dramatic license, because they didn't have the money to shoot the overland escape through Turkey to Greece, which has a *Great Escape* kind of feeling, so they ended it with Billy walking out of the prison after he committed a murder in order to give it some dramatic excitement. We felt he had to kill the fat guy, the commandant who ran the prison, to get out. Actually, the fat guy was a lot funnier than how he's pictured in the movie. He's very solemn and serious in the movie. The Turks are very funny to me because their prison system is so screwed up. When we were shooting in the prison, we would pan down one cell, see some poor guy who's really suffering—skinny and gaunt. In the next cell and you'd see another Turk having hookers and business cronies in and making deals and running contracts from jail. Some of them lived in suites, had all the good food. You could buy anything in a Turkish prison. The whole point about the relativity of the system was a little bit lost in the movie. Everything was for sale—sex. You could have concubines in. We were accused of sensationalism and racism. Amnesty International has always regarded Turkey as one of the great abusers of human rights in this regard. Their prison system is notoriously bad. Years later, when the Turkish prisoner made that extraordinary film *Yol*, about his life in a Turkish prison, he actually shot it in a prison.

"The homosexuality, I dropped. It wasn't even in the book, but I sort of sensed that was going on. Columbia in 1978 was in no position to do a mainstream film with a guy buttfucking or being buttfucked. It wouldn't have gone down."

I asked Stone what it was that drew him to the subject matter of prison.

"I had written *Platoon* a year before *Midnight Express* as an original screenplay. Everyone had read that screenplay, and they were impressed with the writing but they didn't want to make that movie. So they, Columbia, hired me to give it a shot on this film. I was drawn to the material innately because I think it's a great story about justice and injustice, the prison system. And I was drawn to the story because of my own experience in prison, which I used to give it the sense of visceral protest. That all comes from the sense of shock and outrage I had when I came back from Viet Nam. Late in November of '68 I was busted. I had Vietnamese grass on me. Couple of ounces. You know, it was great grass, why not bring some home? I was doing it on a steady basis. I got hooked over there. In a nice way, not in a destructive way.

"I ended up freaking out in America, taking acid on the West Coast. I just had to get out of this country. I wasn't prepared to come home yet—I had to detox. I was not decompressed from the war yet. So I crossed over into Mexico and partied down there because they were a little different from me. I felt more at home in Mexico. On the way back, I was busted at the border with part of those two ounces of Vietnamese grass. Kind of stupid on my part. So the FBI came and got me—handcuffs and all that. I was charged with federal smuggling. Nixon had just declared a drug war on the border. It was the first drug war, which became the precursor to everything that's happened since then. The FBI came and got me and booked me under federal smuggling charges, which was serious. The guys in jail told me that if I got one judge, I'd see three years' probation and probably get it suspended. They said the other guy'll give you twenty years and you'll have to do at least five. It was like a five-to-twenty-year sentence. That was the law, five to twenty years for drug smuggling. So that's what they booked me on. Mugged me and everything. They paraded me through down-town San Diego in the daylight into the courtroom for the indict-ment, chained to the bars. This was ten days out of Viet Nam. I never got to make my phone call. It was a mess. The prison was a fucking mess. It was overpacked, people were sleeping on the floor.

It was San Diego County Jail, a big inner-city prison and it was jammed with people, mostly Blacks and Hispanics, all up on drug charges. Everyone was young, my age or a little bit older. They all hung in gangs. I talked to a lot of these guys and I was just amazed. It opened my eyes. Kids had been in there for six months and they hadn't even gotten a lawyer to come and see them. It was like hard time, but it was preliminary to the trial.

"I think I had spent about two weeks in there and still couldn't get my call in. You're supposed to be allowed a phone call, right? I kept writing notes. At first I didn't want to call my father, I just wanted to deal with it myself. I thought maybe the public defender would come and I could work something out with him myself. But he wouldn't show up. That's the scene from *Midnight Express*. Waiting for some lawyer to get you out.

"Eventually, because of the notes, the guards started to pay a little more attention to me. I got a note out, "Please, I'm a Viet Nam veteran, I haven't had my phone call." Finally, one day they let me make my phone call and I called my father in New York and said I was back from Viet Nam. I hadn't even told him I was back from Viet Nam and here I was in jail on drug smuggling charges. Within a few hours, the lawyer showed up because my father had called and the lawyer knew there was going to be a payment in this matter. He showed up and he was very cheery, like the fellow in the movie. Then he started to work on the process of getting me bailed out.

"Ultimately, to make a long story short, I got out and the charges were dismissed in the interest of justice. I had to stick around San Diego for a week on a probation kind of thing. The lawyer implied that somebody in the D.A.'s office pulled the file. I sensed that money was changing hands. There was something going on. I was sort of detoxed and cleaned out, whatever the word is, and I made it back to New York. Welcome back to New York. It was a weird return. I was twenty-two years old."

"There was that great prison scene in *JFK*," I said, "when Garrison goes to Angola to talk to the Kevin Bacon character. And now, with the horrendous riot sequence at the end of *Natural Born Killers*, you've gone back into prison. Tell us what it was like shooting that riot scene."

"We shot *Natural Born Killers* at Stateville in Illinois, which is a rough prison. It's tough. Stateville was, I think, 70 percent or 80 percent violent criminals. It's the heaviest state prison in Illinois. And I think 80 percent or 90 percent black. So, it was a very interesting view of Chicago. I know it's a violent prison, but I loved the way the warden handled it. He was so cool, just kind of saying, 'They've got it,' meaning the prisoners. 'It's their thing.' He did the minimum, he seemed to give enough leeway to play around and fuck up. I didn't notice a heavy degree of repression, which I saw certainly in Arkansas and in some of the Texas prisons I have visited."

"The Tommy Lee Jones character in *Natural Born Killers* was wild," I said. "Amazing. Tommy was great. Sort of every con's worst nightmare version of some insane geek warden you just know is in there because he really enjoys inflicting pain."

"Yeah? You liked him?" Stone asked with a grin. "In Stateville they had three major gangs, I believe. We shot in several wings of the prison. We had good cooperation. The warden was great, actually. He was the opposite of the Tommy Lee Jones character. He was a very strong guy, he wasn't all that popular, but he knew the right way. He let the prisoners go. He let them have that edge. A lot of the prisoners made cracks about the joint. I'm not going to say it was a perfect prison, but I think that that prison was well run. Imagine allowing us to shoot a riot in there, with real prisoners. It's pretty nutty. Most prisons would never allow that. But Stateville did and I think that ultimately it was a good thing because the prisoners got paid. We also put in a new cable TV system. We hired prisoners to work on the film. They offered us, I think, about 1,000 prisoners and we used most of them. In the first part of the film, we let them use prop guns and beat up our stunt men. They loved it, they were having a ball. Then the press got involved, they heard about it, and they of course went nuts. It hit the papers. Then they closed us down. The governor's office said, 'What is this? Prisoners are walking around making a movie? What if they escape?' The usual. So they closed us down, stopped us from shooting. It was pretty hairy because we were facing a big financial deficit here. We shot some other stuff in Chicago. Meanwhile, we kept negotiating with the prison board to get back in Stateville. Finally, they made a new deal with us. We could use the prisoners, but we had to segregate them from the weapons, rubber weapons. It made it a little more complicated because we needed to use more stunt men which cost us more. But still it worked out. The real sense of violence that you have is those guys going nuts on our stuntmen—beating the shit out of them and enjoying it, climbing the walls, yelling, screaming. Throughout the film, you'll see real prisoners. Sometimes we went to the roundhouse, the real roundhouse, that's a hell of a scene. When you see the uncut version on laser disk, that version will have the uncut riot, which is an amazing scene. People get thrown in ovens. It's all over the top, it's nuts. It's like the music sets in and the riot goes on for about fifteen minutes. The censors went crazy when they saw that.

"A few times during shooting the lights went out. There were a lot of storms and the electricity went out. Our crew got spooked because in the dark, a couple of them got groped. So they saw the real thing, y'know. When the lights go out, things get weird. I like Stateville because you have no security. I mean, once you're in, you're in. They can take you out whenever they want. They could have taken the whole movie crew, if they had wanted to. They knew that we were ransomable, but they were cool. The gangs— one Spanish, one black—were fighting amongst one another and there was a killing while we were there. And then there were the Aryans too, fucking crazies. So there was this whole crazy mix. We had fairly good relations. It's a beautiful old prison, visually exciting. The roundhouse is incredible. Here we were running rampant in it. Claudia Schiffer came to the set one day to do a documentary on us. Schiffer, this gorgeous German model, is walking down the tier and all these black guys are like, 'What the fuck.' The guy who runs the prison system in Illinois was really cool, liked to see these guys have fun. They seemed to be pleased that there wasn't any damage. We were in a long time, shooting riots y'know, and it was tough. I've been to a lot of prisons because I've researched other films about prisons.

"In 1980, I researched *Baby Boy,* which is a beautiful prison novel. And I went to all the prisons in the South. I went to Parchman, and I went to Arkansas and Alabama and Mississippi—that's Parchman. I went to Angola at that point too. It's a good prison, if there is such a thing, it's a much better prison than some of the others I've seen. For example, I remember Arkansas was horrible because the prison was totally regimented, run military style where you walk along the edge of a wall. You're not allowed to even walk in the middle. You shut up and you keep quiet. There were all these rules. I feel like that's the kind of prison that's going to blow."

It was nearly time for us to go to the green room to prepare for the taping. The segment I was to do was about making prisons tougher. I asked Stone what he thought about this whole prison buildup, the creation of an American gulag, a massive prison-industrial complex.

"It's absolute bullshit. It's absolutely the wrong way to go about it. I think it's fascism. The whole concept of fearing crime and creating a monster out of crime is part of the madness of the media. The media has created the fear of crime. Crime itself, violent crime, has remained the same, according to Bureau of Justice statistics, or is actually declining."

"But is it the media creating the fear of crime, or is it the media covering what the politicians in Washington are pushing—their agenda?" I said. "Once we lost the Evil Empire as an enemy, they needed a replacement, some bogeyman to keep the public in fear and get out the vote. Crime, prisoners, prisons—it's a natural. 'Let's pick on them. They can't vote. Nobody gives a shit about them.' To get elected, to get re-elected, they were in a frenzy to see who could pass the toughest laws. 'Three strikes, you're out,' and all that crap. The media picks up on this. The media covers it."

"No, I think the media created this monster because they made a lot of money selling crime shows during the seventies and eighties. It's about money. They created the concept of the bad guy and they terrorized the public with it. The local news is now taking over. Everywhere I go, the local news is tracking a crime around the clock. The average guy stays at home, the passive consumer watches TV and he doesn't want to go out to the supermarket, he wants to stay home and watch the bad guys on TV, which is terrifying. He likes it, he wants to see the violence. But he doesn't want it done to him. Therefore, you have a more passive and consumerist society. Ultimately, they don't want you to leave your house. You can shop on Barry Diller's Home Shopping Network. You can call everything in. You can give them your credit card number for the undertaker. You keep society at bay—it's a repressed society and it's a fear-ridden society. No one thinks for themselves, they can't think through the miasma of images of crime and fear and danger."

"Certainly *Natural Born Killers* has been criticized for its attack upon the media," I said. "But I have to tell you, I didn't see it that way. To me, the movie was really about the culture of violence, the idea that violence begets violence. Ours has always been a violent society. We're a nation founded upon violence. The murder of the Indian in the movie was for me a metaphor of America destroying its heritage by annihilating our indigenous people. You have Mickey coming in and dropping forty pounds of red meat in the middle of the floor, Rodney Dangerfield groping his daughter. By the way, that sequence in the film, the bizarre, over-the-top, sitcom parody with Rodney as the lecherous old man was absolutely amazing. But what I think the movie's saying is: Violence begets violence. This is my whole *spiel*. You want to create a class of super-criminals, people who have no feelings? Treat them like animals, and that's how they will behave. I didn't see your movie as an indictment of the media so much as an indictment of the culture of violence."

Stone flashed me his engaging gap-toothed grin. He took out a pen and began scribbling notes. "Where the hell were you when I needed you?" he asked and laughed. "I think you've said it better than I have in all my interviews. I wish I'd talked to you before the movie came out. I think you've summed it up in a way that I've been struggling to say. The film works on a level which is so hard for people to get. It's a harsh film. It's a savage film. People say they like it or they don't like it. I say that it's irrelevant if you like it or don't like it—it's: Did you get it or didn't you? It's beyond whether you liked it. Who likes this? You can't say you like this kind of culture. It's a crazy culture. It's a culture gone to hell."

A few weeks after the interview, I rented *Heaven and Earth* (1993), the third—with *Platoon* and *Born on the Fourth of July*—in Stone's Viet Nam trilogy. I wanted to round out his oeuvre, get the full sense of where he's been and ponder where he might be going. I watched the film alone late at night, then went to bed to dream on it.

Stone contrasts the beauty of pastoral Viet Nam, the wisdom of its simple, indomitable people, with suburban America, sweet land of TV and obesity. The film is about karma, soul debt, as Buddhists call it. Ultimate justice. The pain and horror you inflict upon others will come back to you. His films are seditious. I wonder if they will allow *Natural Born Killers* to be shown in prison. It should be required viewing in Washington. The riot sequence is your wake-up call. In the nation's prisons, Stone's nightmarish, paranoid vision of America has become reality.

Photo credit: Chris Cozzone

THE RESURRECTION OF EDWARD BUNKER

America's Greatest Living
Convict Writer

Prison Life, Sept/Oct 1995

America's Greatest Living Crime Writer

The best part of running your own magazine is that you get to write about who and what you want. If I had pitched doing a long piece on Edward Bunker to any of the major magazines, most editors would have said, "Who's Edward Bunker?" If you tell them Eddie played Mr. Blue in Quentin Tarantino's Reservoir Dogs *you might get a glimmer of recognition. But if you say he's America's greatest living crime writer, they'll think you mean Elmore Leonard or James Ellroy. The Europeans get Bunker. His books are bestsellers in France, the United Kingdom, and Italy. But in his homeland he's known only to crime-writing cognoscenti.*

When I met Eddie in Los Angeles, he gave me the manuscript of a new novel he'd written called "Men who Prey." The new book had made the rounds of publishers in New York and was rejected by at least half a dozen publishing houses as too hard-core, the characters too unsympathetic. I remember reading what was then the first chapter, about a guy called Mad Dog on a cocaine binge who kills his girlfriend and her daughter, chops them up and puts them in the freezer. I put the manuscript down and said, "Whew, this really is hard-core."

Around this time I had lunch with an editor at St. Martin's Press, Jim Fitzgerald, who wanted to know what I was working on. I said I was writing a piece for Prison Life *about Eddie Bunker. Fitzgerald had heard of Bunker's work and when I told him I had a Bunker manuscript for a new novel I thought was incredibly powerful, he asked to take a look. At Fitzgerald's urging, St. Martin's eventually published "Men Who Prey" as* Dog Eat Dog, *with a new first chapter that introduces the main characters as boys in a California Youth Authority reform school, so that the reader could get some sense of how these boys became who they are by growing up state-raised, as did Eddie Bunker. St. Martin's went on to reprint Bunker's other great crime novels and publish his new book, an autobiography,* The Education of a Felon. *We excerpted Eddie's prison novel,* Animal Factory *in* Prison Life *and it was made into a movie starring Willem DaFoe, directed by Steve Buscemi, with a brilliant performance by Mickey Rourke as a cellblock queen.*

After Dog Eat Dog *came out, it was optioned by the producer Ed Pressman. Pressman threw Eddie a party at the Chateau Marmont in Hollywood. Eddie showed up wearing his Compton baseball cap and when asked to read from the novel, he chose the second chapter, the one about Mad Dog butchering his girlfriend. As he read, I watched the faces of some of the Hollywood types in the audience go from pleasant if slightly condescending smiles to looks of visceral discomfort. The book is disturbing; it's not the inane, gratuitous violence of a Tarantino movie; it's about how we are creating a whole new breed of super-predators in our prisons and how, once released, when faced with laws like three-strikes, these men are going to hold court in the street.*

THE RESURRECTION OF EDWARD BUNKER

TWENTY YEARS AGO, EDWARD Bunker raised from the house of the dead at Terminal Island, the federal pen in San Pedro, California. Bunker was 39 and had spent the better part of his life in reform schools and prisons. Eddie had been a thief, a forger, bank robber and dope dealer. During the sixties he had done seven years straight at San Quentin, and in his last jolt with the feds he'd earned a stay in Marion after refusing to bunk in a dorm at Mac-Neil Island. He was a con's con, as hard-core as they come and a legendary figure in the California prison system, his battered face and scarred body living testament of the brutal beatings he had received at the hands of cops, bulls, and reform school sadists.

Few would have given Bunker more than a couple of years on the bricks before he'd be back in the joint. The chances of a state-raised convict making it in the world are piss poor, and Eddie had no reason to believe that he had undergone the kind of sea change in attitude that might enable him to make it on the streets.

But Bunker's life had changed, though he didn't realize it at the time—it was all still unreal. Bunker was not leaving prison as just another ex-con on parole, like Max Dembo, hero of *No Beast So Fierce*, Bunker's first published novel. Dembo raises from San Quentin wearing ill-fitting dress shoes, with a bus ticket and 65 bucks in his pocket and no family or job waiting for him. Bunker had beaten tremendous odds and transformed himself from a chronic criminal and penitentiary habitué into America's preeminent convict writer.

No Beast So Fierce was published while Eddie was still in prison. Dustin Hoffman bought the film rights to the book and the movie was set to go into production. Bunker had written the screenplay during lengthy sessions with Hoffman in the visiting room at Terminal Island, and now the actor wanted to hire Eddie to work as technical advisor on the movie set. But Bunker was still locked up.

He was also a jailhouse lawyer. "I got a guy out once who was doing a 15-year sentence," he told me. "Got my best friend out, too—who's dead now. He was a good connection, sent me an ounce of junk every month. I was God!"

Eddie made a motion to the court to receive credit for six months jail time he'd been denied by the Bureau of Prisons. "The judge issued a *nunc pro tunc* order. Now for then, it means. So I got credit for the jail time and that was it. They had to let me out.

"I was in the fuckin' hole, D Block, and this is the truth," Eddie remembered of his last day in the pen. "I was doing two sentences, a nickel for the bank robbery and six years on the drug case. I had about six months left and they wanted to ship me out to Leavenworth. But I got a federal court order not to move me. They were so mad, they kept me there in the hole." The convicts were going wild in D Block, setting trash on fire and throwing it out onto the tiers, flooding cells, screaming and yelling—a typical day in the hole. "I burned, I sweated," Eddie said. "Trash in front of the cell, the smoke and the water—when they came to get me I waded out, just kind'a stepped over all the trash and waded out through the shit and the water. I got my street clothes. Dustin sent a limousine for me and the bulls were all coming to work in the morning when that big limo pulled up in the fuckin' parking lot. The convicts are all at the windows and the guards are coming in with their lunch pails. I walk out and get into this long limousine. They rolled back the moon roof, I stood up on the seat and raised both hands in the clenched fist salute. We drove around the parking lot a couple of times and the convicts were yelling, cheering. I was waving back. After that, they coulda dumped me in the bay for all I cared."

No Beast So Fierce is the only one of Bunker's three published novels still in print in the dumb-and-dumber United States. I had to get the real deal on Bunker's work from a French editor, Francois Gueriff, who knows more about American crime writing than most New York literati. I'd heard about Bunker, read about him in H. Bruce Franklin's seminal study of American convict writers, *Prison Literature in America: The Victim as Criminal and Artist*, and I'd seen *Straight Time*, the movie Hoffman made based on *No Beast So Fierce*—just happened to pluck it off the rack at Blockbuster one night and loved it. There is an unforgettable scene in the movie where Hoffman, as Max Dembo, hijacks his twisted parole officer, handcuffs him to the divider in the middle of the freeway and yanks his pants down around his ankles in what has got to be the ultimate parole violation. But it took a Frenchman to educate me on my own literary heritage.

"You *must* read Bunker," Francois said when I showed him a copy of *Prison Life.* He was shocked. "You edit a prison magazine and you don't know Bunker? He is the best!"

Bunker's novels, *No Beast So Fierce,* (W.W. Norton, 1973), *Animal Factory* (Viking, 1977), set in San Quentin, and the extraordinarily moving, autobiographical *Little Boy Blue* (Viking, 1982), all do well in England and in France, yet here he is virtually unknown. It is indicative of how out of touch the publishing establishment is with quality writing that only *No Beast So Fierce,* recently reprinted in the Vintage Black Lizard Crime series, is available.* I had to get in touch with Bunker's agent, have him send me photocopies of the English editions of *Animal Factory* and *Little Boy Blue,* and a copy of the manuscript of Bunker's new book, *Men Who Prey,* in order to read America's greatest living convict writer.

Once I got the books I settled in for two weeks of the kind of concentrated reading I only do when I discover a writer whose work I truly admire. I read Bunker with the same kind of excitement I'd felt when I read Dostoyevsky, Melville, Henry Miller, Norman Mailer and a handful of other writers whose work seemed to possess the power to change my perceptions. First I read *No Beast So Fierce,* an absolutely brilliant portrayal of an alienated convict whose sensibilities, much like Bunker's, have been imbued and tainted with the madness and violence of a childhood in the California Youth Authority at such places as Whittier and Preston, then forged in the animal factory itself, San

---

*Author's Note: Bunker's books are back in print.

Quentin, and finally tempered into hard steel like a shank plunged into the indifferent world he encounters upon release.

The novel opens with Max Dembo polishing his "hideous, bulb-toed" dressout shoes on the night before he is to raise from San Quentin after an eight-year stretch. Against a backdrop of mindless racial hatred and violence, Dembo contemplates freedom. Max has every intention of going straight this time. He's done enough time in joints like San Quentin to know he hates prison and would rather die than continue to live the convict's life of bitter loneliness in a barbaric world crowded with desperate men.

Word had come to the prison that the new jail was worse than the old—that brutality was more freely dispensed—and I remembered being fifteen years old in the other one and having a fight with another juvenile. Three deputies handcuffed me to a drainpipe and took turns punching me in the body. After breaking three ribs they threw me in the hole, a steel box on wheels. It was utterly dark; I couldn't see my hand an inch from my face or know if it was noon or midnight. A quart of water and three slices of bread were the daily food ration. Every three days they brought a paper plate with a gruel of oatmeal sprinkled with raisins. Kneeling in the darkness, I lapped it up like a dog. Nineteen days later they took me back to the reform school (it was when I was captured on the escape) and I collapsed. I had pneumonia. And even if I'd now changed my life, I hadn't changed my loathing for such places and those who ran them.

We follow Dembo on a sentimental bus ride down the coast to Los Angeles, to Hollywood, where he, and his creator Bunker, were born. Max dutifully calls his parole officer, a pudgy bureaucrat named Rosenthal who will prove to be his nemesis—and, in a sense, his liberator from a life of humdrum ass-kissing. Dembo does his best to satisfy Rosenthal's stupid and mean-spirited adherence to rules devised to insure that convicts will violate parole and go back to prison. Then Rosenthal busts Max on suspicion of using junk. Although Max's urine test comes back clean, the parole officer leaves him in the county jail for three weeks while he goes off on vacation.

I stepped into the cell. Steel crashed against steel. I was locked in. The familiar sight of bunk, lidless toilet, pushbutton washbowl and graffiti carved into the paint ("If you can't do the time, don't fuck with crime") combined into a blow that shattered my shell of detachment. Imagine the hurricane of emotions in a man who has served eight years in prison, has been free less than a week, and who finds himself again imprisoned without having committed a crime. A swirl of loneliness, rage, and despair washed me into a tearful, blinded madness. I pleaded silently, "Oh, please help me." The plea was to Fortune, Fate, God, a nameless power, a plea that is torn from every man sometime during a lifetime.

When Rosenthal, still sunburned pink, shows up to get Max and deliver him to a halfway house, Dembo is a whole new animal, though he's crafty enough to keep the beast under wraps until he and the parole officer are in Rosenthal's car headed for the freeway.

We were shooting up a ramp onto the freeway. Traffic was seventy miles an hour. He prattled on, explaining the fullness of his own life in suburbia—golf and bridge and attending football games were enough excitement for any normal person.

"That's good, Mr. Rosenthal. I'm glad you're happy. You know what I really like?"

"I can imagine."

"Speed. Going fast. I've always wanted to be a grand prix driver—vroom, vroom. Ever thought about doing that?"

"Taking unnecessary risks with your life is immature."

"Didn't you like hot rods when you were young?"

"Not really."

"Man, you should see what it's like." I'd been sliding closer to him. Suddenly I stamped my left foot against his right toe, pressing the gas pedal to the floor. The automobile jerked and leaped forward.

"Hey! What!"

I locked my leg straight out as he struggled to pull his foot away. The car was weaving—but gathering momentum. We were going eighty.

"You're through," he threatened.

"Maybe both of us are."

The speedometer rolled across ninety.

"Please," he said, face ashen.

"Fuck your mother."

He reached for the ignition key. I grabbed his thumb and viciously wrenched it back; then backhanded him across the nose. We swerved over the divider line. A horn bleated in protest, and there was a screech of brakes.

My heart pounded. I was afraid—but it was insignificant compared to his terror. We bore down on the rear of a bus. He swerved away just in time. He was whimpering. The sound delighted me.

What impressed me most in Bunker's portrayal of Max Dembo was how he was able to create a hero who has all the normal human feelings, including loneliness, love, despair, fear, guilt, and even pity for his victims, yet whose emotions have been so steeled by the brutal conditions he has been forced to endure in order to survive that he is unable to bow before a dull and oppressive mentality that seeks to stifle his spirit. In essence, Dembo is the embodiment of the convict code: You may rule my body but you will never dominate my character.

On the lam, Max Dembo is thoroughly transformed.

> *I missed Allison intensely. I wished I'd kept her with me—*
> *even being hated is better than being lonely.*
>
> *But I shook off the longing, and by the time I stepped out-*
> *side into the icy afternoon I had the stoicism of accepted hope-*
> *lessness, even glorying in it. The wind was needles against my*
> *cheeks, and I thrust my hands deep into the mackinaw, one*
> *clutching the pistol, my magic wand. The hunger for chaos, for*
> *my life as it was, swelled to swallow loneliness. I walked the*
> *dismal street aware of my freedom, a leopard among domesti-*
> *cated housecats. I felt contempt for the hunched, bundled crea-*
> *tures, all gray and colorless, hurrying desperately toward*
> *warmth and safety.*

The rest of the novel is a Nietzschian hymn to the will to power, an expertly plotted and crafted crime story that does not relent, nor show remorse, up to the final words: "They might get me this time.

"Fuck it!"

THE BEAST CAGED

Animal Factory, Bunker's second book and the consummate American prison novel, was written during Bunker's final sojourn within the walls at a time when his writing career showed promise of salvation. Not only had *No Beast So Fierce* been accepted for publication by a respected publisher, an essay, "War Behind Walls," a controversial and unflinching insider's account of the senseless race wars raging in California's prisons, had appeared in *Harper's.* Bunker had a piece on capital punishment, "Remembering Death Row" in the *San Francisco Chronicle,* as well as articles in other widely read publications.

This was at a time when freeworld Americans seemed to want to hear what their imprisoned brethren had to say. "Yeah," Bunker said when I told him—in answer to his question how *Prison Life* was doing—that the magazine was still struggling. "Nobody gives a shit about convicts anymore. In the sixties when you went by in the prison bus they gave you the V sign for victory. Now they give you the finger."

Bunker, who divides his time between Paris, New York, and the West Coast, was in Los Angeles in early June working on the new Michael Mann film, *Heat*, with his close friend from San Quentin, the actor Danny Trejo. We met at the Holiday Inn in Hollywood. "I like Holiday Inns. They're all the same," Eddie told me. "Kind of like prison cells." Bunker had once been busted at this particular Holiday Inn when he went there to do a dope deal with Squeaky Fromm of Manson Family fame. "The cops let Squeaky go," Eddie chuckled.

He is a mesmerizing jailhouse raconteur, animated, with his constant cigar dangling from his mouth or waving from his hand like a conductor's baton as he orchestrates his tales. He is gentlemanly, almost courtly in manner, and he hits all the right notes in stories he's played before some of the toughest audiences. Convicts know bullshit when they see it, since many are such good bullshitters themselves.

"All the shit I've ever done in my life I've never tried to minimize the facts or alter the facts to make a point," Bunker said when I asked him if he thought of himself as a convict writer. I'm not referring to the narrow sense of the words, but to H. Bruce Franklin's definition of the prisoner writer as the creator of the true tradition of American literature, characterized by realism, pace and plot, and a kind of bloody faithfulness to an outlaw morality at odds with the sanctimonious and hypocritical mass mentality. "I really have brought an extreme amount of integrity to my work. I've never told a lie. I've experienced the truth of the stories I write and I've never distorted anything. No preconceptions. It's always been as true as I can get it, you know?"

Bunker is now stalking through the end of his fifth decade and the beatings are taking their toll. Though he still has a boyish élan and a marvelous twinkle in his eye that belies twenty years of citizenship, his habits are so steeped in prison life that he sprawls on the bed in the hotel room and props his head and shoulders against the bare wall exactly as though he were in a prison cell slumped on the bunk with his back to the concrete. When we were threatened with a traffic jam while out for a ride in Trejo's Caddy, Eddie and Danny panicked at the thought of being stuck in a line and drove all over L.A. on backroads. "I'd rather go around in circles than stand still," they both said at different times.

Remembering my own release from prison five years ago (I also had a novel accepted for publication while still locked up) I brought Eddie back to that time over 20 years ago when the life-long criminal now faced the possibility of profound change.

"The writing gave me hope. I had hope, that was the difference. I'd written like six novels in seventeen years. I'd been out a couple of times, and I'd gotten into a little shit in the joint, but I hadn't really done anything. Nothing published. I decided I'd write a book totally from a criminal's viewpoint and make it as honest, no bullshit a story as I could make it. So I wrote *No Beast So Fierce*. It was for them, the convicts, my brothers. If it hadn't been published, I might have quit. I'd been at it a long time. I didn't write on the outside. When I got out, between those jolts, I got shacked up, stole and carried on. But when I went back to the joint, I'd jump on my typewriter. Other guys do leather," he shrugged, smiled. "I started with no education, no formal education at all.

"I started writing because of Chessman, Caryl Chessman, who wrote while on death row. I was in the hole in San Quentin. The hole used to be behind death row. I kinda knew Chessman, met him in jail, so I talked with him. He sent around an *Argosy* magazine that had published an excerpt from the first chapter of his book, *Cell 2455, Death Row*, and it astounded me, it just astounded me that this convict had his name on a book that had been published. That's when I said, if this motherfucker can do it and he's on the row, what's to stop me?"

I think of Eddie during that period in San Quentin as much like Earl Copen, one of two main characters in *Animal Factory*. Earl is a veteran convict in his 30s with a shaved head, a savvy power broker who reluctantly takes a young, good-looking white fish under his wing. The "youngster," Ron Decker, is a middle-class dope dealer who's been sent to Quentin for a year by a judge who wants to see signs of rehabilitation before he'll consider reducing Decker's sentence. The novel explores the friendship and sense of loyalty that develops between the two men set against the drama of life and death in San Quentin.

The sun had burned off the freezing morning fog, and although the lower recreation yard was still crisp, it was dazzingly bright. Earl sat shirtless on the worn bleachers along third-base line, finishing a joint in the nearest thing to solitude the prison allowed. A red bandanna was tied around his forehead to keep the sweat from his eyes, though it had dried ten minutes after he left the handball court. A still-soaked glove lay limp beside him, and his legs ached from the hard hour of exercise. He played poorly but loved the game. He couldn't bring himself to jog or do calisthenics, because he quit the moment he began breathing hard, but when there was competition he kept going until his body screamed in protest and he had to bend at the waist to draw a good breath. Winter closed the handball courts for months at a time, so he played whenever they were open for a few hours. He sucked on the joint, muttering "dynamite shit" inanely, and the aches went away. He was reluctant to make the long trek to the big yard, and then five tiers to his cell to get a towel to shower with. "Too beautiful a day to be locked up," he muttered, liking the bittersweet ache of longing for freedom. It told him that he was

still human, still yearned for something more than being a con-
vict. He still hoped . . .

He'd decided to follow Seeman's advice and avoid trouble by
avoiding situations. He was keeping to his cell during the day,
reading a lot, and when something happened, it was over before
he heard about it. One of the Brotherhood had killed a man in the
East cellhouse, and the next day during the lunch hour two Chi-
canos had ambushed a third and cut him up pretty bad. If he'd
died, it would have tied the record of thirty-six murders in a year:
the record for stabbings, one hundred and seven, had already been
broken. T.J. and Bad Eye worked in the gym, and he saw them
only at the night movie when the Brotherhood filled two rows of
reserved benches. Earl would have come out during the day if
heroin was on the yard, but the prison had been dry since he'd
gotten an ounce three weeks earlier.

But Earl, and Ron, are drawn inexorably into the vortex of prison
violence as lone psychopaths and packs of predatory men of all
color and stripe vie for dominance or merely strike out to defend
themselves and band together for mutual protection. I won't go
into the absorbing plot of *Animal Factory*, as we plan to serialize
the novel in future issues as a *Prison Life Classics* feature.

Besides displaying Bunker's genius for storytelling, the novel
depicts day-to-day life in a large maximum security prison with an
insight and veracity only a seasoned convict striving to find the
truth could bring to the page. I've never been to San Quentin, never
done time in a state joint, but I spent a few days in the L.A. City Jail
(the infamous Glass House, worst jail I've ever encountered). I was
held for long periods in transit at Terminal Island and Lewisburg,
and I did time in other maximum security federal joints where I
heard war stories from men who had been transferred into the feds
to break up powerful prison gangs that emerged during the sixties
and seventies in the California prison system. Prison life at all levels

and in all prisons bears certain similarities: loneliness in the face of crowds, the humiliation and constant testing of character, and the life of the mind that takes hold once the intelligent prisoner realizes it is all a matter of attitude. Bunker gives us all this in addition to the marrow of life in Quentin, the complexities of symbiotic relationships between prisoners and between convicts and good and bad cops. He shows how smart convicts will ultimately manipulate the rules to suit themselves, the full-time residents of the penitentiary. And he takes us into the ultimate isolation of the hole.

Now he propped a folded blanket as a headrest and webbed his fingers behind his neck, waiting for whatever might happen next. A lifetime of conditioning to bare, dirty cells had given him the ability to endure without letting his mind scream in silent futility at the walls. Such conduct as that was the path to mental breakdown. He didn't care about that either, except that it would give the enemy too much satisfaction. He knew how to be still within his own being.

"In the old days, when I first got there, San Quentin wasn't as violent as it is now," Bunker said when I asked him about those years in Quentin. "There wasn't all the racial trouble, which started with the Muslims. Late fifties. In answer to the Muslims came the Nazis. In the sixties they started getting it on, just between themselves. Then, all of a sudden, George Jackson—the name George Jackson, I remember that plain as day, man, him and maybe six or seven others, they ran down a tier and started stabbing white guys just because they were white. The guys they cut were fish, just arrived off the bus. They were just standing there and these guys came on 'em and started stabbing. That was the first time, that's when it started. Since then, it's been like a war behind walls. And the war still goes on.

"In the sixties the administration started bending over backwards for them convicts, man. I saw so many funny things in that interlude. They had half the joint on fuckin' pill lines. They had fuckin' lines across the middle of the yard, a hundred yards long, givin' them medication, everybody gettin' loaded. They had guys staggering around. They got more liberal and tried to pacify these convicts, but then they started killing guards. When they started killing guards—MAN! Now they've gotten so fuckin' repressive that it's happening all over again.

"Society's attitude toward criminals changed. I remember Eleanor Roosevelt came to San Quentin and gave a speech. If the President's wife went to a prison and gave a speech to the convicts now, society would scream about it. They'd try to impeach him. It's a whole different thing. Back in 1939 and 1940, they had a broadcast from San Quentin, coast to coast, Sunday evening, San Quentin was on the air. There was a whole different social attitude towards crime and criminals.

"The problem is that a lot more people have been affected by crime. Prisons have become more violent, much more racially charged, and there's much more violence in this society. When I was a child, when I was ten years old, I could go anywhere in this fuckin' city on a street car or a bus. Now, middle-class children do not go out alone. They go to play dates.

"Look, they can't stop crime by repression, just by putting people in jail, unless they create a total police state. But, they build more prisons, there's more business for the construction companies, more promotions, more captains—there are big vested interests in all that. It's the prison industry. And the drug laws are insane. I wrote a long article that was in *The Nation* over twenty years ago when Nixon declared his war, mainly about how stupid the whole idea was."

This is one of the many groundbreaking themes in *Animal Factory:* how, because of the insanity of the drug laws, a fairly normal kid like Ron Decker can become transformed into a committed enemy of the society that seeks to rehabilitate him by confining him in an environment where he must either kill or be preyed upon.

The warden had promised that he, Ron, would get favorable action from the judge if he turned on Earl. It was an insulting offer and he'd sneered, refusing to make any statement whatsoever without an attorney—but it also raised hope. Maybe they needed corroboration. Whatever happened, he wouldn't let Earl be convicted of the assault—fuck what Earl said. Yet his own freedom, which had been firmly in hand, was in danger of oozing between his fingers. Either Earl or himself convicted of the crime would face a life sentence or the death penalty, depending on what the jury decided. Even without that, if the judge in Los Angeles found out, he would deny sentence modification, which would mean five long, bitter years before he was eligible for parole, and the chances of getting it would be small even then. He'd already seen too many men psychologically maimed by the indefinite sentences of California. If one year made him capable of plunging a knife into a man's back, what would a decade do?

"I had stabbed a guard in reform school," Bunker went on. "They brought me out to try me in L.A. county, and they put me in the L.A. County Jail. I was still a kid, fifteen years old. I got a famous lawyer to take the case, a guy named Al Matthews who was Chessman's appeal lawyer and sat with him in the courtroom as his adviser—Chessman defended himself. Matthews was great, he put the corrections officials on trial and proved that they had kicked my ass and stomped me, he brought up all the beatings they had given me, tear gas in the face, kicking me like a dog, blah, blah, you know. Meanwhile, the guard wasn't hurt very bad. Talkin' about how I stabbed a guard. Believe me, he wasn't hurt too bad. He was nicked, you know? Gouged him in the leg, mainly, 'cuz he fell on me. I went to stab him and stuck him in the leg."

"What was going on?" I asked.

"I'd escaped from the hole. They chased me around the prison. Strange shit. They took me out of the hole for a disciplinary court line—ya' know how you stand in the line? And the bull turns his head, so I hooked it. I was loose in the prison and they were lookin' all over the joint for me. Anyway, they put me on trial. That's when I first met Chessman. They booked me in violation of California Penal Code, Section 4500. Well, Section 4500 is for inmates serving life sentences and an assault conviction carries the death penalty. I wasn't subject to that because I wasn't doing life. But when the sheriffs saw I was booked with that charge, they thought I was facing the death penalty, so they put me in high power security in the county jail. I'm fifteen years old. Half the motherfuckers there were under death sentences.

"Man, there was this guy with one eye, famous case, he threw a whole family down a well. They made a movie about it. The guy's eye was fucked up, wouldn't close, so when he kidnapped people they didn't know if he was asleep or not. Anyway, he had killed a family in Missouri and threw them down a well. He was murdering people all across the states. Hitchhiking, stealing cars. Crazy shit. And there was Chessman and all these other way-out cases. I remember some guy committed a kidnap-robbery and the broad identified him by his eyes. He had a mask on during the robbery, right? So the lawyer said the bitch couldn't possibly recognize this guy just by his eyes. He put her on the witness stand and brought five guys in with the same hoods on and all dressed alike. She pointed out the right guy, screamed and fainted. The jury was out for about five minutes.

"So, I was in the cage with all these guys. The lawyer got me out. When I hit the streets, I didn't have anybody, no people, nowhere to go. This lawyer had defended a friend of Louise Fazenda Wallis, wife of the producer, Hal Wallis. She had been a silent film star. When she died, in her obituary in the L.A. Times, they called her the "angel of Hollywood" because she always helped people. She didn't do it with a camera, she did it one-on-one. She'd go find people and help them privately. She'd get somebody that was pregnant—and in those days, ya' know? Louise would pay for the woman to have the baby, get the kid adopted by some film star or director. Al Matthews cut me into her and she took an interest in me and liked me. That's how it started. I didn't realize what I had. I'd go see her in the daytime and she'd take me around to meet people like Marion Davies, and William Randolph Hearst. This guy started wars. He ran the world. He was in his eighties and had a couple of strokes by then."

Bunker stayed out about two years that time. At 16, he was selling pot and shoplifting. He got busted after a high-speed chase through the streets of L.A. The judge sent him to the county jail, and he escaped. A year later, at 17, he first walked the yard at San Quentin.

It was during that four-and-a-half year bid that Bunker started writing. Louise Wallis sent the young convict a Royal portable typewriter and a subscription to the *Sunday New York Times Book Review*. Inspired by Chessman's success, Eddie began the long apprenticeship of the prison novelist.

"My friends Paul Allen and Jimmy Posten, the three of us wanted to write. I always thought Jimmy had the most talent. He and Paul are both dead now. I took a correspondence course in grammar so I could learn how to punctuate. Malcolm Braley (author of *On the Yard* and *False Starts*) was another one. He published a couple of paperback books, Gold Medal originals, which I thought was wondrous then. I was into fuckin' up, low-riding, gang-banging and getting drugs. Then I'd go to lockup and for years no one knew that I wrote. When I got powerful jobs in the penitentiary, and when I started with the drugs, everyone was my friend. Braley was like a son to me, just a kid when he came in, and by then I was a veteran and a legend. There was a time in San Quentin when they only called me with major incidents—I was the Major Incidents Clerk. Unless it was a murder or an escape, they left me alone and I had the run of the joint.

"During the first jolt, I could'a killed somebody. I didn't give a fuck. But after I met Louise, then later when I got out on parole the first time, I realized there was a whole other life. I stayed out about three years. I had it good, some of the best years of my life, mid- to late fifties. When I went back to prison after that, I would never cross that line. I was aware of the possibility of getting out. The worst thing they can do to you is take away that hope.

"Louise taught me a lot, man. She taught me that you get out of your own problems by helping other people. She taught me that being concerned with other people is good for your own concerns, lessens your self-focus and increases your self-esteem."

This was Bunker's longest term of imprisonment. He had been convicted of forgery and running a check-cashing scheme, but that is just the bare bones of a criminal career that can only be described as wild and inspired with a kind of edge-of-the-abyss convict humor, like his fiction. One of the reasons Eddie had difficulty getting down to write when he was on the streets is because he was too busy living the fast life. This time he received an indeterminate sentence of 6 months-to-14 years and did 7 straight before being released on parole in the early seventies.

He was 35. He'd had enough of prison life, proved to himself he could survive the worst they had to offer. He wanted to go straight, wanted more of the life he had only glimpsed during his first parole. Before his release he wrote over two hundred letters and sent them out in hopes of securing a legitimate job. No one responded.

THE MAKING OF THE BEAST

Alex Hammond, the child protagonist of Bunker's third novel, *Little Boy Blue*, has just been locked up in the isolation unit at Juvenile Hall for fighting with his only friend until then, a mulatto kid named Chester. He's put in a bare cell with a stripped mattress on the floor and told he'll be given a blanket later. Chester is across the hall.

"Say, Mister," Alex said. "Can I get this window closed? It's cold in here."

"I haven't got the key."

"Well, don't forget the blanket."

"Don't worry."

"I need one too," Chester added, as his cell door was closed and locked.

"I said don't worry," the man said irritably. "This ain't a hotel."

The Man slammed and locked the door; the click of the lock sounded emphatic.

"Jive-ass motherfucker," Chester said, the salty words incongruous in his piping child's voice. "Ah best get me some blankets or ain't nobody sleepin' in this buildin' tonight. What you bet?" His bravado sounded thin.

The slamming door had been like a slap, and Alex also seethed. The blankets were the focus of a wider indignation. It was slowly being etched into his young mind that those with authority didn't care about right and wrong, good and evil— only about subservience.

From somewhere in the city's night beyond the wall came the sound of a siren rising and falling, a lament for human misery. From somewhere else came a terse screech of brakes followed by the bleat of an automobile horn, reflecting the driver's anguish. The sounds were sharp in the stillness, carried on the crystalline night air. Alex hooked his fingers on the wire mesh and stared out at the grounds of Juvenile Hall. The glare of the floodlights—not merely bright but other-wordly—bleached out colors so that the trees and bushes were in stark silhouette, casting impenetrable black shadows, a surreal landscape. Inwardly Alex felt quiet, *cleansed, as if the fight had sweated out angers and drained away bad things that he'd felt vaguely without realizing them. His father's death already seemed to have happened long ago, the heavy pain slowly melting. Clem had been the most important person in his life, and yet Alex had been conditioned to live without a father. Seldom had he seen Clem more than a couple of hours a week, and even then a barrier had existed between them, so they talked little. It wasn't as if something fundamental to his daily existence had been taken. His anguish was less for a lost reality than for a lost hope. Clem had been his one chance to get away from this, and now Alex had no idea what his future would be. Right now things were unraveling too quickly to do more than deal with the moment, but whenever he had a premonition of his tomorrows, it was bleak. He wasn't going home, no matter what; home had no place, even in a dream. An eleven-year-old could see that much.*

Bunker's autobiographical novel of growing up state-raised in California was the first book the prisoner writer would compose as a free man. Like Bunker, Alex Hammond is cast adrift in a harsh, loveless world at age four when his parents divorced.

"My mother was a dancer," Eddie said when I asked him about his childhood. "She danced as a chorus girl in the Busby Berkely movies, and would go flying down to Rio, that kind of shit. My father was a grip and a stagehand with the legitimate theater. Then they divorced and I went from being a pampered only child right into foster homes. A war zone."

He remembered being in a courtroom but nothing about what happened. Then his mother was gone, never seen again, never mentioned. After that began the foster homes and military schools. He couldn't even remember the first one, except that he'd been caught trying to run away on a rainy Sunday morning. His memory images grew clearer concerning later places; he remembered other runaways, one lasting six days, and fights and temper tantrums. He'd been to so many different places because each one threw him out.

At first his rebellion had been blind, a reflex response to pain—the pain of loneliness and no love, though he had no names for these things, not even now. Something in him went out of kilter when he confronted authority, and he was prone to violent tantrums on slight provocation. Favored boys, especially in military school, looked down on him and provoked the rages, which brought punishment that caused him to run away. One by one the boy's homes and military schools told his father that the boy would have to go. Some people thought he was epileptic or psychotic, but an electroencephalogram proved negative, and a psychiatrist doing volunteer work for the Community Chest found him normal. Whenever he was thrown out of a place, he got to stay in his father's furnished room for a few days or a week, sleeping on a foldup cot. He was happy during these interludes. Rebellion and chaos served a purpose—they got him away from torment. The time between arrival and explosion got shorter and shorter.

Little Boy Blue is in many ways Bunker's best book. The prose is understated, proud and poignant in its lack of hyperbole in describing the pain and emotional trauma of a little boy who, like all of us, merely wants to love and be loved. And it is his most accessible novel. Just about anyone can sympathize with a kid who gets in trouble because he misses his dad and won't stand for being threatened or picked on by other kids and beaten by reform school guards. By the time that kid matures into a Max Dembo or an Earl Copen, however, he is too real and scary for the typical American best-seller buyer.

Perhaps this accounts for why Bunker's novels have not

received the wide readership they deserve. He is a cult writer, having found his niche with the reader who wants the truest and edgiest of hard-boiled crime fiction. Bunker is unable to compromise his craft to write novels that are more commercially acceptable. "I tried to write some kind of sexy potboiler, but I couldn't do it," Eddie said when I asked him why he felt his books are not well-known in this country. "After *Little Boy Blue* came out and didn't do too well, I said I'll try to write it commercial, but I couldn't do it. It came out shit. Garbage. I didn't have it in me."

The fact that Bunker's brilliant and still timely novels have been allowed to go out of print also has to do with poor marketing. If a novelist's editor and publisher don't get behind the author's work, promote it and nurture the writer through several books while growing the readership through aggressive marketing, the books will die on the shelf. But big corporate-owned publishing houses spend a fortune promoting and marketing books that don't need it. Viking, for instance, Bunker's publisher for *Little Boy Blue*, is now pushing Stephen King. Yet they won't put out money on an unknown with obvious talent.

Bunker's dialogue is as real and beautifully rendered as the best street blues. There is less plot to *Little Boy Blue* and even more attention to emotional truth. Alex Hammond goes from Juvenile Hall to the state hospital at Camarillo for a ninety-day observation period. There, the young white boy is introduced to a couple of black hustlers, First Choice Floyd and his partner, Red Barzo, who instruct him in the finer points of becoming a career criminal.

> "Boy," Red said when he was ready to go, "ain' no doubt you headin' dead for San Quentin, 'cause you got the devil in you. Ain' no stoppin' it, so it's good you fuckin' with me 'n Floyd 'n gettin' schooled. You gotta decide if you wanna be a pimp, a player, or a gangster."
> "What's the difference?"

"One's slick and the other's tough."
"I think I'd like to be a little of both."
The two black men burst out laughing. Alex couldn't help another blush, but his embarrassment was mixed with pleasure.

Later, Red Barzo sees Alex throwing stones at a demented patient who stands in the yard masturbating every day and has upset the kid with lewd gestures.

". . . the black conman-junky admonished him: "Best freeze on that shit, boy. White folks runnin' this camp will get in your young ass if they catch you teasin' that nutty motherfucker. Ain't no money in it, anyway. You can' go wrong in life, un'er-stan', if before you do somepin', un'erstan', you say, 'any money made here?' That ain't no bullshit. That's the best way to look at the fast life, can you dig it?" The frequently interjected question wasn't really a question but a rhetorical pause. Yet the advice was intended seriously, and the sincere tone impressed the content on Alex. He would always remember and quote it, even if he didn't always follow it.

Alex escapes, Alex always escapes, just as Eddie Bunker was always escaping from one joint or another and getting arrested again, usually after a high-speed chase and the resultant beating by the cops. "What they did to Rodney King," Eddie cracks, "that was just your standard ass-whooping for takin' 'em on a chase." When Alex is arrested again, they take him to Pacific Colony, a California Youth Authority institution and his first reform school. There the cycle is repeated: fights, beatings, the hole—escape. The "code" is thoroughly imprinted in the boy's survival strategies: rats are the scum of the earth: might makes right; strength of character will get you through when all else fails. From Pacific Colony Alex goes to Whittier, and finally to the dreaded Preston School of Industry.

Despite the momentary twinge of fear when he heard about Pre-ston, his mood was jovial. Without being conscious of it, he'd learned to derive pleasure from what was available, and at the moment it was his first ride up the California coast, or at least partly up the coast before turning inland. He didn't probe or try to dissect his unlikely good mood. If asked, he would have replied that it came from getting out of the dirty jail.

I asked Bunker if it had been difficult for him to discipline himself to write once he was out of the can. "No. I'd never done it before when I was out, but it wasn't hard."

"Did you get depressed?"

"Nah. I never got depressed even in the joint."

"He didn't know he was there," Eddie's friend Danny Trejo said. "I'd go to his cell to get him, Eddie would walk out and say, 'Every day is a new adventure.'"

APOTHEOSIS

> Hungry man, reach for the book: it is a weapon.
>
> —Bertolt Brecht

Try as he might, Eddie Bunker was still not quite ready to give up crime. He had written *No Beast So Fierce*, his essays were gaining him serious attention as a writer, but he still hadn't had enough of life on the edge. He quickly got back into the dope business, this time selling Mexican brown heroin to whores in San Francisco. He also planned and executed the occasional robbery with some of his homeboys from Quentin. He was surviving by his wits but not doing much writing.

"The cops were all over me," Eddie remembered. "I got busted for some dope, made a deal to get the connection, but then, as soon as they let me out, I split, went down to Mexico. We had this beautiful set-up. All you had to do was call a number in San Diego and tell 'em, 'I want a kilo of heroin.' And they'd tell you where to wire the money in Mexico. They didn't care, man, these people did not care. You could call up and say, 'My name is Harry Anslinger,' and they'd say, 'Do you have the money?' We used answering services. The connection would call back after they got the money and leave a message: 'Your shit's in the bathroom at the train station under the sink.' It was so easy. They changed the law because of this, made it illegal to wire more than ten thousand. What they eventually began doing was flooding the area. Brought down all kinds of local and federal task force heat.

"When I got back in the country, I called the number again in San Diego. It was an answering service, and the guy I was dealing with, the connection, I told him, 'Man, I don't want to call this number,' and he said, 'Look, it's an answering service, and I own half of it. If they go there, I'll find out about it.' They had already been there. The manager was cooperating on her own in this thing. I didn't think of that. I didn't know how they got me—both times—until I got in the courtroom. They put one of those bumper beepers, one of those tracking devices in my car. They were following me, thought I was gonna lead 'em to the load of dope. They thought I was going to do a drug deal, meanwhile I was on my way to do a robbery."

Bunker had decided to augment his stake by sticking up a plum Beverly Hills bank. Unbeknownst to him, he had several cars full of federal agents and a helicopter following him through the streets of Los Angeles. When he made his move, he couldn't understand how the cops got there so fast.

"The chase was on—from Beverly Hills, Orchard Boulevard, all the way to Farmer's Market. It was a long chase. I couldn't lose them. I'm going through shopping centers, hitting them bumps, them speed bumps, flyin', hittin' my head on the fuckin' roof. I'd turn in another block, and there they'd be! I said, 'Man, what the fuck?' So I go down Fairfax again. There's an alley at the end, I swung in, did a John Wayne, hoping they'd keep going. As soon as I get down there, to the parking place behind this small building, I jumped out, ran through the building, and hit the door on the wrong side. I probably would have gotten away, but the door opened in and I hit it straight on. I see this guy, he sees me, this maniac who runs in with a pistol. I said, 'Lemme outta here!' I looked out a window and they were just going by, the agents, all carrying shotguns. I climbed out the window and ran down the alley, but there were more of 'em waitin' there. I couldn't get away. I ducked back into a doorway. It was a stand-off. One of them comes around the corner with a gun, and another one comes around the corner from the other end. I'm dead, I know it. So I said, 'Woa,' and dropped the gun. I dropped the gun, man. You know, put it down and kind of slid it out with my toe. All my friends said, 'Oh, you punk, you gave the gun up.'

"But I was aware of the possibility of getting out. And I got out. I did an article on the L.A. County jail for the Sunday magazine, called it 'The Human Zoo.' I had a lot of support. This was before Abbott and all those guys fucked up. I had about two hundred letters for the judge. This guy's been rehabilitated, blah, blah. And it happened to be a federal judge that I knew. I fought a state prisoner's *habeas corpus,* conducted a nine-day evidentiary hearing once in front of this judge on a 2255. So he knew me from that thing. Four or five years later I'm back on this bank robbery. The judge appointed a young public defender to represent me. I remember he told this guy, 'Pay attention. You may learn something from Mr. Bunker.' *No Beast So Fierce* was accepted while I was on trial."

The limousine that Dustin Hoffman sent to pick Eddie Bunker up at Terminal Island a few years later delivered him to an entirely different life. He went to work on the set of *Straight Time,* where he picked up a regular pay check of $750 every Wednesday and was introduced to a whole new kind of action—making movies. I remember when I was getting ready to leave prison after eight years I used to worry about what I could do that would give me the same rush I got from smuggling marijuana. When I was hired to work on a documentary about Mike Tyson, I knew I'd found the answer.

Danny Trejo knew it too, the first time he heard a director say: *Action!* Trejo had been out of prison for nearly a decade and was working as a drug counselor when he got a call from a coke addict who said he was afraid he was going to relapse. When he went to see the guy at his job, Danny found himself on the set of *Runaway Train*. There he ran into Eddie Bunker, who quickly got his old prison pal a job on the movie. Trejo, a welterweight boxing champ at San Quentin, was hired to coach Eric Roberts in the fight scenes. But as soon as Russian director Andrei Konchalovsky got a look at Danny's mug, he wanted the ex-con in the movie. Trejo hasn't stopped working in movies since.

The 1985 film, based on a screenplay by Akira Kurosawa, follows two convicts who escape from a maximum-security prison in Alaska and commandeer a train that is soon out of control. Bunker was hired to work on the dialogue, give it more American convict flavor. He rewrote the entire script and helped craft a film most buffs agree is a first rate prison escape/action-adventure movie that transcends the genre to become a symbolic, multi-dimensional drama about survival and character.

Bunker also acted in the movie and coached Jon Voight in his magnificent rendition of a convict who is so feared as an escape risk—and so respected by the other cons as the toughest man in a rough joint—that the warden, in an effort to break the convict's will, has had him welded into his cell in the hole for three years until forced by a court order to release him to general population. The early prison scenes, scripted by Bunker and in which he plays an older Earl Copen character right down to the shaved head, are some of the most realistic Hollywood has ever produced in its long romance with the penitentiary setting. Bunker also wrote all the dialogue between the two convicts on the train, a fine exposition of the convict code: *never give up*, as stated and embodied by the Voight character. From the first frame to the last, *Runaway Train* is spellbinding, as intense, gripping and authentic as Bunker's fiction. Bunker played Mr. Blue in Quentin Tarantino's *Reservoir Dogs*, and when we met he was back in Hollywood yet again working on another movie.

Bunker's life has come full circle. For most of the twenty years since his release from prison, Eddie has been married to the woman who was his counselor in the halfway house. He and his wife, Jennifer, now have a little boy of their own, 17-month-old Brendan Bunker. Bunker works hard, writes every day. "I wish I'd worked as hard when I was in the joint," he told me. "I'd have a lot more done."

In the preface to the French and Black Lizard editions of *No Beast So Fierce* the novelist William Styron wrote, "Edward Bunker is one of a small handful of American writers who have created authentic literature out of their experiences as criminals and prisoners . . . whose work possesses integrity, craftsmanship, and moral passion in sufficient measure to claim our serious attention." H. Bruce Franklin called *No Beast So Fierce*, "one of the finest achievements of prison literature, and, indeed, of that much larger body of literature about criminals."

Bunker's new novel, *Men Who Prey*, has the precision plotting and hard core realism down cold. A chilling, remorseless tale of ex-cons on a crime spree, the story never falters, never gives an inch. The characters are beyond the pale of moral compunction, the kind of men our animal factories produce.

Eddie Bunker is not just a great convict writer. His adherence to the canon that distinguishes the best literature—devotion to truth—places Bunker firmly among the pantheon of great writers, including Melville and Jack London, whose artistic conscience was galvanized by the prison experience. In these times, when prison and crime have become the most politically charged domestic issues, Bunker's work is all the more relevant, all the more important. America fails to recognize this most eloquent and inspired voice at its own peril.

TOP: Richard Stratton at age two, with his mother in Boston Harbor. CENTER: Stratton with a girlfriend, during his smuggling heyday. BOTTOM: Stratton with Lebanese smugglers in Beirut.

TOP: Inmate account card. BOTTOM: Prison love: Stratton and a girlfriend stand in front of a photo backdrop in the visiting room at the federal prison in Petersburg, Virginia.

TOP: Cover of Stratton's novel *Smack Goddess*. BOTTOM: Stratton in Brooklyn Heights shortly after release from prison.

TOP: Stratton with Norman Mailer at the
Smack Goddess book party.
RIGHT: Promotional poster for the film
Slam.

Stills from *Slam*. TOP: Washington, D.C. Mayor Marion Barry plays a judge.
BOTTOM: Saul Williams plays Ray Joshua.

RIGHT: *Street Time* poster.
BOTTOM: Stratton on the set directing *Street Time*, with his sons Maxx and Dash.

Illustration © Fred Ornes

THE GRIM REAPER'S GIRLFRIEND

The Story of the Secret Relationship
Between a Vicious Mob Killer
and a Top FBI Agent

Penthouse, August 1996

King Rat

Another advantage to publishing a convict magazine was that people in the know—people in prison—often leaked me stories before they hit the mainstream media. I was in the Prison Life *offices one day when I got a call from a prisoner being held at the Metropolitan Correctional Center in Manhattan. "I've got a story you're never gonna believe," he said. "But I can prove it. I got the court papers and everything. I'll send 'em to you." Then he whispered, "Greg Scarpa is a rat."*

I'd never met Greg Scarpa Sr., but I knew his son and some of the so-called Wimpy Boys (so named because they hung around a social club called Wimpy Boys in the Bensonhurst neighborhood of Brooklyn) who, with Greg Jr., were busted on a big drug distribution case. I met Greg Jr. at MCC and a couple of the Wimpy Boys ended up in the same penitentiary with me in Petersburg, Virginia. The guy who called me had been arrested with Greg Jr. He and several codefendants were back in court for hearings based on new information that, indeed, the whole time Greg Scarpa Sr. was rising to the top—killing his way to the top—of the Colombo crime family during the internecine war between one faction loyal to imprisoned boss Carmine Persico, and another faction led by acting boss Vic Orena, Scarpa Sr. was an informant working for the FBI.

The story seemed incredible to me then, given what I knew about Greg Sr. He had a reputation as one of the most feared mob killers in

New York. But a few days later a thick package of court documents arrived in the mail and sure enough, Scarpa Sr. was identified as an FBI confidential informant, (CI) or, more accurately, a term no one outside elite law enforcement circles was familiar with at the time, a Top Echelon Informant with a history of working for the Bureau that went back decades. There had been rumors about Scarpa, which I wasn't aware of, and Jerry Capeci identified Scarpa as a rat in his "Gangland" column in the Daily News, but it seemed unthinkable that a mafia capo like Scarpa could be working for the FBI and killing his enemies in a deadly mob war at the same time. When I told the Scarpa story to Peter Bloch, the editor at Penthouse, he wanted to go with it.

The more I dug into Greg Scarpa's history with the FBI, the more incredible—and informative—the story became. Scarpa had been a secret FBI asset going all the way back to the case of the three young civil rights workers who were murdered in Mississippi, the basis for the film Mississippi Burning. Scarpa's involvement made for a whole different scenario on how that case was solved. At the time I wrote my Scarpa piece, Lindley DeVecchio, Scarpa's FBI handler, was still working for the FBI and refused to talk to me. After DeVecchio retired, he did agree to be interviewed by a friend of mine, Fred Dannen, who wrote a long piece on the Scarpa case for The New Yorker, "The Hitman and the G-Man."

But it wasn't until another case involving a Top Echelon Informant came to light a few years later that the FBI's secret program was fully revealed. James "Whitey" Bulger was the preeminent Irish gangster in Boston during the time I was smuggling pot up and down the New England coast and through Logan Airport. I had what is known as a "catch" at Logan, an arrangement either with freight handlers or Customs agents or both, where certain shipments were allowed to pass through the airport without inspection, in exchange for a healthy fee. The men I was working with at Logan, freight handlers, were loosely affiliated with both the Irish mob and the North End Italian mafia.

My understanding was that my guys were kicking up a percentage of the money I paid them, each time we did a trip, to Whitey Bulger.

At a meeting with my catch one day, I was told that a young mafioso wanted to meet me. Over the years, when necessary, I'd done business with organized crime figures in Florida and New York, connected wiseguys and mob associates who took an end out of the profits of certain trips in exchange for providing services, usually arranging for people in authority to look the other way when a trip came in. But the mob never really had a strong foothold in the pot business. Heroin was their drug of choice. I called my mob rabbi, "Uncle George," a Mafia-connected Lebanese businessman, and told him I was being urged to meet this young Mafioso. "Should I meet the guy?" I asked. He told me he'd check with Raymond and let me know.

He was referring to Raymond Patriarca, the boss of the New England crime family, who ruled from his office at the National Cigarette Vending Company in Providence, Rhode Island. Gerry Angiulo, Patriarca's underboss, oversaw the mob's rackets in Boston from his Prince Street headquarters in the North End. A few days later I was told to take the meeting, the young up-and-comer in question was "close to Raymond." We met at a North End restaurant in Angiulo territory.

"The name's Mike Caruana," he introduced himself. "Rhymes with marijuana." Caruana was a good-looking guy, in his late thirties at the time, a former bank robber and rising star in the New England mob. He said he knew of my catch at Logan, he'd checked me out, heard I had a fairly big operation going and said he was taking over all the marijuana distribution on the East Coast, with Patriarca's blessing. I was told it would cost me a million dollars to continue to work in New England and that for paying Caruana the million I would get "protection" and be connected up with other importers and distributors working for Caruana with Patriarca's permission.

"Protection from who?" I asked. "You?" Caruana smiled. I knew enough about mob protocol to tell him I'd have to talk it over with my friend, Uncle George, the Lebanese businessman, and get back to him.

At our next meeting, Caruana introduced me to Jimmy Charga, of the El Paso, Texas, Chagra family. Jimmy's older brother, Lee Charga, was a well-known dope lawyer and both Jimmy and Lee were famous Las Vegas high-rollers. Caruana told me that the million-dollar fee had been waived because of my close connections with the Lebanese, and out of respect for Uncle George's friendship with Raymond. As an indication of Caruana's good faith, and proof of the kinds of people I would meet through him, here was Jimmy Chagra, who was doing huge freighter loads of Colombian pot and wanted me to help him get part of the loads to his people in Canada.

A few weeks after I met Jimmy, Lee Chagra was murdered in his El Paso office. Within hours of the killing, the FBI had sealed off Lee's office and removed all his files. Jimmy Charga was eventually indicted and convicted of hiring actor Woody Harrelson's father, Charles Harrelson, (a Texas hitman who was also said to have been one of the hobos on the grassy knoll in Dallas on the day of the Kennedy Assassination) to kill the federal judge presiding over Jimmy's case, "Maximum" John Woods. The hit was supposedly a vendetta for what Jimmy believed was law enforcement involvement in his brother's murder. I was summoned to another North End meeting with Caruana. He told me that from now on I would have to give him half of every load I brought in through Logan. I refused, said that was impossible. The Lebanese were getting a third, I was paying the catch, so I'd end up losing money. When I walked out of the restaurant after defying Carauana, I was less concerned about him than I was about the FBI surveillance team buzzing around outside.

The next load came in to Logan, some crates of Lebanese hashish on a Japanese Air Lines flight, disguised as engine parts. I got the load out and had it stashed in a garage in my hometown of Wellesley, Massachusetts. Uncle George called me the next day and said Carauana had gone to Raymond and put a contract out on me and that it would only be lifted if I agreed to give Caruana half the load. I told Uncle George to tell Raymond to tell Caruana to forget it, I was keeping the load. I paid the catch and that was it, they could all go fuck themselves, I was finished doing business in Boston and wanted no part of Caruana's so-called protection. "This guy's so hot he's got a whole entourage of feds following him everywhere he goes."

"Too late," George said. "Caruana gave the contract to John Zullo. Unless you give it up, half the load, they'll kill you." For the first time in my career as a smuggler, I started carrying a gun.

A successful real estate broker from Boston's Back Bay was my connection to Whitey Bulger. I explained the situation to him and he set up a meeting for me with Whitey. "You're a good earner, kid," Whitey told me. "Don't worry about the wops. I'll take care of them. You just keep doing what you're doing."

A few days later, in a meeting that was surveilled by the DEA, the FBI and the Massachusetts State police, and recounted in the book, Black Mass, about Whitey's secret relationship with the FBI, Caruana was told to back off. Years later I was sitting in my cell at the penitentiary in Virginia when another Boston homeboy came by and told me there was a new guy on the yard from Boston, "A guy named John Zullo. Ever heard of him?"

Zullo was the kind of killer who would crouch in the bushes outside your home for hours and shoot you in the head as you unlocked your front door. I knew I had to go confront him right away or I'd be perceived as fearful and weak, not a good reputation to have in the joint. I found Zullo sitting in the yard, leaning against a fence, smoking a cigarette. "John Zullo . . . Remember me?"

He looked up. "Yeah, hey, Richie. I heard you was here."

"That thing with Carauana—"

"Forget that. Caruana was a piece of shit. That was out there. We're in here now."

Caruana became a fugitive. Though I don't think his body has ever been found, I heard from reliable sources that he was murdered. John Zullo was shot in the head and killed soon after his release from prison. These guys had huge heat on them from the murder investigation of Judge John Woods. But they were also victims of another secret FBI asset: Whitey Bulger.

If anyone had ever told me Whitey Bulger was an FBI informant I would have said they were out of their minds. Whitey was known as the most stand-up tough guy in Boston. You could get yourself killed calling Whitey a rat on his home turf of South Boston. But it was Bulger's case, as it came out in court proceedings after the FBI took down the entire hierarchy of the New England mob, that exposed the full measure of the FBI's Top Echelon Informant Program. Whitey's younger brother, Billy Bulger, was the President of the Massachusetts State Senate and one of the most powerful politicians in New England all during the years Whitey enjoyed a secret relationship with the FBI wherein he was allowed to continue his criminal activities in exchange for information on the Italian mafia. Because of the embarrassment to the Bureau and to law enforcement in general when the Top Echelon program was revealed, Whitey's FBI handler, John Connolly, was hung out to dry: indicted, tried, convicted and sentenced to ten years in prison for doing exactly what Lindley DeVecchio had done with Greg Scarpa in New York. Such is life in the back-stabbing world of cops and criminals.

Just as Whitey Bulger's secret relationship with the FBI became public ten years ago, he went on the lam and has never been caught. He's second only to Osama bin Laden on the FBI's Ten Most Wanted list. I was hired by former French Connection cop Sonny Grosso to write a mini-series on the John Connolly-Whitey Bulger case for NBC, to be directed by William Friedkin. In my research, I learned that while Whitey was locked up in Alcatraz as a young man, in exchange for a sentence reduction, he volunteered as a guinea pig for LSD tests administered to prisoners under the MK-ULTRA program I wrote about in "Altered States of America." Maybe it was that pure Sandoz acid that gave Whitey the Machiavellian insight to outplay them all.

THE GRIM REAPER'S GIRLFRIEND

AT A SAFE HOUSE on Staten Island, New York City, Greg Scarpa of the Colombo crime family stood staring at his reflection in a full-length mirror. He was unrecognizable, in the garb and mien of an old Hasidic Jew. Reaching for his semi-automatic Tec-9 pistol, Scarpa stuck it in the waistband of the baggy black trousers.

It was Thanksgiving Day, 1991. Carmine "Junior" Persico, the official boss of the Colombos, was in prison, along with the family's other leaders. A bloody internecine war for control of the organization had broken out just days before. Scarpa had triggered it by staging a hit outside his own home. Then he blamed it on the faction led by acting family boss Vic Orena.

Scarpa alleged that a hail of bullets had narrowly missed his daughter and infant grandson. Certainly it shattered an uneasy five-month truce that had been presided over by the other New York families. The 63-year-old mobster was now using the faked hit as an excuse to make his move to take over the Colombo family. Falsely swearing fealty to Persico, Scarpa rallied soldiers loyal to the jailed chief and declared all-out war on the Orena faction.

As one of the wiseguys who was at the Staten Island safe house later told friends, Scarpa was chuckling at the sight of himself and his two underlings in the long black frock coats, black hats, and curling sideburns of the Hasids. The clothes and sideburns would be disguises when they gunned down one of Orena's henchmen. But the plan was abruptly scuttled when Scarpa's longtime protégé, Carmine Sessa, walked in carrying a copy of the New York *Daily News*. He threw the paper on the table, open to Jerry Capeci's column, "Gangland." Scarpa read it.

"What the fuck is this?" Scarpa raged. The reporter had had the balls to call Scarpa—a stone-cold killer and made member of the Colombo family for more than 30 years—a *rat*. Every hood, cop, and federal agent in New York read Capeci's column. Scarpa would have a hell of a time putting this rumor to rest.

Capeci claimed that Scarpa had been targeted for murder because he was a longtime informant for the FBI. The old gangster looked like an angry crow as he stalked around the room in his black outfit, flapping his arms and cursing Capeci. Capeci was full of shit. Who the fuck did this guinea bastard think he was, writing this kind of crap.

But for Scarpa's closest associates the "Gangland" piece revived old doubts and fears about their violent—some said crazy—boss. Scarpa was feared because he was a ruthless killer. He was tolerated by the five families' bosses because he was a top earner. His loansharking, extortion, gambling, and particularly his family-run retail narcotics business brought in millions of dollars. So did his sophisticated mail-, automobile-, and diamond-theft rings, not to mention bank robberies and a host of other rackets run by Scarpa's crew. But there was something else about Scarpa, something that gave him an edge over just about every other wiseguy in town. Capeci had only half the story. Scarpa had long been known in his own circles to have a high-level law-enforcement source he called "the Girlfriend."

During the eighties, according to FBI documents, the Girlfriend had allegedly tipped Scarpa beforehand just as the Secret Service was about to bust the mobster on a phony-credit-card case. Wiseguys grew leery of Scarpa when, despite being called by a prosecutor the biggest dealer in fraudulent credit cards in the New York area, he was sentenced only to probation. A few years later the rat rumors resurfaced when Scarpa's Girlfriend forewarned him about a Drug Enforcement Administration investigation of major drug dealing run out of Scarpa's Brooklyn headquarters, the Wimpy Boys Social Club in Bensonhurst—a largely Italian working-class section of Brooklyn known as Colombo turf.

Scarpa didn't go to prison that time either. He made his son,

Greg junior, take the rap, and then sent junior into hiding. Months later, after a story about Greg junior was aired on "America's Most Wanted," Scarpa's son was arrested and sentenced to 20 years in prison (where he remains). But Scarpa senior's avoidance of arrest fanned the flames of already smoldering suspicions: Why would the man let his son go to prison unless there was a deal to get him out early? Which meant Scarpa was feeding important information to the FBI. And as any half-assed criminal knows, good information flows both ways.

There was only one thing for Scarpa to do to repair the damage to his credibility from Capeci's column. He ripped off the Hasidic garb, loaded his rifle, and went out to cruise Avenue U, a main drag in Bensonhurst, looking for rival goodfellows to kill.

The war for control of the Colombo family was now on. For the next three months, say FBI documents, three months during which Scarpa killed half a dozen fellow mobsters, he and Lindley DeVecchio—a.k.a. the Girlfriend—met frequently. The two had by now reached an understanding that went way beyond the usual quid pro quo between lawman and stool pigeon. In exchange for serving as an FBI informant, according to a legal brief filed on behalf of Vic Orena, Scarpa "could ask for and receive information that DeVecchio had to know was to be used for criminal, possibly even lethal purposes—and DeVecchio would oblige."

Scarpa and DeVecchio had known each other for well over a decade. They trusted each other in a way most men rarely do: with the secret knowledge that each held the other's life in his hands. The Girlfriend, a 25-year FBI veteran, tall, with curly auburn hair and a mustache, usually wore a grave expression. Scarpa was barrel-chested, with salt-and-pepper hair and long front teeth that gave him a rodent-like appearance. He was dyspeptic from the pressures of his double life. Indeed, in 1986 he'd had a large chunk of his stomach removed. And there was an unanticipated side effect that caused the usually hardboiled Scarpa many moments of fear and panic.

At one of their meetings DeVecchio told Scarpa the bureau had information that the Orena faction was forming hit teams to go after Scarpa and his crew. Then DeVecchio did the unthinkable. He gave Scarpa some addresses believed to be of safe houses where enemy mobsters were hiding.

It is hard for most Americans to imagine an FBI agent leaking such sensitive—and deadly—information to a criminal with Scarpa's violent predilections. DeVecchio should have known Scarpa's next move would be to hunt down and kill rival wiseguys. That would have made DeVecchio part of a conspiracy to murder. To fathom the relationship between Scarpa and DeVecchio we must understand the seamy side of law enforcement: the corrupt symbiosis between cops and their criminal informants. The snitch system of law enforcement has its defenders. Most cops rely on informants. But it is easy to see how lines can be crossed. When that happens, the cop begins to identify with the criminal and his milieu, just as the informant comes to think of himself as an agent of the government.

Though DeVecchio refused to be interviewed for this article, it is not difficult to imagine what happened. DeVecchio probably believed that if Scarpa could win the war, he, DeVecchio, would have the highest-placed informant imaginable: an acting boss. With such an ally, DeVecchio would be able to destroy the Mafia.

And Scarpa, what was in it for him? He could ride around Brooklyn settling old scores. He could kill all the pieces of shit who had taken from him or called him a rat over the years. At the same time, Scarpa could help DeVecchio help the FBI, with the understanding that if he got into trouble they would look out for him. Without DeVecchio, Scarpa would be rotting in prison, like his kid, and Scarpa hated doing time. Thanks to this relationship, DeVecchio and the FBI would always be there to bail him out. They always had in the past.

Just five days after the Capeci story appeared, the rat rumormongers were silenced. Scarpa killed one wiseguy and wounded another in a dramatic daytime shoot-out outside a Mafia social club on Bensonhurst's McDonald Avenue. It hardly mattered that Scarpa had murdered the wrong man—a member of another crime family who happened to be in the neighborhood. As one of Scarpa's closest allies, Carmine Sessa, put it a few years later when testifying for the government, Scarpa's brazen action "cleared everyone's mind" of the notion that the old killer was an FBI informant. An unwise naïveté.

That was just the beginning. Lawrence Mazza, a wiseguy who traveled with Scarpa and his men, would later recall another killing that illustrates just how reckless and vicious Scarpa was. Scarpa and his men were heavily armed as they cruised the streets running their rackets and looking for rival gangsters to kill. A couple of weeks into the fray they were en route to a poolroom from their latest numbers pickup. The 1991 Christmas season was getting under way, and as they rode they checked out some of the addresses the Girlfriend had given Scarpa. Suddenly they spotted a rival wiseguy's car parked off residential Bath Avenue. As they slowed to get a good look, Scarpa saw the car's owner hanging Christmas lights in front of his girlfriend's house. "Stop," Scarpa ordered his driver.

Scarpa's men were scared and disbelieving. It was late afternoon, traffic was heavy, no escape route had been planned. Scarpa grabbed his rifle and rolled down the window. His prey was bent over, connecting the lights. When the poor fuck straightened up, Scarpa shot him three times in the back. The man slammed against the front of the house and died clutching a string of Christmas lights.

As Scarpa's car sped away, he cracked a grin and said, "I love the smell of gunpowder."

After the kill Scarpa went home, says Mazza, poured himself a Scotch, beeped his *goombah* (close buddy) Carmine Sessa, the acting *consigliere* of the Colombo family, and gleefully punched in "666." Sessa knew the code: Scarpa had killed again.

Then Scarpa called the Girlfriend and arranged a meeting to report the news. This brought DeVecchio and two other agents directly to Scarpa's home. While the two other agents waited outside, as one of them, Jeffrey Tomlinson, later recalled, DeVecchio and Scarpa huddled in Scarpa's kitchen for close to an hour. The meeting was the equivalent of generals from opposing armies getting together to plan a war. The length of the confab and their own exclusion from it soon became a cause for concern for the two agents, while Scarpa's crew also got hot and bothered that he had strayed over the line.

Inside, Scarpa convinced DeVecchio that only the death or arrest of Vic Orena would bring about peace. DeVecchio believed him, and once again broke a paramount rule. He gave Scarpa an address in Queens where Orena was thought to be hiding.

Greg Scarpa's history as a valued criminal informant for the FBI goes back at least as far as the early sixties. Scarpa, then a tough young turk in his mid-thirties, working to make his name in the crime family run by Joe Colombo, was arrested. He decided to go to work for the bureau rather than go to the joint.

At the time FBI chief J. Edgar Hoover was under intense pressure from Attorney General Robert Kennedy's Justice Department to solve the disappearance and suspected murder of Andrew Goodman, Michael Schwerner, and James Chaney, three young civil-rights workers, in Mississippi.

Greg Scarpa, who thought of himself as a patriotic American, was enlisted to find out what had happened to them. The case would years later be dramatized in the controversial 1983 Alan Parker film *Mississippi Burning*, starring Gene Hackman as a willful FBI man ready to do whatever was necessary to get the bad guys. What is missing from the Hollywood version—apart from other distortions—is the role played by Scarpa.

After his release from custody, Scarpa flew with his mistress from New York to Miami Beach, where he registered at the Fontainebleau Hotel to establish an alibi. Then he left the woman and continued alone to New Orleans, where he met with agents from the FBI's New York office. They drove Scarpa to the small town of Philadelphia, Mississippi, gave him a gun, and directed him to an appliance merchant who belonged to the local Ku Klux Klan and whom they believed to be a weak link. Posing as a newcomer in town, Scarpa went to the store, left a deposit on a TV set, and told the clerk he'd be back later to pick it up.

He returned to the store just before closing. Scarpa paid for the TV and asked the merchant to help him carry it out and put it in the trunk of a car rented for the occasion. Outside, as the fellow struggled with the TV set, Scarpa clubbed him over the head with a length of pipe. He tied the man up, threw him in the trunk, and, leaving the TV set on the street, drove to a prearranged location. While the FBI agents squatted outside the window of a shack deep in the pine woods of eastern Mississippi, Scarpa tied the Klansman to a chair, slapped him around, and demanded, "What happened to the three kids?"

At first the Klansman tried to lie his way out. But Scarpa held him captive while the agents went to check the information the Klansman was supplying. When a first and then a second story proved false, Scarpa lost patience. He beat the Klansman, stuck the gun barrel in his mouth, and threatened, "Tell me the fucking truth or I'll blow your fucking brains out." The terrified Klansman gave up the location of the bodies, an earthen dam where they'd been buried under 17 feet of red clay, and provided Scarpa—and the FBI men listening outside—the names of the killers.

Scarpa returned to New York to resume his criminal career. The full extent and value of his assistance as a high-level informant for more than 30 years may never be known. So far, the government has consistently refused applications for release of the full Scarpa file. What is known is that all during the sixties, seventies, and eighties, as he robbed and extorted, as he moved massive amounts of drugs, as he muscled, murdered, and ratted his way up in organized-crime circles, Greg Scarpa enjoyed extraordinary protection from the FBI.

During the eighties Scarpa helped the bureau and the United States Attorneys' offices in Brooklyn and Manhattan to bring major racketeering cases against the hierarchies of all five New York crime families. When Colombo boss Carmine Persico, who had a long-standing feud with Scarpa, supposedly over a woman, was convicted and sentenced to 139 years in federal prison, the entire upper echelon of the Colombo mob was jailed along with him, clearing the way for Scarpa. And as Scarpa rose within the family he was able to provide DeVecchio with the rarefied intelligence needed to make cases against the mob brass of all five New York families. Thus was DeVecchio able to rise in the toughest "mob" of them all: the FBI.

The wiseguy and the G-man were a natural. Scarpa knew exactly how to play DeVecchio—coming on strong as a vulnerable tough guy willing to put his life on the line for his Girlfriend. The two grew so tight over the years, it was difficult to tell who was running whom. In 1986, according to testimony given by FBI agent Howard Leadbetter, an immediate subordinate of DeVecchio's, agents of the FBI appeared before federal Judge I. Leo Glasser (who later presided over mob boss John Gotti's culminating trial) to convince the judge to allow Scarpa on the street after Scarpa pleaded guilty in the credit-card case. While out on bail awaiting sentencing, Scarpa was hospitalized for a bleeding ulcer and required emergency surgery. Sessa says FBI agents even visited him at the hospital.

The hospitalization was fateful for Scarpa. He needed a transfusion, but he rejected the hospital's prescreened blood in favor of blood from relatives and fellow wiseguys. One of the latter was a young underling named Paul Mele, whose blood was infected with HIV and who is now deceased. Soon Scarpa was back on the street.

It was during 1992 in the struggle for the Colombo family that the sub-rosa relationship between Scarpa and DeVecchio blossomed. In January of that year Scarpa had stunned Orena's crew with the brash killing of Nicky "Black" Grancio, a feared Orena *capo*. The Grancio hit was a turning point in the war and a major victory for the Persico faction—i.e., Scarpa and the FBI. Vic Orena and his men went scurrying for the mattresses in remote safe houses, cowering in terror of "the Grim Reaper," as they had come to call Scarpa.

Scarpa seemed invincible. By the spring of 1992 the war was in its final throes. In May its last killing took place; once again Scarpa was the triggerman. FBI agent Chris Favo, who worked under DeVecchio as coordinator of intelligence for the bureau's Colombo squad, heard of the hit early the morning it happened.

At 9:00 AM Favo went to DeVecchio's office to give him the daily war briefing. DeVecchio was seated at his desk when Favo informed his supervisor that there had been a shooting, that an Orena soldier had been killed, but they had no information on who had done it. The tip he added, had come from Scarpa.

DeVecchio slammed a hand on his desk and blurted out unexpectedly, "We're going to win this thing!" To Favo it was a shocking outburst that betrayed how far over the edge DeVecchio had gone. "He seemed like he didn't know . . . we were the FBI or that [Scarpa] was not on our side," Favo testified at a recent Colombo racketeering trial. "A line—it was like a line had been blurred . . . over who we were and what this was. . . . I thought there was something wrong. He was compromised. He had lost track of who he was."

Finally, in July 1992, DeVecchio arrested Vic Orena. Throughout the war Scarpa had believed that only if they killed Orena, or if Orena were arrested, would Scarpa's faction emerge victorious.

Scarpa and his men had tried to kill Orena a number of times. When Nicky Grancio was hit, Orena went into hiding. He kept changing locations, hoping to fend off Scarpa by using underlings for protection; one by one, Scarpa killed them all. At the time of his arrest, Orena was hiding at the home of a girlfriend on Long Island. Later a proud DeVecchio paraded the captured acting boss like a big-game trophy before waiting news photographers.

At last the war was over. Most of the soldiers who died or were wounded on the streets of Brooklyn had been hunted down and shot by Scarpa. Surviving *capos* and rank-and-file button men were rounded up and herded into holding cells on charges of having participated in the war—with the notable exception of Greg Scarpa. Once again, the FBI's criminal operative was allowed to roam free. Even after a number of Scarpa's men flipped and began cooperating with the FBI, naming Scarpa as the shooter in nearly all the killings attributed to the Persico faction, DeVecchio, to the alarm and dismay of his subordinates, continued to protect his canary.

For Scarpa and the Girlfriend the war had resulted in total victory. Indeed, they did "win this thing." There was no one left to oppose Scarpa. Orena was in custody, charged with conspiracy to commit murder, and those loyal to him were either dead or under arrest. Scarpa made certain that anyone who had ever had the poor judgment to call him a rat would never speak on the subject again—except, that is, for columnist Jerry Capeci.

In the end DeVecchio could no longer shield Scarpa, and he was arrested on August 31, 1992. But he still got special treatment. After an appeal to Judge Glasser failed to overturn a magistrate decision to grant bail, Scarpa was released. The government, though fully aware of Scarpa's role in any number of homicides, did not appeal Glasser's ruling further.

Scarpa remained as bold as ever. Because he was supposedly under house arrest, he was monitored by an electronic ankle bracelet. During this time, says a former member of Scarpa's faction, the Grim Reaper was shot in the head in a drug-related gun battle down the street from his house. Scarpa, hit in the eye, drove home. Leaving the body of one of his victims lying in his car, he went inside, poured himself a Scotch, and with blood dripping down his face, called his probation officer to report that the reason the ankle monitor had gone off was because the alarm had somehow been triggered in the shower.

The truth of Scarpa's dual role as hit man and FBI agent provocateur might never have come out had it not been for Jerry Capeci. Within a week of the gunfight, Capeci's "Gangland" column declared that sources from both law enforcement and the mob had confirmed that Scarpa was a longtime snitch for the feds. The reporter revealed other startling news. Scarpa was dying of AIDS from tainted blood received during the 1986 operation on his stomach.

In May 1993, Scarpa was allowed to plead guilty to racketeering and weapons charges. He faced life imprisonment without parole. But it was clear to all parties that he was rapidly deteriorating. The Grim Reaper looked grim indeed—ravaged by disease, his new glass eye staring blindly around the courtroom. All the while that Scarpa was out on the streets committing murder with the knowledge of DeVecchio and the FBI, he had known that he was under a death sentence himself.

Scarpa's attorney asked the court to let the sick old man serve a one-year penalty for a misdemeanor gun charge at the medical facility for prisoners with AIDS on Riker's Island. The date for sentencing on federal charges was adjourned until December, when Scarpa would come before federal judge Jack Weinstein. In a sealed proceeding Scarpa's attorney, acknowledging that his client's reputation "precedes him into the courtroom," asked the judge to depart from the guidelines which called for mandatory life imprisonment. When Weinstein asked Scarpa if he had anything to add, Scarpa told the judge he had nothing to say "other than I expect to go home." Then the judge asked Scarpa if he wished to say anything in mitigation of his crimes.

Scarpa replied tellingly, "I tried to help, Your Honor. I am sure you're aware of that." When Weinstein persisted, asking for a statement from Scarpa that he had cut off "all ties to organized crime," Scarpa responded, "I thought that there was a possibility of me going home. I'm just saying I thought that, and when I was thinking that, Your Honor, I already knew that I was retiring from everything."

The judge told Scarpa his request was impossible, his crimes were too serious. Though he pled guilty to three murders, Scarpa got a mere ten years. The killer who hated to do time would never see the streets again. Scarpa died 18 months later, at the age of 67, in the federal prison hospital in Rochester, Minnesota, of complications from AIDS.

Supervisory Special Agent Lindley DeVecchio appeared as an expert witness in the first series of racketeering trials resulting from the Colombo wars. In answer to a defense attorney's question, DeVecchio testified, "[W]e don't condone criminal activities by informants, any more than we do by anybody else." He added that he had never gone to special lengths to keep an informant on the streets knowing the person was committing crimes. Vic Orena, who had never fired a shot during the so-called war and had spent most of the time hiding from Scarpa, was convicted of conspiracy to murder and sentenced to life imprisonment.

The final unraveling of the relationship between Scarpa and DeVecchio began in the most-frequented mob hangout in the world: the attorney conference room at the federal holding pen in downtown Manhattan. Despite Capeci's allegations in "Gangland," the FBI and government prosecutors were successful in covering up Scarpa's informant role—and DeVecchio's leaking of sensitive information to a known killer—until dozens of wiseguys and associates were convicted of participating in crimes perpetrated by Scarpa.

One Colombo member convicted of murder asked a smart young attorney named Alan Futerfas to look into his case. Futerfas heard the rat rumors, he read the "Gangland" columns, and he called Capeci, who stood by his story. Still, Futerfas could hardly get the case back in front of a judge based on innuendo and a newspaper article. He hired a private investigator to go to the courthouse in Brooklyn and pull the sealed records on Scarpa. The minutes of Scarpa's sentencing in front of Judge Weinstein, where the mobster said, "I tried to help, Your Honor," gave Futerfas the evidence he needed to make a motion for a new trial.

Gradually the story came out. When juries at later trials learned of Scarpa's true role, they acquitted Carmine Persico's son, Alphonse, and a number of others charged with engaging in the war.

DeVecchio, still with the FBI, is reportedly under investigation for his handling of Scarpa. When I let the FBI know I was doing this article, spokesman Joe Valiquette said, "I can't discuss the investigation, not even to say whether it is ongoing. All I can say is, DeVecchio is still in the FBI."

DeVecchio's attorney, Douglas E. Grover, told *The New York Times* in July 1995, "There is no evidence that DeVecchio leaked anything to anybody at any time. Everything he did in dealings with Scarpa [was] made known to his superiors at all times." Grover refused any further comment for this article, adding that when it comes to granting interview requests, DeVecchio is "an equal-opportunity denier." We therefore have to settle for a recent appearance the agent made as an on-camera personality in a PBS documentary, *Inside the FBI*.

There, looking grave and fatigued, DeVecchio hosted the show's segment on the FBI's tireless pursuit of organized crime. Sitting in an Italian restaurant, he lamented the added costs patrons must pay for wine and clean linen, not to mention garbage removal, because of the mob's bite. DeVecchio's loathing for such rip-offs seems so sincere it is palpable. But he failed to mention the costs to society and to the rule of law of running criminal informants like Greg Scarpa.

For that we must turn to a 25-year veteran of the Drug Enforcement Administration, Michael Levine, who has written and testified extensively on relationships like that of the Grim Reaper and his FBI Girlfriend. "The illegal use of sleazy criminal informants," says Levine, "is tantamount to firemen starting fires to get themselves headlines. It has made a mockery of the justice system, and costs the taxpayers tens of billions each year. With protectors like these, who needs enemies?"

LOCKDOWN!

Penthouse, February 1997

Father of Abu Ghraib

Qui custodiet ipsos custdodes *is a Latin phrase that means Who shall keep the keepers themselves?*

In Arabic abu means father-of. The father of Abu Ghraib is Alcatraz. Pelican Bay. Corcoran. Marion. Americans who were shocked by the prisoner abuses in Abu Ghraib are living in fantasyland. Better wake up, what happened in Abu Ghraib was child's play, kids dressed up as soldiers mistreating a bunch of Iraqi prisoners. Big deal, say George W. and his policy wonks. We are over there for the greater good, to teach these backward sand-niggers about freedom and democracy, American-style. They better learn to bend over, take it up the ass and keep their mouths shut.

The thing I feared most when I was locked up was a riot. Almost any other situation that came about, I figured I had a fighting chance to survive. But in a riot, the beast is unleashed. You could be minding your own business and get your head chopped off. Men locked in cages and treated like animals become worse than animals. Animals don't humiliate and torture each other. But men do. Given a little power, they revel in it. The main reason I quit working on the prison TV series Oz was because I couldn't get Tom Fontana, who created the show and wrote every episode, to understand that the key relationship in prison is not between the prisoners but between the keepers and the kept. Of course there is violence and tension between prisoners, but it's usually set up and exacerbated by the guards.

Guards were complicit in nearly every prison murder case I've worked on as an expert witness. It's only natural that men and women who work in institutions designed to degrade and crush the spirit of their fellow man will become even worse than their charges. There is more nobility in suffering than in inflicting pain.

What I found shocking about Abu Ghraib was how much media coverage it got compared to the widespread October, 1995 crack cocaine riots in our federal prisons that were virtually ignored by the mainstream press. The story was kept alive on the Internet by family members of prisoners, mostly African-Americans. These men were beaten and tortured, not for anything they had done, but to warn them against even thinking of protesting the harsh sentences they received for small amounts of crack cocaine as compared to much shorter sentences given for powdered cocaine. That's freedom and democracy, American-style. Better learn to love it and cower before those in power or you too could end up with a plunger handle shoved up your ass.

LOCKDOWN!

WITH MORE THAN 1.5 million men and women locked up in the United States, we now imprison the largest percentage of our population of any nation in the world. A record 90,000 new prisoners entered state and federal correctional institutions in 1995. A whole raft of politically driven get-tough-on-crime measures—mandatory sentences for petty drug offenses, three-strikes-you're-out laws, the abolishment of parole and time off for good behavior, the elimination of education and rehabilitation programs—has turned our prisons into pressure cookers full of angry, desperate people who feel they have been singled out to suffer for society's sins.

In October 1995 rioting broke out at more than 20 federal prisons—the most widespread and costly uprisings the American penal system has ever experienced. Seventy federal joints across the country were locked down in a state of emergency. The unprecedented rash of violence resulted in dozens of injuries to prisoners and staff, and cost tens of millions of dollars in damages, overtime, and lost revenue from closed Federal Prison industries factories. Touched off by Congress's rejection of proposed modifications of mandatory drug-sentencing laws, the riots afford a frightening look at the impending crisis in America's burgeoning prison-industrial complex.

But why should we care about these low-life criminals, you ask; who gives a damn about a bunch of vicious, predatory animals? Let them rot in cages. Don't do the crime if you can't do the time.

The issue is more complicated than that.

Increasingly our proliferating prison population is made up of nonviolent, first-time drug offenders serving sentences that are longer than those given to rapists and killers. Women in jail on drug charges, mostly minor players caught up in a life of addiction and low-level dealing, are the fastest-growing incarcerated segment. People serving time for drug-related crimes now account for nearly three-quarters of all those locked up.

The Russian novelist Dostoyevski, who himself served time as a political prisoner, wrote, "The degree of civilization in a society is revealed by entering its prisons." We want our prisons to confine violent, predatory psychopaths. But do we want merely incapacitation, isolation, and punishment for each and all of those whom we label criminals? Because the prison business is one of our fastest-growing industries, we need to ask ourselves what product these institutions are turning out. Are prisons actually making people worse rather than better? If so, then prisons are doing us all more harm than good.

Last year marked the 25th anniversary of the uprising at Attica in New York state, still this country's deadliest prison riot, with more than 40 inmates and staff killed by state police retaking the area—the largest number of Americans killed by American gunfire since the Civil War. After Attica a number of reforms were instituted across the country. Now, with the recently passed Prison Reform Litigation Act and the whole slew of get-tough mandates, the message from Washington is clear: No mercy. Except when it's one of their own. Oliver North skated through on evidence that would have brought a conviction and life sentence to someone without government connections. Gang warfare rules at the highest level as well as the lowest levels of our society, and if you are not with the right gang you can be killed or go to prison. (Remember, these are the same people who gave us the Cold War and Viet Nam.) The well-connected make a lot of money while the less fortunate are sacrificed and the average taxpayer gets fleeced.

I spent eight years—from 1982 to 1990—in federal maximum- and medium-security prisons for smuggling pot. I was lucky. Originally sentenced to 25 years without parole, I became a jailhouse lawyer. Because the judge had stipulated on the record that she was giving me more time for my refusal to "cooperate" with the government—in other words, rat on my friends—I was able to persuade an appellate court that my sentence was coercive rather than punitive. Had I been sentenced under mandatory guidelines enacted during the years I was locked up, I would have received life with no parole for a nonviolent conspiracy to traffic in weed.

I was a middle-class white boy who grew up in the suburbs of Boston, steeped in the marijuana subculture of the sixties—an exception to the rule of who usually winds up in prison. When I was locked up I had all the advantages of education, money, friends and family who supported me, and the emotional and intellectual wherewithal to make the best of a bad situation. Since my release from prison a little more than six years ago I have been active in criminal-justice and prison reform. I married ex-convict Kim Wozencraft, a former undercover narcotics cop who fell while fighting on the front lines of the drug war. Together we put out a magazine, *Prison Life, the Voice of the Convict.* We stay in close touch with a number of convicts and ex-cons around the country, and publish their art, writing, opinion.

During my sojourn in the American gulag I learned that crime pays. It pays for the hordes of lawyers, cops, and other law-enforcement agents, judges, and prison officials who make their living off the men and women in penitentiaries. It pays for the people who build prisons, for the companies that provide goods and services to prisoners, and for the politicians who win votes by whipping up public fear of crime. And it pays big-time for drug kingpins, mob killers, and millionaire white-collar criminals willing to trade the lives of others along with a portion of their own illegally gotten gains for reduced prison time.

I learned during my stint in some of America's most notorious joints that most of our prisons are far from the country clubs we hear denounced by get-tough-on-crime politicians. More and more prisoners must pay for every aspect of their upkeep, including soap and aspirin, and their wages are docked for fines, court costs, resti-tution. Meanwhile educational programs that once offered a glimmer of hope to convicts looking for a way to turn their lives around have all been cut. Our prisons are awash with drugs and weapons, and riddled with bribe-taking guards who smuggle drugs and weapons to prisoners and encourage violence.

My first weekend as a prisoner I spent at the infamous Los Angeles City Jail, named the "Glass House" because the walls of the holding tanks are made of thick Plexiglas so guards can see what's going on inside without having to enter. There I lived for three days in one of those tanks with more than a hundred other men, all of them black or Mexican except me and another white guy. The tank also held two open, overflowing broken toilets amid a big puddle of piss and shit. At breakfast the second day guards used their truncheons to beat bloody a crazy guy who sat laughing to himself over his food; he was breaking the silence-at-meals rule.

On Monday, after the judge set my bail at $15 million, I was taken to "the hole" at Terminal Island, the federal prison in San Pedro, California, where I spent two days in a dark, filthy, slimy, damp cell listening to detoxing junkies retch and howl day and night. In eight years I never got used to having guards order me to strip, bend over, and "spread 'em" so they could look up my ass hole. I did learn to stifle any sign of emotion that might cause guards or other prisoners to perceive me as weak.

In the late eighties, as the prison population exploded, I was transferred, with several busloads of other prisoners, from Petersburg, Virginia, to Raybrook in upstate New York. It was a grueling trip, 20-plus hours in handcuffs, shackles, and chains. On one of the buses, according to a widely told story, a lieutenant wrapped a mouthy prisoner in a thick layer of masking tape to shut him up. The man died of suffocation. (When asked by *Penthouse* to comment on this, Bill Bechtold, public-affairs spokesperson for the Bureau of Prisons, said he had heard about the incident and believed the guard in question had been prosecuted, but refused to give further details, citing the Privacy Act.)

When we arrived I and several other high-security prisoners— I was considered a "sophisticated" criminal, and my long sentence made me an escape risk—were thrown in "the hole." We were kept there 24 hours a day for a week just to let us know that in case any of us were thinking of complaining about the treatment we received in transit we could expect even harsher retaliation.

For what may be the first time in the history of U.S. prison riots, the October 1995 uprising was a protest not just about prison conditions but also the political forces that put people there. According to letters and affidavits I've received from convicts at different joints, what began as nonviolent work strikes to protest disparity in crack-versus-powdered cocaine sentencing erupted into full-scale rioting when Bureau of Prisons staff overreacted, ordered an emergency lockdown, and sent in black-clad, baton-wielding Special Operations Response Teams. My correspondents, most of whom had not participated in the demonstrations—told of beatings, gassings with tear gas and Mace, and hours of torture.

"After we were handcuffed and shackled," Joseph L. Davis, a prisoner at the Federal Correctional Institution at Greenville, Illinois, wrote in a letter he sent to me as well as to various members of Congress and B.O.P. Director Kathleen Hawk, "the officers at Greenville, in the presence of two prison officials, called out inmate Tommy Scott from the bullpen and beat him with a baton and sprayed him with pepper Mace. After he passed out, they carried him to the front of the bus and threw him on the ground, where they had another 15 or so inmates that had been beaten and sprayed with pepper Mace. . . . I thought Greenville was bad, but nothing could have prepared me for what awaited us at U.S.P. Leavenworth."

From Greenville, hundreds of prisoners, mostly African-Americans, were trussed up in special handcuffs (known as the "black box"), leg irons, and belly chains, put on buses, and shipped to the famous Kansas penitentiary. Upon their arrival at Leavenworth, they were treated to a traditional welcome known as "the gauntlet." Another Greenville prisoner, Richard Pruden, a white bank robber with more than half of a 13-year sentence under his belt, sent me his account of the Leavenworth beatings. Pruden says that when he hobbled down from the bus at Leavenworth, two guards dressed in combat fatigues grabbed him, one on each arm. They yanked him off his feet and ran him through a series of doors into the bowels of the penitentiary. At each doorway the guards veered to the side, smashing Pruden into the concrete-and-steel doorjambs. "There were a few old guys, a few lames, and one guy who had no teeth and no stomach and weighed about 120 pounds at five feet three," Pruden says. "They beat them just like everyone else." Pruden says he was carried to a holding cell, slammed against the wall, and told not to move or he would have his head bashed in. "I stood there as unmoving as I could for several hours."

Joseph Davis, who was on a bus that arrived before Pruden's, told in his letter of a similar reception. "I was dragged off the bus by my handcuffs and through this gauntlet of men with batons and gloves on," he wrote. "I was punched and beat as I passed, and after reaching the inside I was slammed into a brick wall and told to keep my nose on the wall. And the statement was made: 'So you want to riot, nigger?' I went to say I had nothing to do with the riot. I was told, 'Nigger, shut the fuck up, *now!*' Still being held by my handcuffs, I was slammed into an iron gate. Now there were people all around me, begging and crying for them not to beat them anymore."

The "welcome" lasted at least five hours. Pruden wrote that he was then "transported by two officers who more or less carried me briskly through the penitentiary and placed me in a cell." Later he got a visit from the warden, who told him, "Lie down and lick your nuts. You were lucky they didn't break your wrists."

The worsening of a bad scene all began on October 18, 1995, when the House of Representatives voted overwhelmingly to reject a recommendation by the Federal Sentencing Commission to modify the great disparity in sentences for crack and powdered cocaine. Bureau of Prisons officials had informed members of the Sentencing Commission (as well as their own staff) that there could be trouble if inequities in cocaine sentencing laws were not eliminated. The congressmen were unmoved. Under current federal law, possession or distribution of five grams of crack cocaine will get you a mandatory minimum five-year sentence, with no possibility of parole. To get the same sentence for cocaine powder, you would have to be caught with 500 grams. (A recently reported 20-year clinical study finds virtually no difference in the effects of crack and powdered cocaine.) In 1993 nearly 90 percent of offenders arrested for crack crimes and sentenced to lengthy mandatory prison terms were African-Americans.

The day after the Sentencing Commission's proposal was

defeated, a fight broke out in a federal joint in Alabama. Two days after, on Friday, October 20, B.O.P. Director Hawk issued panicky orders for a nationwide emergency lockdown of all 70 federal prisons. Although most of the joints had remained calm, wardens and B.O.P. officials called the lockdown a "precautionary measure."

Locking down a penitentiary is the equivalent of slamming a lid on an already simmering pot. The federal system operates at about 150 percent of capacity; in most state penitentiaries and county jails the overcrowding is even worse. Cells made for one man have been doubled up, and in a number of institutions there are men sleeping on bunks in common areas. Tensions are exacerbated by the lack of privacy, the inescapable, constant noise and smell of other people, and, above all, the fear of violence, which can erupt at any time.

In 1995 frightened authorities did exactly the wrong thing. A lockdown means just that: You are locked in your cell 24 hours a day. Guards come by three times a day and toss in a bag containing an apple and a bologna sandwich, or a couple of hard-boiled eggs. By law, prisoners are supposed to get one hour of exercise a day, but during an emergency lockdown these regulations are suspended. During the nationwide lockdown B.O.P. staff were also stressed out, because they were required to work 12-hour shifts.

David Correa, a Cuban-born former pilot with Eastern Airlines who's now doing life with no parole for cocaine possession and distribution, sent me a detailed account of the lockdown and subsequent riot at the medium-security prison, F.C.I. (for Federal Correctional Institution) Marianna, in Florida. "You would not believe what is going on," Correa wrote. "I see all hell breaking loose down the road, and I want no part of any of it. The crowd coming in is younger. They have no education, there is no education to give them, and they all have so much time [to serve]! They are mostly blacks and Hispanics."

Correa added that the riots were not race- or gang-related, as many people supposed, and another inmate who called in a report to me from F.C.I. Memphis said the same thing. "The feds are saying it's racial, but it's not," he said. "During the riot, you had Crips and Bloods from L.A., you had gangs from Chicago, you had white guys, all in this together."

At Marianna, Correa reported, prisoner fury was exacerbated by the way the lockdown was handled. Staff told the prisoners that there would be a "special count" at 4:00 PM, which meant that they would be locked in their cells for 15 minutes instead of being allowed to stand in cell doorways. Before the count, prisoners who, because of crowding, had been housed dormitory-style in a common room were added one by one to every regular two-man cell. It was two days before cells were unlocked and the men allowed out, and then only to the common indoor areas of their units.

"At this point," Correa wrote, "everyone was outraged at the lies, no showers, and, for those men who normally live in the common area who were stuck in a room, they had to do [without] fresh clothing or personal articles, plus they had to sleep on the concrete floor. This was the beginning of the security tightening at this institution, where there was absolutely no indication of any pending trouble."

With the men out of their cells but still confined to their cell-blocks, Correa said tensions mounted as staff began treating the men with overt hostility and verbal abuse, and enforcing rules and regulations no one had ever heard of.

Correa claimed that early on the morning of October 25 he saw Marianna staff meet in the parking lot outside the prison with members of a Special Operations Response Team. At 6:00 AM prisoners were released from their cellblocks for the morning meal and work call, in what was supposedly a resumption of normal activities following the lockdown. Marianna has what is known as "controlled movement." For ten minutes each hour the compound and outdoor recreation area are opened to allow convicts to move from one secure section to another. At the end of the move the compound is closed. Correa, already at his assigned job, saw the move through the window. He said a group of black prisoners in the yard refused to report to work. They were "voicing their complaints, making hand gestures only," Correa said "No one had weapons, and no violence was being demonstrated."

He added that he was standing near a female staff member who had a radio. He heard the compound officer say, "It has started."

"Shortly thereafter," says Correa, "the SORT team was running across the rooftop of the administration building that connects to the gym roof. SORT members took up positions with high-powered automatic weapons inside the compound and on the rooftops. The SORT people were wearing full riot gear, dressed in black with face shields and helmets. The weapons they carried into the compound were AR-15 machine guns, Remington 12-gauge riot-type shotguns, tear-gas guns, and tear-gas foggers and sprayers. They also carried shields and electric batons. There was a total of about 35 SORT officers, not counting the ones on the roof. They lined up shoulder to shoulder facing the rec yard, and assumed a defensive stance. When the inmates saw this massive show of force they took up any object that came to hand: weights, pool sticks, weight bars. There was no attempt at all to talk to the inmates, who at this time totaled about 30 men, all African-American, and only trying to be heard."

The prisoners began breaking windows in the gym with weights, setting fires, and trashing the recreation area. Now the riot had really begun. Correa continues, "The SORT team stormed the yard, firing tear gas and setting off percussion devices among the crowd."

Another Marianna prisoner, Ignatizo Giuliano, a non-participant in the strike who reported for work in the recreation area and got caught in the riot, corroborated Correa's account of how the disturbance had begun. Giuliano told me in an affidavit of watching as the SORT team fired tear-gas canisters at the protesters, who picked them up and hurled them back. "Meantime a guard on the other side of the perimeter fence was shouting, 'Everybody down, with your hands on your heads!' while at the same time the SORT crew were yelling from on top of the gym for all non-participants to go to the right side of the field of the rec yard and lie down by the fence. This contradiction in orders was making the guard on the perimeter fence furious because he wanted everyone to lie down where they were."

Giuliano and around 230 other prisoners did lie facedown with their hands on their heads. They were ordered to strip to their underwear and march by twos through rows of armed SORT members, who tied their hands behind their backs with plastic straps and herded them into a caged outdoor recreation area. The straps work on a ratchet principle. The more you pull on the strap, the tighter it gets. "My straps were so tightly bound, my hands turned a deep purple and went completely numb," Giuliano wrote. "After approximately ten hours of having my hands bound behind my back, I could not stand the pain any longer. I was desperate to have something done with the straps since one of my friends told me that my wrists had started bleeding."

The caged area where the men were kept had no toilets. Prisoners were urinating on the back walls, and before long a large puddle of piss covered the floor. None of them had food or clothing, except undershorts, for 16 hours. The temperature dropped to the low forties. "We were freezing," wrote Giuliano. "We were all yelling for some clothing to wear and finally they brought out short-sleeved jumpsuits, which proved to be better than nothing. As the night wore on, the concrete floor, which was the only place to sleep, became bitter cold. Then, to top it all off, the guards brought out cardboard boxes for the inmates to defecate in. At this point the smell was unbearable. Every time someone would urinate or defecate, we all had to move closer together. At approximately 5:00 PM on the following day, two guards came and escorted me back to my unit. My feet were so swollen from standing on the cold concrete floor for over 30 hours that I couldn't get my shoes on."

When I called B.O.P. Director Hawk for a statement on allegations of prisoner abuse following the October riots, I was told by spokesperson Bill Bechtold that there were allegations made and that some were found to be true. However, he refused to discuss specific cases or the allegations of specific prisoners because of limitations imposed by the Privacy Act.

Like all of federal law enforcement, the bureau has militarized its attitudes and operations over the past 15 years as our society's philosophy has shifted from rehabilitation to punishment. During the crisis Director Hawk wrote in the bureau's weekly newsletter, *Monday Morning Highlights:* "I am extremely impressed and very proud of the extraordinary manner in which Federal Bureau of Prisons staff have responded to the difficult and dangerous challenges of the past week. B.O.P. staff have demonstrated strength, resourcefulness, heroism, and the highest standards of professionalism in handling the many incidents that have occurred, protecting inmates, fellow staff members, and surrounding communities from serious harm, and preserving the security of our institutions."

Hawk went on to say that the incidents were under investigation. "We are assessing the causes and will work to ensure that further unrest is averted."

If we believe Correa and Giuliano, the rebellion at Marianna consisted of 30 black prisoners voicing anger over crack laws, and the SORT team's presumptive retaliation that led to violence and destruction of government property. No staff were injured. A number of prisoners, including many who had not participated, did require medical attention. The warden ordered a second lockdown that lasted for 15 days. That has restored peace for the time being.

Police brutality is one of those evils that is magnified

grotesquely behind bars. If prisoners are society's rejects, the men and women who guard them are at the bottom of the heap in a law-enforcement system riddled with sadism and corruption. To make matters worse, most prisons are built in poor-white boondocks, where racism and distrust of cultural differences are rife. "Right after the disturbance, a group of officers who had participated in the 'roundup' were standing by the front gate of the unit, right by my window," Correa wrote. "These men were openly bragging to each other how they slammed this guy to the ground, how they roughed him up. They were discussing how much fun it had been, and that they wished it would happen again soon."

During the riots at a minimum-security prison camp in Atlanta, according to letters and reports from prisoners and family members, SORT troops randomly beat dozens of prisoners, including one who is blind. Like the gauntlet, a general ass-kicking is considered a good way to keep prisoners who merely watched the riots from even thinking of joining in next time. Guards and prisoners all agree there will be a next time.

Lockdowns and SORT assaults have become the penal management tools of choice for the nineties. Prison officials are relying more and more on fear and force to control the populations of young prisoners who have no hope of getting out for decades, if at all. Where parole and time off for good behavior—or for participation in educational, job-training and treatment programs—once shortened sentences and were incentives for prisoners, now nightsticks, machine guns, tear gas, and expensive lockdowns struggle to keep an ever-more-tenuous order. Long sentences, the injustice of the disparity in the drug laws, and the rapid deterioration of prison conditions have given birth to a bitter, vengeful new breed of prisoner who knows that his plight means nothing to the people in power. As Malcolm X said, this man is dangerous because he has nothing to lose.

The most recent assault on prisoners' rights came in the age-old form of censorship. Inmates in the federal system were slated, as of December 1, 1996, to no longer be able to receive any "commercially published material that is sexually explicit or contains nudity." The bureau-wide ban is the first of its kind. Normally the feds leave it up to the warden of each individual prison to determine which books and magazines prisoners are allowed to read. This time, however, in keeping with the federal government's self-appointed role as moral guardian, the B.O.P. cited the Ensign Amendment, a rider to an appropriations bill, as grounds for a system-wide ban that originated with lightning speed out of the bureau's central office in Washington. The Ensign Amendment, named for the Nevada Republican congressman who drafted it, forbids disbursing federal funds to distribute or make available information or material that contains, in the words of a bureau spokesperson, "nude female breasts or genitalia or other pornographic material." Welcome back to the Dark Ages.

At the present rate of incarceration, there will be more than seven million people locked up by the end of the century—more than are enrolled in colleges and universities. Most of these people will someday get out of prison. Then it will be payback time.

Photo credit: Fionn Reilly

ONLY IN AMERICA: THE GETBACK OF DENNIS MCKEE

Prison Life, February 1997

The End of *Prison Life*

Prison Life *died a slow, agonizing death, kicking and screaming all the way to the grave. I'm a Capricorn, our zodiac sign is the goat, and Capricorns can be stubborn. I don't take failure or defeat easily. Like Dennis McKee, the bank robber turned entrepreneur we profiled in our final issue of* Prison Life, *I subscribe to the convict mantra,* Never give up. *I sunk all our available cash into the magazine, got a second mortgage on our home, borrowed from friends, trying everything to keep us afloat, hoping some angel would come along and bail us out, give us the financing we needed to keep publishing until the magazine became profitable. I was all too aware of how much* Prison Life *meant to the prisoners who saw it as their only means of contact with the outside world. I will never forget how winning a PEN Prison Writing award changed my life.*

We sponsored an annual Art Behind Bars contest and the work kept getting better and better. I used to love to go to the post office and see what treasures were in the mail. There was hope. Creativity had the power to tame the wild urge toward criminality. We'd seen it happen with men like Rock Dutton, Eddie Bunker, Danny Trejo, Jimmy Baca, just to name a few lost souls who were saved by language and art. Prison Life *helped fill the void. We tried everything to keep it alive. We shut down the New York offices, ran the magazine out of a post office box with editorial offices in the basement to save money. But even with the stipend coming in from the HBO* documentaries, we couldn't keep up the printing and mailing costs and eventually we were forced to surrender.

That was eight years ago. The magazine has been dormant for as long as I was in stir. There are now well over two million people locked up in our prisons and jails, even with the war on crime and drugs taking a crowded backseat to the enemy with a thousand faces, known today as the war on terrorism.

Conditions in the prisons are no better. The private prison companies are in deep trouble. Trying to cut costs to maximize profits they cut corners, hire poorly-trained staff, build inferior facilities. But prison is a two-way street. As veterans on both sides of the fence will tell you, you need to go along to get along. No one wants to do hard time. Being locked up is the punishment, being separated from the family of man and woman, shunted into the dark parallel world of imprisonment. Of the world but not in it, lonely as hell, that is the punishment. You're not supposed to be degraded, tortured, fucked with constantly until you go off and start killing people—or you get out and start killing people.

The best argument against making our prisons gladiator schools is that some day many of those behind bars will come out. The result of bad conditions, overcrowding, abolishing education programs is always the same: riots. People on both sides get slaughtered in riots. Society suffers when convicts come out of prison better criminals and avowed enemies of society. Super-maxes breed super-criminals. Men with nothing to lose. Homegrown terrorists. The states are running out of tax money to run their over-burdened corrections departments. The feds are shutting down military bases and turning them into prisons. We're creating a dangerous new enemy within.

Dennis McKee's story is a combination of one of those irresistible American stories of success against all odds, and a wacky version of Runaway Train meets One Flew Over the Cuckoo's Nest with an upbeat Hollywood ending. Miraculously, Dennis got away. He made it out alive.

ONLY IN AMERICA: THE GETBACK OF DENNIS MCKEE

MANY IS THE CONVICT who lies on a bunk in a cell after lockdown dreaming of what he will do once released. Ah, sweet freedom, goes the fantasy; anything is possible if only I could get out of prison. And even if he may never get out, and if freedom was not so sweet to begin with, he remembers the good times, or he imagines what it would be like to be happy, to be loved, to have a decent job and a good income, friends, maybe even a family.

Most convicts hope never to return to prison. Contrary to what *Reader's Digest* might say, and what the majority of disinformed Americans might believe, our prisons are not plush resorts where depraved criminals lie around doing bench presses and plotting new assaults on society. They are houses of pain, warehouses of despair, and nearly everyone in prison is in constant emotional anguish, even if they don't always admit it. The duress of captivity and alienation from free humanity will penetrate even the hardest body and soul armor.

If the convict was state-raised, brought up in institutions of pain, the reform schools and juvenile joints that serve as prep schools for the penitentiary, his cellblock dreams are distorted. Chances are he does not know what it is like to be loved; he has no context for happiness except maybe a few cherished childhood memories. Most of these men and women are lost to us. They fulfill our darkest expectations by running afoul of the law, hurting themselves and others, and returning to prison. People despise the convict writer Jack Henry Abbott because he got out of prison, after spending nearly his whole life locked up for petty crimes, and killed a man over a perceived slight. Yet that is how he had learned to survive in prison.

The state-raised convict is a special breed brought up in houses of hatred, violence, and torture where they have been trained like junkyard dogs to be suspicious, mean, ferocious. They can be some of the toughest, most merciless people you will ever meet. If, through it all, they somehow manage to retain a connection to the human family and are able one day to break free of institutional life, these convicts can be some of the sweetest people you will ever meet. All those years of oppression and strife turn them deep within themselves to mine whatever goodness is there, perhaps a mother who once loved them, then forge a strong character from this meager ore. I usually recognize these men when I meet them; often I feel a respect and love for them that comes from having seen where they spent their lives and knowing what inner work they have accomplished to survive with their humanity intact.

I knew Dennis "Rex" McKee was such a man the first night I met him Houston, Texas. He was wearing a T-shirt, shorts, a pair of flip-flops with a lot of miles on them, and a cockeyed baseball cap. True to his breed, he smoked pretty much constantly, drank coffee or Pepsi steadily, and told epic war stories about his seventeen years in and out of some of America's toughest federal pens: Alcatraz, Atlanta, Leavenworth, Terre Haute, El Reno. Dennis makes no bones about the fact that he is an ex-convict and a former bank robber. He's proud of the transformation he has made, proud that although he never went further than the fifth grade and he reads and writes with difficulty, he can sign his name on a check for tens of thousands of dollars drawn on a bank he once robbed.

I met Dennis when I went to Houston to do Ray Hill's prison radio show. Dennis was introduced to the listening audience as an example of a man who had become a successful self-made businessman despite his checkered past. On the air, Dennis told the story of how he once borrowed $20,000 from University Savings Bank to launch himself in a video-trading business he had conceived. He had no credit history, he was just out of the halfway house and working for an attorney who helped him get out of prison—hardly an ideal candidate for a bank loan.

"I went to University Savings, talked to some loan officer, and they turned me down flat," Dennis told the listeners. "So I went higher and they turned me down again. Then I called the bank president, man by the name of Paul Yates, and he listened to me. I went in to see him and asked him for a loan, and when I was all finished asking, Paul Yates said to me, 'Now, Mr. McKee, aren't you the same Dennis McKee who once robbed this bank?' And I told him, 'Yessir, that's me.' And do you know he went and loaned me that $20,000 unsecured because he felt that any man who had the nerve to go into a bank he'd once robbed and ask for a loan to start a business was either crazy or one helluva man." For Dennis, the incident confirmed a fundamental tenet of the convict code he had learned the hard way.

There is a picture that sums up the theme of Dennis McKee's extraordinary rise from the dungeons of our penitentiaries and mental wards to the good life and the realization of those lonesome convict visions. I saw it on the wall of Dwayne Sherlock's room at Steven's House, and Eddie Bunker has the same picture on the wall of the cell-like room he writes in. It shows a frog being swallowed by a long-legged, long-necked bird. The frog is disappearing down the bird's throat, but it has grabbed the bird in a choke hold and is strangling it. The caption under the picture says: Never give up.

DENNIS THE MENACE

The all-American saga of Dennis "Rex" McKee begins in the backwoods of Alabama. Born to a fifteen-year-old mother who worked as a waitress at the time, Dennis was raised by his grandmother in a house that rented for $9.25 a month. By the time he was two, his father was gone, shunted off to the penitentiary. When he was a little boy, Dennis' grandmother beat him so badly he had to be hospitalized twice.

It was a hardscrabble life but Dennis was an enterprising kid who refused to succumb to the deprivations of poverty. His mother worked to support him and pay the rent, but there was nothing left over to buy toys for Dennis and his younger brother. Dennis learned to steal at an early age.

"We were dirt poor," he told me during a visit to his home near International Video in Katy, Texas, one of two huge movie rental emporiums Dennis owns. "I never had a tricycle, so I stole one. Never had a bicycle, so I stole one. Never had a car, so I stole one."

Some of his most vivid childhood memories were of the beatings his grandmother gave him when he acted up.

"My grandmother was a drunk," he said when I asked him why she abused him. "Plain and simple. She was mean, too. She would walk up and down this dirt road in the little town where we lived and she would scream, 'I'm drunk as a skunk and I don't give a goddamn who knows it!' Back then when you died they'd embalm you and then take you back to your house. Two doors down from where we lived they had a dead woman in there and my grandmother took a can of kerosene and went down and kicked in the door. There was a bunch of people in there mourning. My grandmother walked up to the casket, she poured kerosene all over the body and said, 'Somebody is going to fix me some goddamn soup or I'm sending her straight to hell right now!'

"One time she beat me real bad because I wouldn't come in to eat when she called. She came out on the porch and I was riding a bike I had stolen from the kid next door. She told me to come in and eat and I wouldn't. I was looking at her and riding and trying to get away but I ran off the damn road, rolled into a ditch, and broke my arm. Had a compound fracture with the broken bone sticking out of my arm," he remembered, touching one of the many scars on his arms. "My grandmother came over to where I was lying in the ditch and she beat me. She grabbed the end of the bone that was sticking out and she yanked on it and said, 'You little bastard, you come in the next time I tell you to.' "

I asked Dennis if he thought it was the circumstances of his youth that caused him to make an early, inauspicious try at crime as a career. Dennis claims he knew what he was doing was wrong but he just didn't give a damn. He wasn't bad so much as he was full of mischief and daring. He takes full responsibility for the choices he made in his life, refuses to cast blame on his family or his background and feels he got into trouble because he was rebellious and he refused to knuckle under. His stealing soon went from play to livelihood.

"One of the first things I stole for money was a car battery, me and another kid, and we wrapped it up in my coat so we could carry it. We took it to the junkyard to sell. On the way, we dropped it and the battery busted inside my coat and all this water—I didn't know it was acid at the time—spilled on my jacket. Next day I wore the same clothes to school and my jacket was all full of holes and just started coming apart. The other kids thought that was pretty funny. I was about eight or nine at the time."

When Dennis was thirteen, the family moved to Phenix City, Alabama where Dennis pulled his first B&E. "I broke into a drug store and stole all the comic books and marbles because back in them days whoever had the most marbles and comic books to trade was king of the hill. But I got busted and they sent me to the Alabama Boys Industrial School in Birmingham. I stayed there for about four months—then I ran off. I got to Columbus, Georgia and stole my first car."

Dennis hot-wired a '52 Ford at a small roadside used car lot, Bill Heard Car Sales, now a major Southern automobile franchise with dealerships in Texas. Twenty-five years later, Dennis walked into the Bill Heard car dealership in Sugarland, Texas and, savoring the irony, bought the first of three brand-new Corvettes. Over the course of a year he also bought three fully decked-out custom vans for his video trading business, and a Mustang convertible. In total he spent $128,000.

"To this day they do not know that the first car I ever had, I stole from them. So I went from the thief of the smallest magnitude to one of the biggest customers they've ever had and I've always thought about stopping by there and telling them, but I never have."

For the car theft Dennis caught a bid at a reform school in Alto, Georgia.

"That was the first time I'd been to a place where they had real guards in uniforms, bars on the windows and armed cops watching the fences," he told me. It took him eight months to get out. In what would become a pattern during those years, Dennis stole another car and fled. This time he made it Houston, Texas. Inspired by gangster movies, he armed himself with a stolen .45 caliber Tommy gun and decided to try his hand at robbing banks. He was just 15 years old when he sauntered into University Savings lugging the machine gun.

"While I was trying to rob the bank," Dennis recalled, "one of the tellers, a lady, looked at me and just sort of patted me on the butt and said, 'Why don't you go home, little boy.' I didn't know what to do so I turned and ran out of the bank with the Tommy gun."

"Was it loaded?" I asked him.

"Yes it was loaded. Hell, it weighed about sixteen pounds."

"Did you get the money?"

"Shit, no. I turned and ran out the bank. I was scared to death. I had never fired the gun, so two days later I decided to try it again. I went back to the same bank and this time when I walked in I decided I was going to pop a roll of caps to get somebody's attention. But I lost control of the gun because it pulls real hard when you fire it and I was popping holes in the ceiling. I finally got it under control and this time nobody patted me on the butt and told me to go home. They gave me the money."

Emboldened by his success, Dennis packed up his Tommy gun and returned to Alabama a professional bank robber. He always worked alone; he'd steal a car, leave it running outside while he ran in to stick up the bank. In a Birmingham robbery he made off with around 18 grand, more money than he had ever dreamed of, but he was shot by a cop as he fled and, although he got away, he was wounded and needed to find a doctor to patch him up. The doctor called the cops and two days after the robbery Dennis was arrested at the doctor's office.

THE PENITENTIARY YEARS

Because of his age (he was just fifteen) Dennis was sentenced in federal court to an undetermined length of time and sent to the National Training School in Washington, D.C. His second day there, he walked off and was caught later the same day. This time they sent him to Chillicothe, Ohio to a reform school that was supposedly secure enough to hold him. Again, Dennis took off. When he was arrested a few days later, they sent him to the federal penitentiary in El Reno, Oklahoma.

"El Reno at that time was more like a high-grade reform school, a gladiator school where everybody fought. I decided that I wasn't going to work. They put me in this broom factory and told me I had to work making those damn brooms. My attitude was if I was going to work in a factory, I wouldn't be in the penitentiary to start with. They would roll the cell doors open and tell me to get up and go to work and I'd say, 'Fuck you. I'm a bank robber, not a worker.' They would roll back the doors and get everybody out of the block because if one convict says he won't work then pretty soon two or three others will say they're not working either. They can't have that. So they would beat me unmercifully, throw me in the hole and leave me there. At some point after they beat you enough—because the guards get tired of beating you just as much as you get tired of it—they put you on the 'pay him no mind list.'"

When he refused to program at El Reno, Dennis was certified insane by the penitentiary shrink and shipped off to the U.S. Medical Center in Springfield, Missouri. "I'd never been in a nut house and they have rules there that I didn't know about. When you first come in they put you in a strip cell until a doctor can evaluate you. I got there on Labor Day weekend and there weren't any doctors around. Back in them days at Springfield the guards wouldn't even talk to you. If they thought you was a nut, they just stripped you naked and threw you in a cell. I was maybe sixteen years old and I think that is the only time I ever knew fear. I'm thinking, 'What the fuck am I going to do, spend the rest of my life in this cell?' "

It was a small, dark cell with a solid metal door, an observation window that could be shuttered closed and a "beanhole" food trap the guards would open to shove in the food tray.

"The guard would come by and look in on you ever' 15 or ever' 30 minutes. I'd been in that cell maybe an hour when I heard all this commotion out front and I looked out and here was the biggest man that I'd ever seen in my life. He was at least six four and weighed around 300 pounds and there was some fat but it was a lot of muscle. This was the first time that I'd really seen a goon squad in action. There had to have been eight or ten guards in this hallway and they had these pads like mattresses with straps on the backs and they were using them like bodybags and they were pushing this guy and he was whipping guards like you've never seen and they kept stabbing him with these syringes and finally he dropped. Later I found out that they hit him with Paradol and it dropped him down. So I see all this stuff and then it goes silent again and two hours later they just opened the beanhole, fed me and *adios amigo*, they was gone again."

In desperation, Dennis tried what he called "sympathy suicide." He worked a piece of metal off of the bunk, waited until he heard the guard's key jingling and knew he would be discovered, then he slashed his forearm. "I figured he would see me bleeding and open the door. I didn't think they would let me bleed to death. But, when the guard got a few feet from my door, some fuckin' convict started banging on his door and hollering and the guard turned back to see what the fuss was and here I am shootin' blood all the way to the ceiling. There was blood everywhere. I hit an artery and it was spurtin' out and there I was just knowing I'm going to die 'cause I've never been around anybody even tried suicide and so I start banging on my door and they come and see all the blood and in a minute or two here comes the same goon squad.

"This doctor threw me on a gurney, took me upstairs and said, " 'Son, you wanted to commit suicide, you wanted to die, well, you might as well be dead because I can't do nothing for you.' I became unglued, I begged that doctor to do something and he said, 'I'm going to try but I don't think there is anything I can do.' And they took me to surgery and they put me on this bed that had a board sticking out for the arm and they strapped my arm down to it and this doctor took like two pairs of long tweezers and where I had cut the artery it shot back in the arm like a rubber band and he reached down and got the artery and clamped it off and I'm screaming at the top of my lungs and the doctor said, 'Shit! I forgot to give you anesthesia.' So he stopped and deadened the arm and then went ahead and put a tube in my arm and I think that was the best thing that ever happened to me."

"How's that?" I asked.

"Well, cured me of ever wanting to try suicide again, that's for damn sure."

Dennis pointed to the scarred gash across his thick forearm. "You see that one scar? You don't see them scars all up and down the arm like you do on somebody who tries a lot of them sympathy suicides. Now, if that doctor had said, 'Son, why'd you do that?' and just sewed me back up, I'd've said, 'Fuck, I'll just do that again.' No, once was enough."

"How did you lose your little finger?" I asked Dennis as he sipped his coffee and lit another Benson and Hedges. He cracked a grin and said, "Oh, that. That's another story. I chopped that finger off to leave the penitentiary because if you lost a limb, they would take you to an outside hospital. So I cut it off with a tin can lid and they rushed me to the hospital and I left. And as you can see it's a real bad job but I stitched my finger myself like Patrick Swayze in *Roadhouse*."

The brush with death at Springfield convinced Dennis he had had enough of the nut ward. He behaved himself long enough to be put in population at the Medical Center and was eventually decertified, pronounced cured, and sent back to El Reno. This time, Dennis did not object to working in the broom factory. He studied operations in the warehouse and devised a plan to hide in a shipment of brooms.

"I stayed in there, in them brooms, what I think was close to two days. And then when I finally figured I could come out because it wasn't moving anymore and there were no more voices, I busted the case open and got out. I seen this building, this real familiar looking building and it had bars everywhere and, well, I walked around two minutes and figured out I hadn't gone after all, I'd just transferred myself from one penitentiary to another. It turned out I was in the warehouse at the penitentiary in Leavenworth."

"What did you do?"

"There wasn't much I could do. I didn't want to get shot. Back then when a guard got in trouble the emergency code for the telephone was 222. The guard could dial 222 and it activated phones ever'where that indicated he was in trouble. I didn't know what to do so I dialed 222 on the phone and said 'I'm out here in some kind of factory and I've gotten out of El Reno.' And they came over to get me. They thought it was funnier than shit. They didn't beat me or nothin', they just laughed. They threw me in the hole for five months and then they sent me to Atlanta."

Atlanta was a real penitentiary: Dennis, not yet twenty, had finally made it to the Big House and he was scared to death. In the fifties and sixties, Atlanta housed some of the most notorious criminals in the country. "It was a spooky joint," he remembered.

"Real spooky. Big walls, right there in the middle of town. Long corridors and big cellblocks. They put me in a single cell. They always put me in a single cell, for refusing to work and other things in my record like being insane. I think it was A block, but I don't remember. I know I was on the top of a four-tier cellblock, but that was over 30 years ago and I've been in so many of those places since then. Later on, they classified me as a security risk and sent me to Alcatraz."

At twenty-one, Dennis was the youngest man at the fed's most secure joint on a rock island in the middle of San Francisco Bay. They were building Marion, the underground super-max joint in Illinois at the time, and getting ready to close down the Rock. In the 18 months Dennis spent in Alcatraz he says he never tried to leave. There were rumors that the Rock was being closed and Dennis bided his time to see where he would wind up next.

"One of the nicest people I met in Alcatraz was a guy named Joe Schultz. He shouldn't have been in the penitentiary in the first place. He was a professional fighter and his manager overmatched him and he got beat half to death. He went to a bank and robbed the bank and demanded an exact amount of money like $397 or something, and then went out to the bank steps, sat down and started counting his money. And they gave him 25 years.

"This had to be around '63 because they recertified me back in Atlanta after we all got shipped out of Alcatraz. I went back to the Medical Center in Springfield and it was a couple of years after the Bay of Pigs when JFK happened. You know that when the Americans decided not to attack Cuba, all the doctors, lawyers and Indian chiefs got out and all the doctors, in order to practice medicine in the United States, they had to have a one-year internship. That one year of internship ninety percent of them took in public health which is military and which is also the prison doctors and they brought some of the most horrible methods of treatment of insane people back over here. It was awful. Now Springfield quit doing lobotomies back in '57 or '58, but they were doing electro-shock therapy and I wound up getting over 50 shock treatments before they were done with me."

"Good Lord," I said, studying the scars on his head. I imagined him with electrodes stuck to his temples and then I realized who it was Dennis reminded me of: Randall Patrick McMurphy, the malingering hero of Ken Kesey's great novel, *One Flew Over the Cuckoo's Nest*. Dennis hadn't just flown over the cuckoo's nest; he'd crash landed in it and been forced to undergo treatment that would have driven a lesser man stark raving mad.

Dennis had told me about the shock treatments and other unorthodox procedures he was subjected to over a dinner at a Mexican restaurant after the radio show. It was then I decided I wanted to do a story on Dennis. For some time I have been doing research and writing about a variety of experiments conducted by agents of the U.S. government on its citizens, particularly prisoners, over the last 50 years—everything from dosing people with LSD and radiation to the latest reports of sensory deprivation, organ harvesting, and computer chip implants. If it all sounds like a bad sci-fi flick, remember, prisoners and crazy people make excellent guinea pigs because they can't complain and even if they do, nobody believes them or has any sympathy for them. During my years in the system I met some truly demented people who had been treated worse than laboratory animals. The very nature of prisons turns them into horror chambers no matter how spotless the corridors are and how crisp the uniforms of the guards. Dennis was locked up before Attica, before there was any real scrutiny of what goes on inside these joints. And even now that we know prisoners are subjected to unbelievable abuse and torture right here in our own country, the prevailing attitude is: So what? They are scum and they deserve it.

But Dennis seemed like a good man to me, just a wild country boy who got off on the wrong tack. He certainly had turned his life around, proving he had it in him to do the right thing. During the next couple of days we took a tour of his operation. I was impressed with how his staff at the video stores got along with Dennis and Rebecca, his charming and lovely red-haired wife. Man, I kept thinking to myself, this guy is doing okay. It's a wonder he's even alive, let alone out here taking care of business, driving around in a brand-new Lexus, and doing major promotions for Pepsico, one of the largest corporations in the country. And rather than hiding his past, he holds himself out as an example for others. There is hope yet for ex-cons, I thought. Condemn them, lock them in cages and treat them like a subhuman species, then clutch them to you breast once they strike it rich. Only in America.

"What happened in Atlanta that made them recertify you?" I asked. Lives like Dennis's document a dark aspect of recent American penal history that needs to be examined in light of where we are going with our present punishment binge.

"Penitentiaries don't want to put up with you unless they have to," Dennis said, "when all they need to do is get a doctor to come in and spend three minutes with you and say, 'He's crazy,' certify you and send you to Springfield to get you out of their way."

"Plus," I said, "they look at your jacket and say, 'The guy is a nut job. He's already been certified once.' "

"That's right. I've been certified insane five times. I tried to get life insurance with Aetna and about a month later I got a call from a vice president at the company and he says, 'Mr. McKee, I'm working on your policy and I've run into a problem. We find you've been certified insane five times and only decertified four times.' And I said, 'Does that mean I'm still crazy and can't be held responsible so I don't have to pay all my bank loans and ever'thing?' And he said, 'I would think so.' I told him I thought he was kidding and he said, 'No, I'm no kidding. We've even checked with the State of Texas to get you decertified again. You have to commit yourself for 30 days so you can be observed and they can decertify you.' I just laughed and told him, 'Well, sir, I don't intend to do that.' "

Dennis pointed to his head and said, "There's whole parts of my memory of those years that are just wiped out, fried. Some years I hardly remember. In Springfield they put me in what was called 21 East Section, and people from many years ago will remember what 21 East was. That's where the bad crazies were. I stayed one length of time 17 months in a cell and all I had was a roll of toilet paper. Had a hole in the floor that you piss and shit in. You got out once a week to take a bath and shave and stayed out as long as the guard let you. They gave me all the cigarettes I wanted, four, five cartons at a time, but no matches. You couldn't have open flame. A guard would give me a light for a cigarette and I would just keep one going off another until I fell asleep. You could smoke all five cartons and just ask for five more and they would bring them to you. You know, sometimes you got decent guards and sometimes you got asshole guards. They had me on Thorazine, 200 milligrams four times a day. All the convicts there was on Thorazine or Stelazine or some shit and I'd be doing the Thorazine shuffle from one wall to another and feel something like a sixth sense and turn and look and there was all these pretty faces of girls and guys looking at me and it turns out they're from the university criminology or sociology department or whatever and if I could, if these people came during feeding time, I would turn and stare and take my paper plate—they fed me on paper plates with no utensils of any kind—and put it on the floor, then I'd stomp my foot down on the food and squish everything between my toes and rub it all over my face. That wasn't insanity. I thought that's what those assholes were there to see so I was gonna give 'em their money's worth.

"They come and got me one day and put me in this bathtub that was maybe four foot deep, two-and-a-half foot wide and they had a net in it because it would be over your head if you sat in the bottom. And they had canvas covering me and the only thing out was my head and there were three buttons on the wall: hot, cold, and empty. And they reached up and pushed the cold button and ice cubes and ice water came in on me and they filled that tub up and let me sit there for three minutes but felt like three days and you just turned blue. And then they reached up and pushed the button that said empty and what happened the whole bottom of the bath tub dropped out, but you're on a net so you don't drop with it so it emptied in seconds and then it'd close back up and they would push hot and scalding hot water would pour in and you'd sit there till you turned beet red and they did that three times, cold then hot. I couldn't move a muscle in my body for days. Since I've got out and been in places where I've met doctors and nurses I've asked them about those treatments and ever' one of them says, 'Fuck, Dennis, all that will do is kill you, you know, make your heart stop.'

"When you're like me and uneducated, you come from a real poor background, that's the people they experiment on. I remember they sent my mother a letter on the shock treatments saying I needed it, and it wasn't called shock treatments, it was called electro-therapy, a big name that my mother didn't understand and the letter had all these seals on it and all these doctors' names and your mother or your father they know that you fucked up or you wouldn't be in the pen so they believe these assholes, because these are doctors and we are brainwashed to believe that when a doctor tells you something it's true. And my mother probably signed the letter. But even if your family wouldn't sign it, then the fuckin' warden will sign it as an emergency. One way or another, it don't matter, 'cause they're gonna do what they're gonna do."

Dennis's *modus operandi* was to get himself classified insane and transferred to a nut ward, or he would pull the medical emergency ruse, feign injury or illness or actually maim himself to get moved to a medical facility from which he would immediately begin plotting his getaway.

While out, Dennis would live out his adolescent jailhouse fantasies, packing whole years of intense experience into a few weeks or even a few days as he led the bloodhounds, the FBI and the U.S. Marshals Service on some of the most action-packed manhunts of the sixties and seventies. "Every time, even if it was only for a few days, I got married," Dennis told me. "Real young girls. Always real young. And then I'd go back to the penitentiary and they'd get on with their lives."

Often, Dennis would be apprehended by the feds in some remote Southern town where he would have to be housed in a county jail until the marshal could transport him to a federal joint. It became a sort of game to see how long it would take Dennis to break out so the chase could be continued.

"One time they took me to the Scottsboro, Alabama jail where I was put into a cell with two other prisoners. I hadn't been in the cell more than a few minutes when one of them said, 'Hey, if you had the chance, would you take it?' I said, 'Shit, yes.' The guy walked to the window and pulled out two of the bars they'd already cut through. 'We were headed out the window and we heard all the commotion when they brought you in,' he told me. He laid the bars on the cell floor and all three of us climbed out that window and took off. I was outta there before the deputies that dropped me off finished filling out the paperwork."

It was to be Dennis's most spectacular flight, and when it was over Rex McKee would be famous locally as the man who led the FBI, the U.S. Marshal, the Georgia State Patrol and the Rome, Georgia cops on a 180-mile high-speed car chase that was broadcast over the radio. On the run from the Alabama, Dennis broke into a Pontiac dealership in Dalton, Georgia and stole a brand-new souped-up Bonneville convertible. He was headed for the interstate when he noticed a pickup truck following him with its lights off. As

Dennis accelerated and hit the entrance ramp onto the highway, the truck braked and pulled a U-turn. Dennis would later learn that the man driving the pickup was the customer who had ordered the Bonneville; he was on the way to the dealership to admire his new car when he saw Dennis driving it down the road.

The man alerted the police and by the time Dennis roared into Rome there was an all-points bulletin out on him and the Bonneville. The Pontiac was too fast for the cop cars, but they had their radios and were using the local taxis to relay Dennis's location. He left a trail of wrecked police cars and damaged property in his wake as he sped around Rome and environs desperately trying to shake his pursuers, all the while listening to a play-by-play description of the chase on the car radio.

Dennis was one of those outlaws who liked to taunt his trackers. "I was hiding in downtown Rome—trapped because they had all the roads out of town blocked, but they didn't know where I was. I called the police station and spoke to the sergeant.

"Sarge, this is Rex McKee,' I told him—my usual opening line. 'I'm sure you know who I am.' The sergeant said he did and added he knew I'd left a mental institution. 'Rex, we know you're sick and we want to get you some help. Tell me where you're at I'll come get you.' I laughed and told him I might be crazy but I sure as hell wasn't stupid. I said I knew the taxis were reporting my location and I told him he better call off those taxis or I was gonna ram my car into the very next one I saw. The sarge told me that if I didn't give myself up, they was going to start shootin' at me."

A few minutes later Dennis was back in the Bonneville with police cars in hot pursuit. When the cops lived up to the sergeant's threat and started firing at him, Dennis sped off. One of the cop's bullets shattered the Pontiac's windshield and glass cut his face. He pulled the car into a driveway, shut off the lights and fled on foot. He ducked into a church during a service and tried to lose himself in the congregation but the shocked parishioners screamed when they saw his face streaked with blood. Dennis ran through the church and jumped out a rear window.

He cleaned his face at an outside faucet, stole a clean sweater off a clothesline, and wandered around on foot looking for a way out of the police dragnet.

Dennis went to the door of a home in the neighborhood and convinced the man who lived there to drive him to the emergency ward of the nearest hospital. He ducked out a rear door and was trying to steal a car in the parking lot when he was spotted and chased back inside. The cops finally captured him hiding under a sheet in the morgue trying to pass himself off as a stiff. Two more escape attempts during the same spree earned him an all-expenses-paid trip to sunny California and a cell with no view on Alcatraz Island.

RETURN FROM THE LAND OF THE LIVING DEAD

If Dennis's life is like a movie, it's a Hollywood movie complete with upbeat ending. He's an unsung American hero who survived incredible hardship and abuse and has now prospered by living up to the best of that unwritten canon known as the convict code. He still operates under the tenets of the code that became a means of survival for old-time convicts: loyalty to those who look out for you; refusal to knuckle under to the iron fist of authority; and a kind of tenacity of spirit summed up by the Nietzschean lines: That which does not kill me makes me stronger.

Dennis's persistence in pursuing his first bank loan also comes from a deeply ingrained institutional survival tactic: never take no for an answer until you have gone all the way to the top; and even when the boss says no, keep after him until he relents. His loyalty, perseverance, boldness, and imagination—qualities that enabled him to survive nearly two decades in our worst prisons—have paid off handsomely. Dennis has fulfilled many of his cellblock fantasies. He is successful running his own business and doing something he enjoys. He lives well, drives a nice car, and has a beautiful home with a swimming pool. He is happily married to an intelligent, attractive woman who helps him run the business. But he is still a country boy at heart, still a convict in the best sense of the word: a man whose true wealth is his character.

Yet, even with his incredible will to survive, even with his pluck and toughness, Dennis might never have made it back from the land of the living dead that is our penal system if it hadn't been for help he got from caring people. Ironically, the man who rescued Dennis from oblivion was a criminal lawyer.

"I was walking around the yard one day and this attorney who had come to see some other convict looked out the visiting room window and saw that I just kept walking around and he said to the convict, 'What the fuck is wrong with that guy? He's been walking around in circles like that since we've been here.' And the convict told him a little about my situation. For some reason the attorney—and his name is Bob Tarrant of Houston, Texas—he told the guard he wanted to visit with me also. And I think he just visited with me because I never got visitors or never got a letter while I was in the pen. And so I visited with Tarrant and ever' time he would come to see whoever he was representing, he would spend time with me. And then Bob Tarrant started to fight the system for me and he pointed out that a lot of the crimes I had committed took place when I was certified insane. I would be certified, I would leave, I would commit the crime—and a lot of them were car thefts and the cars would have credit cards and I would be charged with credit card fraud or interstate flight or some other damn thing. So Mr. Tarrant got my case back in court by saying, 'This is ridiculous. How can you certify this man insane, then decertify him, try him and give him 20 years, then certify him again three days later and send him to the nut house?'

"The government let a lot of the charges go and Tarrant finally got me a shot at parole. Tarrant offered me a job in Houston and I went to work for him for about two months. I was put in a halfway house, New Directions Halfway House, and New Directions had a rule that you could not have a car while you were there. Mr. Tarrant was taking me back to the halfway house one night after work and stopped at a video store to get some movies for his family. Now I'd never seen a video store. It was something new out there on the market, and at the halfway house I got to thinking like back when I was a kid trading comic books. I wondered what happened to all them movies 'cause at some point ever'body had seen them or they didn't want to see them in that neighborhood. So ever' time I got the chance I would stop at ever' video store to try to find out what happened to those movies and I found out that nothing happened to them. They just sat there for two or three years. So I came up with this idea to become a movie trader based on the comic book idea.

"And Bob Tarrant told me it wouldn't make it, you couldn't make a living doing that. And my parole officer told me, 'Dennis, you can't make a living doing that.'"

Dennis had been told he couldn't do things all his life, but that had never dissuaded him from trying. Again, he got lucky. He had a decent parole officer who was willing to take a chance and go to bat for him.

"I had a parole officer by the name of Ray Friedman and he was the kind of parole officer that, after he interviewed with me, he took his business card out and he wrote his home phone number. And he told me, 'Dennis, if your mind starts screwing up—because you're not a bad person—you call me at home. One o'clock, two 'clock in the morning, I'll meet you. We'll drink coffee or we'll drink whiskey. We'll do whatever it takes to work with you.'

"The first month I did like $800 in trades. I wound up getting 175 movies and I would go into a video store and say, 'Mister, I'm Dennis McKee and I'm a Texas video trader. You don't know what that is but I have 175 tapes. You go through these tapes and if you find any that you didn't buy or you've never had, I'll start trading with you for tapes out of your store that haven't rented for a few years and I charge seven dollars to trade. So, when you've rented a movie two times you're back even.' The idea caught on but both Tarrant and Friedman were sure I couldn't make a living doing it. Bob Tarrant told Friedman, 'Dennis is working his butt off on this. I will continue to keep Dennis on my payroll just like he was working here.' And Friedman said, 'Well, you can't beat that. I'll let him continue.'

"Well, the second month I did like $2,000, and by the sixth month I did $15,000. Before that, I went to University Savings Bank that I had robbed a hundred years ago and I told Paul Yates my story. They give me the loan, I paid them back, and they loaned me more money. When Mr. Yates helped me, I opened up my own video store and in neon I would put inside my store, on each side of the wall or doorway, the big University Savings logo and then the word, 'Thanks.' And it was my way of thanking University for helping me but what happened it was working so well that people thought I was a branch of University Savings and that I had ATM machines in there. And some woman came by, a Regional Manager and told me, 'Mr. McKee, you have to take those signs down because that's a copyrighted logo.' I called Yates and he said, 'Fuck her. We're proud of those logos in there.' About two days later they called me up and said they wanted to do a pamphlet explaining the logos and the connection."

Dennis's next big break came when he struck up a conversation with a supervisor from Pepsi Cola who stopped by his store one day to rearrange the Pepsi display. Though he had been out of prison less than a year, Dennis had two vans stocked with movies to trade out making the rounds of video stores all over East Texas. He had opened his first store in Pasadena, and he was about to forge a lucrative relationship with one of America's mega corporations.

"I was doing like five or six cases of Pepsi a month. And that's nothing to a big company like that, but I got real loyal to Pepsi because they had stepped up and took an interest in me. They put a Pepsi machine in my store and a new display. With their help I went from selling six cases a month to selling about 130 cases a month. So it wasn't a thing where they was just helping me out. They was helping me make money for them, too. By this time I was making a lot of money and I was getting a little more arrogant. I was trading movies in a 750-mile radius. I had five vans that would go out and I created my own policy."

"Do you still trade movies now?" I asked.

"No, because the movie companies dropped the prices on the movies to cut people like me out of business. But in the year 1986, the second year I was out of the penitentiary, I deposited $1,300,000 into University Savings from trading and most of that was profit. You leave home with 1000 movies and you trade 500 of them at $7 apiece and you've still got 1000 movies. Then I started telling people, 'I can't trade movies with you if you have a Coke machine in here or a Dr Pepper machine in here. I just won't trade with you.' And I actually have pictures where I had 27 Coke and Dr Pepper machines taken out of video stores because I was the only video trader in the country. Pretty soon the people at Pepsi was getting calls from video stores saying Pepsi can't tell us we've got to do this or that and after several calls they knew who it was doing this and they would tell people, 'Dennis McKee is an individual person and he doesn't represent Pepsi Cola nor does he work for Pepsi Cola and we can't tell him what to do.' Around then I started doing bidding on promotional stuff for Pepsi. If Pepsi was going to buy 2,000 T-shirts or 50 or 100 TVs or bicycles or whatever, I'd say to them, 'I can beat them prices. Let me bid on some of this stuff.' And I would beat the prices Pepsi was getting anywhere from 20 to 70 percent. I've had other major companies come to me and ask me to price for them but I won't do it because I'm loyal to Pepsi. You see my video stores, my cars' license plates, I got Pepsi 1 for me and Pepsi 2 for Rebecca. You see my house. I got a Pepsi machine in my kitchen. Pepsi Cola became like my father because they were straight with me. Even when they found out about who I was—and I never hid it; there was stories in the newspapers and ever'thing—they called up and said, 'Dennis, is that you we've been reading about?' and I said, 'Yes, sir, that's me.' And University Savings became like my mother 'cause when you're kids you always go to your mother to get money to buy candy or whatever. And I've had 51 loans with University Savings, which is now Nations Bank. At least eight of them have been six-figure numbers. In eleven years I have never missed a payment. Sometimes my payments have been $27,800 a month. Never been late on a payment. I'm pretty much where people know that what I tell them I'm going to do, I'll do. One of the Vice-Chairmen of Nations Bank called the main branch and said, 'I'm new here. Dennis McKee wants to borrow six-figure numbers. I know he was a bank robber but I know he's done business and you were his loan officer. Tell me who Dennis McKee is.' And they told him, 'Sir, if I was his loan officer and hadn't been transferred, I would give him the money because Dennis McKee would go out and rob a Texas Commerce Bank to pay Nations Bank before he would even miss a payment.'"

The last day I was in Houston hanging out with Dennis for this story, I had a vision of a cover for the Christmas issue of *Prison Life*. Santa in the slammer. "But who to get for a model?" I wondered aloud, eyeing Dennis. I said I needed someone with a face that could be believable peering out of a jail cell. Dennis got the hint and said he was game. We spent the next few hours tracking down first a Santa suit, which proved easy enough, then a location—not so simple. Dennis cracked that it had never been hard for him to find an accommodating jailer back when he was stealing cars and robbing banks. He was reminded of the story of how he had once been captured by the FBI, who warned the sheriff running the jail in Huntsville, Alabama, where Dennis was to be housed for a few days, that Dennis was an escape artist.

"They put me in a bullpen and there was a convict in there I had done time with at one of the pens. We were deep into old stories when the sheriff showed up and asked for the federal prisoner. He called me over and said, 'McKee, I thought you were some kind of Houdini. What the hell you still doing here?' and he laughed and walked away. Ever' so often he would come around and laugh at me and say, 'McKee, you still here? The way those feds been talking about you, I thought you would have gone by now.' Then he looked at his watch and said, 'You been here three whole hours,' and he thought that was funnier than shit. Finally, to shut him up, I told him, 'Sheriff, I just drove all the way from Miami and I'm dog tired. But if you'll let me get a few hours sleep, I'll make you happy. I'll get out for you.' He didn't like that. He got red in the face and yelled at me, 'McKee, you son-of-a-bitch, I promise you one thing: your soul may leave this jail but your body never will!'"

Early the next morning Dennis left using one of the oldest known ruses. He got hold of a hypodermic needle from his jailbird friend, extracted several syringes full of blood which he held in a peanut butter jar. He drank the blood, keeping the last gulp in his mouth, then smashed the peanut butter jar and smeared blood and broken bits of glass all over his face. His friend shouted for the guard, and when he showed up Dennis duly puked more blood. His friend told the guard Dennis had tried to kill himself by eating glass. They rushed him to the local hospital and Dennis fled through an emergency ward window. He stole a car in the parking lot and headed out of town. "A few miles down the road I stopped at a phone booth and called the sheriff. 'Hey, buddy, this is Rex McKee,' I said when he answered the phone. 'Where the hell are you, McKee?' he shouted at me. I said, 'Well, sir, since you don't have telephones in those cells, I guess that means I must've escaped. Body and soul.'"

Finally we located a suburban lock-up where the cops agreed to let us borrow a jail cell. The sergeant on duty told us that last year they actually had to tank Santa and a couple of his elves for imbibing a few too many egg nogs. Dennis was a good sport throughout the photo shoot. He hammed it up for the camera, he put up with my whims and photographer Fionn Reilly's relentless quest for the perfect photograph.

Unlike the biographies of most state-raised convicts, the Dennis McKee story has a happy ending. In the last year-and-a-half Dennis's life has taken another major turn for the better. Dennis is the kind of person you want for a friend if you are going through a tough time—another characteristic of the best long-term convicts. Rebecca, whom Dennis had known for years, was involved in a nasty divorce from an attorney she had met through Dennis. In an effort to help her through her difficulties, Dennis wired her some money. Rebecca refused the money but she accepted Dennis's moral support and after a courtship of long, heart-to-heart phone calls, Dennis told Rebecca he felt they were good for each other and they should get together and keep each other company. Rebecca came to Houston to meet Dennis, took one look at his exotic S&M ex-convict bachelor's bedroom complete with wall-to-wall mirrors, chains and handcuffs suspended from the ceiling, whips, and even a fog machine for added atmosphere, and she understood that what Dennis needed was woman who loved him instead of some sex toy to fulfill his erotic jailhouse fantasies.

The final ingredient in any formula for happiness is love. Dennis had lost all contact with his mother and brother during the dark years he was doing the Thorazine shuffle in prison cells or out leading carloads of cops on cross-country car chases. One of the best times in Dennis's life took place last Christmas when Rebecca got in touch with Dennis's mother and brother and had them come out to spend the holidays at the house in Katy.

"She's seventy-four years old now," Dennis said of his mother. "She lives in Columbus, Georgia. We went back to where I was born, where all the stuff happened, and I went to see my grand-mother's grave. Then my mother and brother came out to spend Christmas with us and it was the happiest I've ever been. My mother is a real good person, basically she was always a real good person. She was just a kid when she had me and she didn't have no fuckin' money."

Money and success haven't changed Dennis McKee. He's been out of prison a little over 11 years now and has made enough money in that time to live comfortably without ever having to work again. But like the little boy who started out as a comic book thief and then graduated to robbing banks, Dennis keeps coming up with new ideas for money-making ventures. All those years in the slammer taught him to survive by using his wits. The American entrepreneurial spirit that has turned imprisonment into a business and prisoners into a product ultimately becomes a survival tactic for the prisoners. As the gonzo ex-convict capitalists hit the streets, all I can say is: Watch out corporate America.

THE MAKING OF BONECRUSHER

Esquire, September 1999

A Place You Never Want to Be

The year Prison Life *ceased publication I was back in jail. The D.C. City Jail, known in the system as one of the roughest stops on the circuit. But this time I was back inside not as a prisoner but as a filmmaker. We were shooting the documentary,* Thug Life in D.C.*, part of the* Prison Life *TV series that continued and aired after the magazine folded. It was a unique time in the history of Washington, D.C. Department of Corrections. The embattled mayor, Marion Barry, himself an ex-con, was losing control of the capital city to the federal government. One of the first departments to be taken over by the feds was corrections.*

I was also writing a piece on Marion Barry for George *magazine, about how the mayor and his aide, Rhozier "Roach" Brown, had rallied the ex-con vote to get Barry reelected after he was set-up by the feds in a crack cocaine sting with a former girlfriend and sent to prison. While working on the documentary, we established a close relationship with the warden, Pat Jackson, who became the unofficial Executive Producer of* Slam. *She wanted us to tell the real story of one the most despised and feared elements in the federal prison system, known collectively as the "D.C. niggers."*

I cast Mayor Barry to play the judge in Slam. *We were sitting in his office talking about his crack case, how he had given up smoking crack at the time and refused the pipe seventeen times before he finally gave in. "I just went up there to get some pussy," he said.*

I asked him if he'd try playing the part of the judge in the movie we were making.

"What's it about?"

"A talented kid from South East who gets busted for a small amount of pot and is caught up in the criminal justice system."

He thought about it, smiled. "Okay, let's do it."

Washington, D.C., our nation's capital, has the highest incarceration rate in the country that has the highest incarceration rate in the world. At any given time, one out of every two young black men in D.C. is either in prison, in jail, on probation or parole. The D.C. blacks have a reputation in the system as being loud, unruly, violent, and volatile. The ghettos of South East D.C., known as Anacondia, where most of the D.C. prisoners were reared, are some of the worst in the nation.

But I had been locked up with D.C. blacks, many of them at the penitentiaries in Lewisburg and Petersburg, and I knew that, like most stereotypes, upon closer scrutiny this myth didn't hold up. Some of the quietest, most intelligent, respectful, sweetest men I met in the joint were black men from Washington, D.C. who had been doing time pretty much their entire adult lives. They were just like anyone else except that they came from an environment that prepared them for only one thing: prison.

That is the story Warden Jackson and Mayor Barry wanted us to tell. The Mayor gave us the unofficial run of the city, and in the window of time between when the local government lost control of the Department of Corrections and the feds took over, Warden Jackson opened her jail and let us shoot not only the documentary but a dramatic feature film using real prisoners and real guards to tell a universal story of salvation through art.

I was in Los Angeles to accept an Emmy for Thug Life in D.C. when the story of the gladiator fights at Corcoran Penitentiary broke on the front page of the L.A. Times. Catherine Campbell is a Fresno attorney who was hired by the family of one of the prisoners killed in one of the human cockfights staged by a gang of prison guards for their entertainment. Catherine contacted me in L.A. and I took the

*train up to Fresno. On the way, I passed Corcoran, a massive com-
plex of bunker-like buildings surrounded by high-security fencing on
what was once farmland outside Fresno. Catherine wanted me to
meet a former Corcoran guard, Roscoe Pondexter, known as The
Bonecrusher, who had a change of heart after he was fired for a minor
indiscretion, admitting he slapped a prisoner.*

*Corcoran is a super-max, a special prison designed to contain pris-
oners with known gang affiliations or those who have had disciplinary problems at other institutions. You don't just get sent to
Corcoran, you have to earn your way in.*

THE MAKING OF BONECRUSHER

IN THE GLADIATOR DAYS, just a couple of years ago, there was
a guard there known as Bonecrusher.

The Bonecrusher was a very large man, and he tortured prisoners, and he perfected a strangulation technique that he liked to
call "deep-sixing." He boasted that, despite his name, he never
actually broke bones.

Bonecrusher had a seat in the "car," which means that he had
earned a position of respect among the gang of guards that ran
Corcoran State Prison in California, the gang that from 1989 to
1995 forced prisoners to fight in the yard like Roman gladiators.
Bonecrusher was part of this gang of guards that was said to wager
on these fights, part of this gang that shot and killed seven of the
gladiators when the fights didn't go as planned, or shot and killed
them just for sport. Forty-three more Corcoran prisoners were shot
and seriously wounded, some paralyzed.

After each killing, an internal-review board would determine
that the use of force had been necessary, that the shooting had
been a "good shoot," and then things would carry on as usual.
Bonecrusher says that nothing would have ever changed for the
guards at Corcoran but for one particular investigation following

a gladiator killing that with one small exception had been indistinguishable from all the others. Just another dead convict. Nobody special. Who cares?

"It didn't matter to us," Bonecrusher says. "Who we killed, who was killed. It didn't matter, and everybody got cleared."

Maybe it says something about American justice that Bonecrusher has never been considered criminally liable for any of his actions during his time as a guard at Corcoran State Prison. He has, in fact, been granted immunity from prosecution in exchange for his testimony in two upcoming trials—those of the Corcoran Five and the Corcoran Eight.

Maybe it says something more that Bonecrusher's story begins after it ends, after he has been stripped of his power, his Bonecrusher status, and fired from his job. There likely would never have been a story had Bonecrusher not found himself out of a job with a wife and three kids, fired for the minor infraction (by Corcoran standards) of beating up a prisoner.

No, there likely would never have been a story at all had Bonecrusher not found himself sitting in a college classroom, trying to remember where he had left off with his bachelor's degree twenty years before, trying to salvage something from a life that had in the intervening years gone very wrong.

The class is Sociology 143: Deviance and Control at Cal State, Fresno. The students are discussing prison violence. In the front row sits a huge black man slid down low in his chair with an air indicating that this is a subject with which he's familiar. Not hostile. Knowing.

The big man is still not entirely sure how he got here. It's a bad joke, he thinks, the way he was forced out of a well-paying job for doing what he was trained to do. Now he's in a classroom with a bunch of naïve kids, working for his B.A. so he can go out into the world and see what opportunities are available to a forty-four-year-old black man starting over from scratch.

"The guards are trained to shoot for the outer extremities," says Tom Quinn, an investigator who is speaking to the class about the rash of prisoner killings by guards at nearby Corcoran State Prison.

"Center mass," contradicts the giant student, Roscoe Pondexter. Roscoe is six seven, 270 pounds of hard muscle. The twenty years he has on most of the other students does not show. A former professional basketball player, he's still in great shape, with a shiny shaved head, a riveting basso profundo, and a no-bullshit style as striking as his physical presence. He's never really talked about his former job in public before.

"Outer extremities," Quinn says. He's got the training manual to prove it.

Pondexter slides up to his full height. He looks at Quinn for a second without saying anything, leans forward in his chair, then repeats slowly, "Center mass."

Quinn: "I'll defer to Mr. Pondexter's superior—"

"We were trained to shoot for center mass," Pondexter interrupts. "But we were told to say we were trained to shoot for the outer extremities."

After class, Pondexter approaches Quinn and his wife, Fresno attorney Catherine Campbell, who represents the family of Preston Tate, one of the seven prisoners shot and killed at Corcoran. Campbell and Quinn are interested in what he knows and invite Pondexter to their home. When he shows up two weeks later, they sit in the kitchen over coffee. "I was taught better than that," he tells them. And then it just pours out, a four-hour confession of the violence Pondexter saw and participated in while walking the tiers of the Security Housing Unit at Corcoran State Prison.

He tells them about the "Corcoran way." The Corcoran way, which included routine beatings and the torture of prisoners; the Corcoran way, which brought on the gladiator days for the entertainment of the guards; the Corcoran way, which meant turning bad shoots into good shoots with silence and lies.

Roscoe will tell one of his stories and then stop, gaze at Quinn and Campbell for a few moments, as though to let them absorb what he's saying. He figures that people will take his word for it about the violence because people always want to believe horror stories. And besides, he's telling on himself. But it is important to him that they understand something: He was just doing his job. It's going to be a pretty hard sell, but that's his story. He was doing his job. The guards with the guns, doing the shooting, they were also doing their jobs. People, higher-ups, knew of what he and the others were doing at Corcoran, and they approved. These people told him he was doing a good job. And he thought he was doing a good job, too.

Given what you know about him, meeting him is a surprise. Roscoe Pondexter greets you with raucous, quaking laughter. He has an engulfing smile that feels like a blessing. He has an impossibly deep voice, a voice that makes you understand how he could dominate any man, but his countenance is earnest, comfortable, and confident, and makes you think of a benevolent African king. But as he extends his massive hand, you can't help but look down at it and think what it might feel like wrapped around your throat.

"I always wanted to set the example, not be made an example of—that was my mantra," Pondexter says of his youth in the tough West Fresno neighborhood where he grew up. He comes from a hardworking family. Roscoe could spend a Saturday out chasing jackrabbits with the greyhounds he and his friends raised, stretching his long legs for miles on end over the surrounding farmland, and know that when he got home, his mother would have a full meal on the table. His father worked construction; his mother cared for the extended household.

Roscoe set his example by becoming one of the most outstanding athletes to come out of the San Joaquin Valley. Along with his younger brother, Clifton, Pondexter made his name playing basketball. In those days, he was known as the Machine. His state scoring record of 2,228 points, set while he played at San Joaquin Memorial High, still stands. He was a high school all-American, and after he graduated in 1971, he was recruited by Jerry Tarkanian at Long Beach State. Drafted in the third round by the Boston Celtics. He wound up signing with the American Basketball Association, and after that league went under, played for ten years in Europe and South America.

For Roscoe, the years abroad were a "beautiful, glorious time." In Europe, being black didn't really matter; he was accepted for who he was. He was doing what he enjoyed most and getting paid for it. He married lovely Doris from back home in California, and they had three kids. Life was good.

But a man can't play ball forever. When the legs lose their spring, the game becomes work, and it's time to find a real job. Roscoe brought Doris and the kids home to Fresno and went out to look for work. There were a few things available, but nothing that would bring home a decent wage. There just weren't that many openings for an ex-basketball star.

They did need guards at the county jail. Roscoe had some qualifications, his "stature and authoritative voice," he says. He called a friend who worked for the Fresno County Sheriff's Department and was hired. Being black worked to his advantage, because so many of the prisoners were black or Hispanic. "I think most of my community, kids that I grew up with, ended up in trouble with the law or in prison," he says. He even had relatives who were locked up there. Ironic, he thought: I manage to beat the odds and make it out of West Fresno without a record, but I still wind up in the joint.

But he was on the other side of the bars, wearing a guard's uniform, keys jangling from his belt. Hack, turnkey, bull, pig: Those were just some of the names the prisoners called him. It could have been hard for Pondexter, having to lock up people he'd known from the street. They might think they had something coming.

Turned out just the opposite. They were glad to see a familiar face, a black face, and they knew they'd get a fair shake from Roscoe.

He quickly moved up in the field. He signed on to become a California correctional peace officer, joining the most powerful labor union in the state, and went to work at Soledad penitentiary at a higher wage. As a prison guard, Pondexter could earn as much as a professor at a state college. And there was plenty of job security. California, like the rest of the nation, was in the middle of an unprecedented prison boom. From 1982 to 1988, the state's incarcerated population had more than quadrupled. The state now had the largest prison system in the Western industrialized world. With 160,000 men and women behind bars, California has more people locked up than France, Great Britain, Germany, Japan, Singapore, and the Netherlands combined. And the San Joaquin Valley, once said to be so fertile it could produce enough food to feed the entire world, had become the heart of the state's emerging prison-industrial complex. Yield was now measured in beds, not bushels.

In 1988, Corcoran opened. By that point, Roscoe had passed the probationary period at Soledad and was just the kind of man the state wanted to walk the tiers at the new place. At a cost of $272 million, set on a thousand acres of prime farmland just an hour's drive out of Fresno, Corcoran was conceived as a model of total control. Five gun towers stood ringed around the complex like lighthouses warning of the lives run aground inside. Charles Manson, Sirhan Sirhan, and mass murderer Juan Corona are housed in high-tech, high-security cellblocks. Corcoran was the "first prison in California built with a separate Security Housing Unit—the SHU, a prison within a prison built to house the "baddest of the bad," prisoners who had been charged with new crimes in other institutions, troublemakers, and ranking members of the notorious California prison gangs: the Grips, the Bloods, the Mexican Mafia, Nuestra Familia, the Black Guerrilla Family, the Northern Structure, the Aryan Brotherhood.

For Roscoe, this would be a much different prison experience. At Soledad, there were official policies, and the guards generally followed them. Those who didn't were disciplined. At Corcoran, there were official policies, and then there was the way things were done. Although it was against the rules, Corcoran's SHU was a "hands-on" unit. Hands-on meant that guards could manhandle a prisoner without having to write a report; it meant a guard could escort a prisoner by carrying him, by putting him in a chin hold or a control hold with his cuffed hands wrenched up behind his back and dragging him from one place to another. It meant, essentially, no holds barred. Total control.

To be accepted by the powerful posse of guards that ran the SHU, Roscoe had to make his bones. In order to get into the group, "everybody did something that was seen as in the gray area," Roscoe says. "There was a guy who was a chronic masturbator and who would not program with female staff." Roscoe and another guard beat the prisoner, dragged him out of his cell, marched him before the other convicts, and Bonecrusher deepsixed him while his partner yanked on the guy's testicles.

After that, the other guards were more open with Pondexter. They taught him what he needed to know in order to get a seat in the Corcoran car. Most maximum-security prisons have a car run by tough guards who make their own rules. The Corcoran car had guards with shaved heads and tattoos and gangster walk and talk, just like the convicts. By enforcing the unwritten code that determines how the joint functions on a day-to-day basis, the car runs the prison. At Corcoran, the dominant guards were known as Sharks, because they struck fast and without warning. It didn't take Pondexter long to figure out that as a guard working the SHU, you were either in the car or you were out— ostracized, not part of the team, which meant you had no one watching your back as you walked the tiers, particularly if you were black.

Being in the car meant job security, plenty of overtime, choice watch assignments and days off, and respect from both fellow officers and convicts. You had to be aggressive; you had to be a tough and disciplined team player in order to survive. And it paid to be distinctive. Demonstrate how dedicated you were to the group endeavor. Again Roscoe set the example.

There was a weekly ritual the guards in the SHU all looked forward to. It was called "Greet the bus."

Here's how it worked: Let's say you're doing time at another prison, but you've done something bad and they want to punish you for it. So you're transferred to the Corcoran SHU, where they are quite prepared for you.

You've been on the cramped, overheated Department of Corrections bus for hours. You're shackled at the ankles; your wrists are tightly cuffed and fastened to a belly chain looped around your waist. The muscles in your shoulders ache, your hands are swollen, your fingers are numb from the cuffs, and your gut is knotted with hunger and fear.

No one speaks as the bus passes through security gates festooned with coils of razor wire glinting like millions of tiny knives in the bright California sun. The prison hunkers in squat, fortresslike cellblocks. For a moment, you might think you're actually glad to have arrived somewhere, anywhere. Then you remember seeing seasoned convicts break down in tears at the prospect of being transferred to Corcoran; you remember hearing them beg not to go.

As the bus pulls up inside the prison complex, you look out the window and see rows of black-suited guards whipping their batons around. They're pulling on leather gloves, doing stretches, calisthenics, yelling like a football squad getting psyched up to kick ass. This little ritual is the guards' way of letting you know that you have arrived in a different world and it's your ass they're about to kick. But you are not about to show your fear, because showing any weakness at all will only bring on more violence.

Guards might wear tinted plastic shields over their faces and black tape covering their identification badges as they storm the bus and drag you and the other trussed-up prisoners to the door. There, two guards take you, one on each arm, and they lift you off the steps, and you feel the handcuffs bite deeply into your wrists. A third guard grips your balls and drags you off the bus.

The rest of the guards have formed a gantlet. They might punch you hard with their gloved fists, take full cuts with their batons at the backs of your legs, kick you with steel-toed boots. At the end of the line, you meet Roscoe Pondexter. The Sharks have taken to calling him Bonecrusher.

With his huge mitts, Bonecrusher snatches you in a chin hold. He growls at you with that voice. "Look skyward!" he commands. You're all about complying; this guy is so intimidating, you keep your mouth shut and look up at the bleached sky. "Welcome to Corcoran SHU!" Pondexter bellows. And then, quietly into your ear, intimately, "This is a hands-on institution." And you feel his hands gripping your throat, cutting off your breath until you are about to suffocate. You are being deep-sixed, friend, by the expert. He lifts you off your feet, holds you like a puppet, then yet another guard grabs you by the balls again and pulls hard. The guards learned to focus on the balls at Corcoran. It's a hands-on institution.

Bonecrusher's face is in your face.

"Don't go passing out on me, you hear? Punk ass, you in our house now!" he yells as he squeezes your neck a little harder. Blood vessels begin to burst in your eyes. His powerful hands now compress your trachea, which causes unbearable pain, and his thumbs actually begin to crush your larynx. You won't be able to speak very well for several weeks.

Bonecrusher delights in the skill it takes to leave a scumbag just enough breath to remain conscious enough to hear his words.

"Whatever your life in prison was before, it's over! Welcome to hell!"

Pondexter sits forward, stares down at his hands. "It was what I did for a living," he says. "I mean, for us, when something like that happened, it was just overtime. Just the job. Just normal." Somebody gives you a shovel—your *boss* gives you a shovel—and says *dig*, you dig. That's the way the world works. Not exactly playing ball, but Roscoe was on the team, in the car. Bringing home that paycheck. "They were using me and another black officer to discipline inmates at random all over the prison, all over the four yards. All right, they had a problem anywhere in the unit, I was being used to come and discipline inmates, to intimidate them, to use pain compliance to get them to go along with the rules of the prison." He says that except for when he greeted the bus, he never administered a beating to a handcuffed prisoner. "Never a cheap shot, once the handcuffs went on, right, I don't break no bones. I could still be in control because of my power and my strength." If he beat the guy up, if he broke bones or hurt him too badly, Pondexter might have to take him to the infirmary. Then there would be all the nuisance paperwork to fill out. Who needs that? At the end of a long day walking the line inside the SHU, deep-sixing assholes, Roscoe just wanted to get into his car and get the hell out of there. Go home.

But it got harder and harder to leave the prison behind. The kind of things Pondexter saw and did every day in the SHU stayed with him in ways he wasn't even aware of at the time. As he left the vast prison compound for the drive back to Fresno, past the miles of scorched cotton fields stretching in either direction, the same fields he used to run through chasing jackrabbits as a boy, Pondexter began to feel numb. Detached. His wife, Doris, could see it in his eyes, feel it in his sullen moods. The Roscoe Pondexter she married had been a different man, kind and respectful, with a good sense of humor, fun to be around. People liked Roscoe.

Now he had become distant and paranoid. He didn't like to go out in public. He might run into someone he'd met on the other side of the wall. He wanted to stay home when he wasn't at the SHU, sit in front of the tube for a few hours in a stupor.

Corcoran's warden, George Smith, was nicknamed Mushroom George, because "he liked to be kept in the dark and fed shit." It was Associate Warden Bruce Farris who ran the Corcoran car. Farris was a handsome, cunning man who had the confidence of the guards and had been seen as a talent with a bright future in California corrections. He set the hands-on policy and covered the gray areas for the warden.

At Corcoran, the classification committee determined work assignments and living quarters and assigned counseling for all Corcoran inmates. Under Farris's stewardship, the committee became a second court in which the inmates would be tried. Housing and work assignments would serve as forms of punishment.

In March 1993, the classification committee made a decision about an inmate named Eddie Dillard that would prove fateful for Roscoe. At the time, Roscoe couldn't have cared less about Dillard. He was just another punk, a twenty-three-year-old first offender doing time for assault with a deadly weapon. If he had had any sense, he would have done his bid somewhere else in the system and gotten out without ever coming to Corcoran. But at another joint, he'd kicked a female guard. As always, Roscoe says, the guards were made aware of what Dillard had done to wind up in the SHU.

Dillard had been at Corcoran for about a week when two guards appeared outside his cell. "Roll up your crap," they said. "You're moving."

"Where am I going?" Dillard asked as they escorted him away.

"We got a little surprise for you," one of the guards answered.

"Remember your old pal Wayne Robertson? We're gonna put you in his house."

Dillard freaked. He pleaded with the guards, told them to check his jacket, the file that follows a prisoner through the system. Robertson was listed as a personal enemy from a beef he and Dillard had had at another prison. The guards laughed. On the way to Robertson's cell, they ran into Roscoe and a sergeant named Allan Decker. Dillard began to cry and grabbed at Roscoe's sleeve, begging him and Decker to intervene. But Roscoe thought Dillard was a fool who needed to learn to show some respect. And Sergeant Decker, forget it—he was the one who had put in for the cell transfer in the first place.

Robertson, six three, 230 pounds of penitentiary beefcake, was a convicted murderer and serial inmate rapist called the Booty Bandit. The guards in the SHU used Robertson to teach punks like Dillard how to do time. Depending on how he was feeling, Robertson would either beat Dillard or rape him. Since he'd been locked up, a dozen assaults and rapes had been documented in Robertson's file.

"You know better than to be kicking female officers," Robertson told Dillard after he'd been locked in. Dillard tried appealing to Robertson's street loyalties; he reminded him that they were both convicts, both from the same neighborhood. But Robertson was unmoved. He enjoyed his work, and he received extra food and sneakers from the guards for checking fools like Dillard.

After lights-out, Robertson made his move. He grabbed Dillard and threw him down on the bunk. Dillard fought back, but Robertson was too strong. Dillard screamed, banged on the cell door. No one came. Hours later, Officer Joe Sanchez showed up. When Dillard told him he feared for his life, Sanchez laughed at him. During the next two days, Robertson raped Dillard whenever the mood struck him.

• • •

When you're behind the walls and on the tiers every day of the week, you might not notice, but things change over time. At first, Roscoe didn't see the changes in himself. He lost count of how many times he almost strangled one of those punks. Routine, slipping a little every day. In the car, one bad thing makes a slightly worse thing possible. So turning the prisoners into gladiators, forcing them to fight, and then carting out the bodies didn't come as a shock to anyone riding in the car.

In the SHU, convicts are locked in their cells twenty-two and a half hours a day. By law, they are entitled to ten hours a week of fresh air and daylight. Following a 1985 directive from the California Department of Corrections called the Integrated Yard Policy, guards at Corcoran and other California SHUs began to mix sworn enemies from the major California prison gangs together in confined exercise yards. The theory was that gang members would be forced to get along, preparing them for a return to the general population and, ultimately, the outside. "It sounded good if you said it real fast," said Warden Smith.

The Corcoran SHU yards are narrow, concrete-walled pits attached to the housing units like dog runs. Gunners, armed with two rifles—a wide-bore 37mm crowd-control gun that fires non-lethal wooden "baton" blocks, and a 9mm assault rifle—hover above the yards in a fortified nest that the guards call the shooting gallery. Shooters have an easy shot at prisoners in the yards below. Video cameras mounted above the yard record events. In the first year the SHU was in operation, shots were fired at prisoners more than seven hundred times.

Prison regulations call for guards to use firepower to break up fights "any time the gunner perceives the possibility of great bodily injury or loss of life." Gunners are required to give verbal warnings first, then shoot the riot gun if the convicts keep fighting. The carbine is to be used as a last resort if the fighters refuse to stop after they've been shot with the wooden blocks, or if the gunner believes a convict has a weapon and may kill or maim a staff member or another prisoner. The way Roscoe remembers it, you could tell what time of day it was by the number of gunshots going off.

Gang members, men like Vincent Tulumis, a six-four, 280-pound gladiator, are released into the SHU yard at Corcoran knowing they have to fight or surrender. Doing time on a low level drug rap, Tulumis had just a few months left to serve in May 1993 when his gang affiliation landed him in the SHU. For a gang-banger like Tulumis, being housed in the SHU is a badge of honor; it gives him a measure of respect, which is the most valued penitentiary currency. Shot callers, the omnipotent prison gang leaders who provide protection for men like Tulumis, demand total loyalty. They instruct their subjects that to break weak and refuse to fight would violate the code and bring disgrace on the whole clan. If you surrender, you're a bitch, a punk. Bitches are cut loose, cast out of the group to become prey for other gangs. As a member of the Northern Structure out on the yard with a member of another Mexican gang, Tulumis has to be ready to go to war. The enmity goes back decades.

He and another gang member named Alberto Beltran had been in a fight and were denied yard privileges for ten days. Tulumis knows that after the ten days are up, he will be called to go back out to the yard with Beltran, and that again he will have to fight. For the first few days, he relaxes in his cell. He sleeps well, eats. But as the days pass, he begins to wonder: Will Beltran go out? Will I?

On the morning of the tenth day, Tulumis can't eat. He hasn't slept, up all night pacing in his cell, waiting for this moment. His homeboys in the nearby cells whisper encouragement: "All right, homes," they say. "Do it, brother." Then he hears the guard shout his name: "Tulumis! You going out to the yard?"

Silence in the unit. Everyone waits to hear how he will respond. "Yeah, I'm going to the yard."

"Beltran!" the guard calls. "You going out to the yard?"

"Yeah," says Beltran. "I'm going out."

It's on. The guard escorts Tulumis to a holding cell, where handcuffs are removed and he is strip-searched. Another guard looks in his mouth, behind his ears, under his balls, and up his ass, and then he is scanned with a metal detector to make sure he hasn't hidden a shank under his skin. The Sharks are excited because it's fight day.

An officer, Bruce Brittsan, looks at Tulumis. "Today's the day," he says as Tulumis passes and steps out into the bright sun.

Tulumis is one of the Sharks' prize fighters. When he wins, he is rewarded with the Corcoran bounty of extra food and sneakers. He might even get a decent ham sandwich. But Brittsan has spooked him. Tulumis turns and looks up into the shooting gallery, sees the guards crowded around looking down at him, then he sees the 9mm.

When the door opens and Beltran comes out into the yard, Tulumis looks at him and flashes: *You better stop when they say stop.* But he has no time to dwell on his fear. Beltran comes at him and they trade wild roundhouse punches.

They've been at it for eleven seconds, inflicting little real damage, when suddenly, without a verbal warning and without firing a warning shot from the riot gun, Brittsan fires the 9mm rifle and hits Tulumis just below the back of his head with a soft-tip dumdum bullet that fragments on impact. Tulumis drops immediately, hard, spread-eagle on the concrete floor. The whole yard hits the ground when the shooting starts, and Tulumis's homeboys are down, looking to see if he's still breathing. Finally, the watch sergeant orders the other convicts to remove Tulumis from the yard. They drag him out by the head and shoulders.

"If an inmate got shot, you know, oh, well, we just went on with the program," Roscoe says. "And that goes for the guy that got paralyzed. He stayed in the hospital here for three weeks. Nobody cared. It was just another inmate shot. And when Preston Tate got shot, the physician's assistant came on the yard and said, 'Hell, if he wasn't an asshole and didn't rape people, he wouldn't be in prison.' Fuck him. So what? Another dead-ass inmate. Who cares?"

Tulumis's spinal column was shattered and he was paralyzed from the neck down, confined to a bed and a wheelchair. When doctors realized the extent of his injury, he was given an early release. He can't understand why he, one of the Sharks' favorite gladiators, was shot. And why in the neck? Why destroy him?

One of the last things Tulumis remembers about that day is the guard's voice: *You going out to the yard?*

And Tulumis remembers the voice he heard when he woke up in the hospital with a useless body. The state had a guard there in the room with him to make sure he didn't run off. And Tulumis asked the guard, Why did they have to destroy me? Why *me?*

"You played the game," Bonecrusher answered. "You knew the rules."

When the Sharks killed Preston Tate, they violated Corcoran State Prison Rule No. 1: Never kill your own kind.

They didn't realize it at the time, but it was their undoing when they broke this rule.

Every penitentiary in the country has an unwritten tribal code that governs the conduct of its prisoners. At Corcoran, the Sharks also adopted this convict code. Whites look out for whites, blacks look out for blacks, Hispanics look out for Hispanics. And this code held true for the relationships between guards and convicts. "At the time I came into the system, no black officers had ever been killed in prison, because the Black Guerrilla Family wouldn't allow it," Roscoe says.

That's the way it was, at least, until the day Preston Tate was murdered. Tate was black, twenty-five, and a few months short of freedom when he was shot in the back of the head during a fight in the yard with two other inmates in April 1994. The officer who killed him, Chris Bethea, was also black. Roscoe believes that Bethea shot Tate by mistake, that the bullet was intended for one of the other gladiators. Or that the Sharks were testing Bethea's loyalty, seeing how badly he wanted to keep his seat in the car, finding out if he was more Shark or more black.

The day of Tate's death, another officer, a straight arrow named Steve Rigg, saw Bethea off in a corner of the shooting gallery surrounded by three or four white guards, Sharks, who were all telling him what a good thing he had done and coaching him in how to write his report for the Shooting Review Board. Rigg is an ex-marine, had recently been assigned to the SHU, and was in some ways Pondexter's opposite: short, compact, white, a by-the-book career corrections officer. So of course he was trusted by no one.

Rigg is also a certified range master and police firearms instructor, and he believed that what the gunners at Corcoran were being told to do was way out of line with Department of Corrections procedures. Rigg believed that it was, in fact, murder. When he learned that there were three separate reports written on the Tate shooting, all of them different, he began his own investigation.

The Sharks were a white boys' club, and Roscoe was getting worried about what was going on with Bethea. There's a small fleet of golf carts that the guards use to get around the Corcoran complex, and one afternoon in the week after Tate was killed, Roscoe and Bethea took off in one of them to talk about the shooting. Bethea was shaken up, so Roscoe drove. "They were slapping me on the back and acting like shooting a brother was such a great thing to do, like I was a hero," Bethea said. "They'd probably like it if I shot myself, too."

Roscoe told Bethea that he had violated the code and killed one of his own, so he could never work in population again. Bethea's job was in jeopardy, and so was his life.

The heat was coming down fast now. Rigg went to the FBI and told the feds about the Corcoran way. Brave man, he was taking his life in to his own hands. And Preston Tate happened to have come from a family that cared that he was now dead. On his behalf, his parents pursued a wrongful-death suit against the California Department of Corrections. Seemingly out of nowhere, investigations were rampant at Corcoran, for every little thing. *Infractions* being added up. What's an infraction? the Sharks on the tiers joked to one another. And with everybody finding *rules* all of a sudden, Pondexter was one of the first to go. One day, a female officer who had it in for the Sharks saw Roscoe and six others manhandling an inmate and reported him. When questioned about the incident, Pondexter admitted slapping the prisoner. It was nothing he hadn't done a thousand times. "All I had to do was lie and I could've kept my job," he says. "They said, 'He told on himself.'"

He was given the option to quit or be fired. He couldn't believe it, but less than four months after the incident, he was on the street. And he was mad, furious. And lost. But still, Roscoe couldn't help but feel like a convict who had just gotten out after a long bid.

I was taught better than that.

Roscoe sits in the kitchen at Catherine Campbell and Tom Quinn's house, and he tells them everything. He did not expect to talk so much, or to talk at all, and after a while he can't talk anymore.

Bonecrusher could easily have been among the indicted. Instead, Roscoe is finding his redemption as a witness for the prosecution. After telling his story to Campbell and Quinn, he told a grand jury about the Corcoran way, too.

"When Roscoe Pondexter came to Corcoran, he was an excellent correctional officer," Steve Rigg says. "He appeared to be a caring professional. During his tenure there, he completely changed. He became a Shark. He disliked inmates, didn't care who he hurt. Yeah, he's responsible. But so is this department. They did that to him."

Sergeant Dale S. Drakebill, Sergeant Robert Allan Decker, Lieutenant Jeffrey A. Jones, Officer Joe Sanchez, Officer Anthony J. Sylva. All have been indicted for conspiracy and sodomy for the repeated sexual assault of Eddie Dillard.

Sergeant John Vaughn, Sergeant Truman Jennings, Lieutenant Douglas Martin, Officer Christopher Bethea, Officer Michael Gipson, Officer Jerry Arvizu, Officer Timothy Dickerson, Officer Raul Tavarez. All have been indicted for multiple counts of civil rights violations, including the murder of Preston Tate.

"I need to emphasize this," Rigg says. "A handful of dirty employees, dirty peace officers, who held significant rank within the department, caused this at Corcoran. It wasn't your line officers, it wasn't your sergeants, for the most part. It was upper management, starting from the director of corrections and working all the way down to the associate-warden level. Those are the individuals who need to be answering to civil rights violations. Those are the individuals who need to be indicted. We've got the little minnows indicted, but the big sharks are still out there."

Warden George Smith has retired. Associate Warden Bruce Farris was dismissed for his role in organizing a particularly brutal "greet the bus" incident. The former driver of the Corcoran car was through. At least that's what everybody assumed, anyway. Word had it that he had taken himself out on the road and gotten lost, touring the country in a Winnebago.

But on July 1, Bruce Farris was reinstated. On that day, he reported to work as an associate warden at the state prison in Susanville, California.

This fall, at forty seven, Roscoe Pondexter will receive his B.A. in sociology from Cal State, Fresno. He is now working as an assistant in the athletic department there.

He says he has doubts about his former career, but he keeps them mostly to himself. He will say only this. "A lot of people thought that I would never turn on them because I never told on anybody. If they retaliate on me for telling the truth, man, so be it. I have the same phone number and address as always. They could find me easy. So be it."

He and his wife have started going back to church with their kids. So Roscoe takes his doubts to church with him. He sits there at Fresno's Family Community Church every Sunday. He sits there and clasps his hands, those hands, and prays very hard, and with his praying hands, he sends all of his doubts into heaven.

THE MAN WHO KILLED DUTCH SCHULTZ

The Story of Joe Stassi

GQ, September 2001

Original Gangster

"Bring me Arnold Stone," Joe Stassi said when we asked him who, as he neared death, he wanted to see. Not his daughter, with whom he had become estranged, disowning her over a dispute about property when Joe's wife died. Not his son, Joseph Junior, who was still in the wind, living somewhere in the Caribbean. No, Joe wanted to meet face to face with the former Kennedy Justice Department attorney who had overseen the investigation and prosecution that resulted in Joe spending most of the last thirty years of his life in prison.

It was like bringing Moriarty and Sherlock Holmes together at the end of their lives. Arnold Stone, in his seventies and still sharp and fit, a lawyer in private practice in North Carolina, looked at the ancient Mafia don who had been his quarry and asked him, "Mr. Stassi, are you a made member of organized crime?"

A long pause, then Joe replied, "Yes and no." Prosecutor Stone asked Joe to tell him about the yes and about the no.

The answer is that Joe was grandfathered in. He went back to the days before there was a Mafia, when it was the Black Hand and a bunch of loosely affiliated ethnic gangs. It wasn't until after Prohibition made them all rich and they wanted to protect their turf that the gangsters decided to get organized. Joe sat in at the meeting when the bosses established the National Commission and structured what became known as The Outfit, La Cosa Nostra, the American Mafia, Organized Crime. There was no need to "make" Joe; he came pre-made. He made his bones when he produced and directed one of the outstanding hits of the era: the murder of Dutch Schultz, among many others.

Joe wanted to kill me after this article about him appeared in GQ. I had his permission to publish the piece. In fact, he wanted to do a book and tell the whole story of his life and times in the highest circles of organized crime to "set the record straight," and as a cautionary tale to young men attracted to the gangster's life.

I was in Toronto producing Street Time when the GQ story came out. For three years, Marc Levin and I had been filming my sessions with Joe for a documentary about his life. We had the meeting between Joe and Arnold Stone on film. We brought Joe from Florida back to the Lower East Side where he had begun his life of crime, stealing ribbons from pushcarts after a teacher made him wear a dunce cap and sit in the corner because he stuttered. We put him up in the Warwick Hotel where Joe had his run-in with Joseph Kennedy. As I rolled him into the hotel in a wheelchair, Joe freaked out; he grabbed a handrail and held on, afraid the staff would recognize him and call the police.

"Joe, that was fifty years ago. No one is still here from those days."

He wanted to kill me because he felt I'd abandoned him and gone off to make some bullshit movies when he was ready to tell the inside story, how it really happened, after years of stony silence in prison with nothing but his self-respect. And he was pissed because he had misread the caption under one of the photos in the magazine, a picture of Meyer Lansky and Charlie "Lucky" Luciano, that read, "two of the powerful gangsters for whom Stassi worked—and murdered."

"What the fuck is wrong with you? I never said I murdered Meyer and Charlie Lucky! They were my friends! Are you out of your fuckin' mind, writin' that shit?" He was still fuming even after I explained that was not what the caption said. He demanded that I get on a plane and fly down to Florida to see him immediately. No matter that I was in the middle of production. Marc and I took a long weekend and flew to Orlando, met our camera crew and drove to Joe's for the sit-down.

Joe was eating a bowl of macaroni when I walked in. He rattled his plate threateningly, motioned me to a seat and went off. "You're a liar, I don't trust you. You're a rat . . ." He went on and on, railing at me, calling me all sorts of names, saying I had made him out to be a rat.

I sat there and took it, remembering Joe's advice to me from his good friend, Meyer Lansky. Lansky once instructed Joe that when you were called to a sit-down you should never interrupt, let the bosses or whoever was beefing say what they had to say and keep your mouth shut because usually, if you let them talk, they'll say something wrong. Then you can catch them and win your argument. When he was finished, Joe said, "So now you can talk,"

Joe was intimidating when he got angry. He may have been a frail old gangster, hardly able to walk, but he had years of experience running a far-flung, multi-dimensional criminal enterprise and knew how to emote anger. I knew he wouldn't respect me if I didn't stand up to him. I reminded him that he was the one who wanted to tell his story. I hadn't pursued him or tried to get him to talk. I went right back at him, knowing he'd get off on the drama.

"Everything I wrote in the article you told me and we have it all on film. I don't give a fuck who you are, you know fucking well I'm no rat or liar. We were in the joint together, Joe. You know what it means to call me a liar."

"I never called you a liar," Joe said, proving Lansky's theory.

He died soon after we finished filming, a lonely, bitter old killer groping around looking for his little black book to call some hitman who'd probably been dead for thirty years to tell him to whack me. By then he'd succumbed to Sicilian Alzheimer's; he'd forgotten everything but the grudge. During one interview with Joe we asked him what he'd learned in his long life. "I learned to stay away from family and friends," he seethed. "They'll fuck you every time."

Even though he claimed he wanted to tell his story, and I believe he did, getting him to talk was always an ordeal. Some great stories he told over and over, other things in his past he skirted or said he'd come back to later. It was only after I sprung him from the hospital in Miami that he opened up about the professional killings he'd done on orders from his bosses. He never came clean on some of the most notorious mob hits I'm sure he was involved in. What Joe did for bosses like Lansky and Longy Zwillman was to produce and direct major mob hits. He'd take weeks planning them, hiring the killers, gathering the weapons and getaway cars, setting up the hit and, most important, mapping the escape route.

He was also, according to his son, brilliant at coming up with solutions to Mafia-related disputes. He'd hear both sides of the argument, sit with it for a few days, and then come back with a compromise that usually settled the score. If that didn't work, there were other ways.

I had documents from Joe's FBI files showing that he was staying at the Park Sheraton Hotel where Albert Anastasia was shot to death in a barber's chair while getting his morning shave. Joe arrived a few days before the hit and left the next day, back to Havana where he had a couple of casinos.

Did he have anything to do with the Anastasia hit, I asked Joe. No. Just a coincidence he happened to be there? Yeah. And the Kennedy assassination. Joe knew a lot more about that hit as well. He was believed to have been involved in smuggling some Sicilian shooters into Texas from Mexico. Bobby Kennedy wanted desperately to talk to Joe about who killed his brother. The Kennedy name was all over Joe's case. When Joe refused to come in and talk to Bobby, he was indicted for supposedly smuggling heroin into Texas from Mexico, a charge Joe always denied. Joe was one of the first gangsters to make Hoover's Top Hoodlum list, but he kept such a low profile over the years that few people realized how close he was to Lansky and Zwillman.

People ask me how I could befriend a confessed killer of more *men than he could remember. At first it was forced proximity; for three years we lived in neighboring cells at the prison in Petersburg, Virginia. I came to admire the way he did his time. He kept to himself, he was respectful of everyone, he never bitched. In time I began to see Joe as a soldier, then a lieutenant, following the orders he received from his commanders. He wanted to succeed. It was kill or be killed in the ranks. And Joe never delighted in what he did; he was a professional, not a psychopath. It tortured him. He wanted to confess, he tried, he told me much more than he told anyone else in his long life. But in the end, the dictates of omerta meant more to him than unburdening his hopelessly damned soul.*

THE MAN WHO KILLED DUTCH SCHULTZ

FOR SEVEN DECADES, JOE Stassi moved in the highest circles of organized crime in America. He has a lifetime's worth of stories about the likes of Meyer Lansky, the Kennedys, Bugsy Siegel, and others. And for the first time, he admits to orchestrating one of the great unsolved murders of the twentieth century.

Joe says he can't talk about the killings. Not yet. There is no statute of limitations for murder; the government won't give him immunity, and he doesn't want to go back to prison, not at his age. He's done enough time already—more than thirty years, counting the strict Special Parole and the year he did when they locked him back up, at 88, for associating with known organized-crime figures.

Now 95, Joe Stassi, also known as Hoboken Joe and Joe Rogers during his forty-year criminal career, may well lay claim to the title Oldest Living Mafioso. The crimes Stassi has agreed to talk about include some of the most infamous events in gangland history. And Stassi was there. Stassi's life spanned the heyday of organized crime and intersected with all the major players. Though he was accorded what the Justice Department called ambassadorial rank and classified as a Top Hoodlum by the FBI, few outside law enforcement know anything about Joe Stassi. Now, after nearly a century of dedication to the rigors of omerta, Stassi has agreed to go beyond the thousands of pages of government documents chronicling his life of crime and tell his story.

"I'm only talkin' about what I know," he says, and reaches for a sparerib. We are at Christine Lee's, a Chinese place in North Miami. Joe's voice is a raspy whisper, sibilant echoes of Marlon Brando's in *The Godfather*. "What I seen with my own eyes," he says. "And what I done. Not what they write in books or what you see in movies. That's all bullshit. That's rats and agents talking." At the mention of rats, he looks at me with a fierce glint in his eye, and I see the throttled rage and intense criminal passion that earned Stassi an underworld reputation as the most dangerous man in La Cosa Nostra.

Joe falls silent, gnaws on the sparerib using the upper set of his dentures and his lower gum. His false teeth, the ones that were made for him while he was locked up in the federal penitentiary at Marion, Illinois, are the best he's ever had. The trouble is, he has only the uppers because his dogs keep stealing the lower set and burying them in the garden out behind the house.

"You can't believe these fuckin' stool pigeons." He practically spits the words. "They're only saying what the agents and prosecutors want them to say." I have to lean in close to hear him. "What I'm saying is the truth. I'll take a lie-detector test, I'll swear an affidavit, I don't care. What I'm telling you is the way it really happened."

The check comes, and Joe nabs it, pays with a crisp $100 bill, leaves a hefty tip. As we get up to leave, I help him stand and steady himself on his cane. Scoliosis has curved his spine into the shape of a question mark.

In the parking lot, I ease him into the low-slung rental, and we drive off into the soft Florida night. Joe hunkers down over the console; the lights from the dashboard glow red and green on his wizened, white-bearded face as he looks up at me and allows the intimacy of the car to relax a lifetime habit of secrecy. "We never talked about what we did," he says. "Not even to each other. They killed you if you talked." He licks his flinty lips several times. "I've never told anyone what I'm telling you. No one."

But the killings are off-limits, at least for now. Except to say that there were five. Five that stand out.

When I met Joe Stassi at the federal prison in Petersburg, Virginia, he had already served more than two decades in some of America's toughest penitentiaries. For three years, I lived in the cell next to Joe's. I saw him every day, many times a day, in the forced proximity that is prison. I found out who Joe was by chance. Someone loaned me a book, *Gangster #2: Longy Zwillman, the Man Who Invented Organized Crime*, by Mark A. Stuart. Leafing through the photos of gangland legends such as Charles "Lucky" Luciano, Frank Costello, Meyer Lansky, Benjamin "Bugsy" Siegel, and Joe Adonis, I came upon a group shot taken at the wedding reception for one of Longy's people. Seated at a table were Longy, New Jersey Mafia boss Gerry Catena, Longy's close associate Joseph "Doc" Stacher, and a well-dressed, good-looking man identified as "Joe Rogers, who ran the numbers for Zwillman in Union County." Joe Rogers looked an awful lot like a young Joe Stassi.

"Yeah, that's me," Joe admitted when I asked him. But he wouldn't tell me any more than that. By that time, I had become a jailhouse lawyer of some repute. It was only when he asked me to look into his case after he was refused parole—this after twenty years of good behavior—that I began to get a sense of just how important an organized-crime figure Joe was. Much of what I know about Stassi and his various cases I learned while digging into his paperwork for the elusive loophole. Eventually, I found a mistake: Joe had been denied fourteen months of "meritorious good time" that when added to his time served would spring him from prison. I was in another prison when I heard through the grapevine that Joe had been set free and that he sent me his gratitude and regards.

In 1990 I was released after serving eight years for smuggling marijuana. I settled in Brooklyn and began working for a criminal lawyer in Manhattan. One day while riding the subway to work, I looked over and saw an old man accompanied by two large characters who looked like muscle. On second glance, we recognized each other. "Richie!" Joe exclaimed, and hugged me. I asked him what he was doing riding the subway; he said, "Gotta keep a low profile. FBI's all over me."

A couple of weeks later, Joe and I risked violating our respective paroles when he took me to lunch. He asked what I was doing, and I told him that in addition to writing legal briefs, I had written a novel and was publishing a magazine, *Prison Life*. Joe invited me to his home in Brooklyn to examine the dozen cartons of legal papers he had accumulated and stored in his basement. "There's a story in there," he said. "A hell of a story. I'm not saying a goddamn word. Your story is in the documents."

But before I could take him up on the offer, the Feds grabbed Joe yet again. He was caught having breakfast with another organized-crime figure. Joe's parole officer photographed the get-together, and quicker than you can say "Two over easy," Joe's parole was revoked and he was locked up again for "association."

During that stint at the Metropolitan Detention Center in Brooklyn, Joe began to reassess his life of crime. Frances Paxton, his wife of more than sixty years, a former Miss California who waited for Joe while he was locked up, died of throat cancer just a month after his release after the parole violation. Joe sold his home in Brooklyn and moved to Florida. Soon after settling in the land where paroled gangsters go to die, Joe urged me to come down to Miami, pick up where we'd left off.

Talking to Joe, listening to his life story, is like setting out on an archaeological dig. Newly released FBI documents, obtained under my repeated Freedom of Information Act requests, prove Stassi is a bona fide gangster and stimulate more digging.

"The Jews made the mafia," he states resolutely as we cruise along Collins Avenue beside the huge hotels lining the beach. "Without the Jews, the Italians wouldn't have gotten anywhere. The Jews were the ones that done the work." Joe says he means the series of hits carried out in the early '30s by the mostly Jewish killers of Murder, Inc., that opened the way for the modern Mob to take control of the rackets under the planning and leadership of the affiliated East Coast bosses known as the Big Six: Meyer Lansky, Abe Zwillman, Ben Siegel, Frank Costello, Joe Adonis, and Charlie Luciano. Stassi knew them all.

Joe was born on New York's Lower East Side in the early 1900s, when hoards of tough immigrant Jewish and Italian kids took over the streets from the Irish gangs. He graduated from being a street urchin stealing quarters from tenement gas heaters to heisting craps games and sticking up payroll deliveries. Arrested for robbery, possession of a weapon and other petty charges while still a kid, he says it was the connections he made with older criminals in jail that gave him entrée to the beer barons and bootleggers of Prohibition. Though Sicilian, Joe forged a series of close bonds with top Jewish gangsters who trusted him and served as his criminal mentors. The most influential of these men was the undisputed boss of the New Jersey rackets, Abner "Longy" Zwillman.

Just two years older than Joe when they met in the early '20s, Zwillman was already well established as the smartest, if not the wealthiest and toughest, of the brash Jersey bootleggers. Abe was born and raised in Newark's predominantly Jewish Third Ward. His father died when he was 14, and Abe took it upon himself to become the breadwinner; he quit school and went to work selling fruits and vegetables from a pushcart. When the Irish kids would roam into the Third Ward to harass the peddlers, the cry would go out in Yiddish: *"Reef der Langer!"* Go get the Tall One, the Defender. Longy would come running and chase off the outsiders.

With Prohibition, Zwillman went to work for Joseph Reinfeld, owner of Reinfeld's Tavern. Reinfeld bought whiskey from the Bronfman brothers' Seagram Distillery in Montreal and began shipping directly to the Jersey shore, where Zwillman would oversee the off-loading and distribution to speakeasies all over the East Coast. By 1922 Newark had become the bootleg capital of the country, and Zwillman, though just 19, presented Reinfeld with an offer he couldn't refuse: fifty-fifty partnership or Longy would go out on his own. Reinfeld knew that to spurn Zwillman would mean war, and Longy had the gunmen. Reinfeld swallowed his pride; they shook hands. Before Prohibition ended, the Zwillman-Reinfeld partnership made them both millions in tax-free cash.

"Right around this time, there was a war going on," Joe says. "There was always wars, but this one I remember was the war between the Jews and the Italians to control Newark. Newark, Elizabeth, Union City was where we had all the big breweries. Tugboats would bring barges up the river with tens of thousands of gallons of molasses and pump it into the stills. We owned everybody in Jersey—judges, police, politicians. Nobody bothered us. Except other mobs."

We pull in to the driveway of a house that is a low-end version of the anonymous suburban Miami home Lee Strasberg, as Hyman Roth (a character based on Meyer Lansky) in *The Godfather II*, was living in when he was visited by Michael Corleone. Joe says it was through Zwillman and his partner, Gerry Catena, that he became friendly with the men who conceived and ran the national crime syndicate. Both loyal soldier and downrange thinker, Stassi learned early on to follow Lansky's first law: Retreat to the background and turn over the high-visibility street activities to others. Joe became a master of the low profile. He never used his real name; he moved from place to place. "All the mobs knew I was connected," he explains, "but no one knew exactly how or why. I was the only one who was free to go wherever I wanted, meet whoever I wanted, without having to report. Because I was with Abe and Meyer."

Joe remembers that around this time, Lansky and Ben Siegel had their headquarters in a building on the Lower East Side. They were at war with the four Fabrizzo brothers from Brooklyn. One of the brothers, a killer known as Tough Tony, climbed onto the roof of the building where Siegel and Lansky had their office and dropped a bomb down the chimney. One man was killed, and Siegel was injured; Tough Tony was seen fleeing over the rooftops. A few weeks later, as Tough Tony was having dinner at his parents' home, a couple of Siegel and Lansky's men showed up dressed as cops and demanded to talk to Tony. When he got up from the table and went to the door, the men barged in and shot him to death right in front of his parents.

In the forties, Stassi was one of the first men invited to invest when Siegel began to explore the possibilities of founding a gambling empire in the Nevada desert. Siegel and a guy named Little Moe Sedway were partners in a small hotel in what was to become the Mob's richest jackpot. "Moe was buying up property, and they tried to get me interested. I had a place in Lake Tahoe with Lou Walters—that broad Barbara Walters's father. I was looking at Cuba and the Dominican Republic. Ben came down and visited me in Havana a couple of times," Joe says. Then he adds, almost as an afterthought, "When Ben was killed, everyone was shocked. They thought it might have been Little Moe that had it done."

"Who thought that?" I ask.

"Meyer and Abe," Joe answers.

"You're saying Meyer Lansky never OK'd the hit on Siegel?"

"Please. That's all nonsense. Meyer loved Ben. I was the one who looked into it. I went out to California; I investigated it for Meyer and Abe."

"So who did—"

"Excuse me. Listen to me. I'll tell you."

Joe says he hired an ex-detective, Barney Wozinski, to investigate the Siegel killing. "There was a cigarette girl Ben was always talking to. Virginia Hill [Siegel's girlfriend] was jealous of this girl. One day Virginia Hill got that cigarette girl and beat the bejesus out of her. When Ben heard about it, he went out and got Virginia Hill and beat the hell out of her. Virginia Hill left for Switzerland.

"The night Ben was killed [June 20, 1947], there was Al Smiley and Swifty Morgan with Ben when they drove in from Vegas. They stopped for dinner at Jack's, the fish place on the pier in Santa Monica. They dropped Swifty off at the hotel, and Al and Ben drove to Virginia Hill's house. I talked to Al. He said they only just sat down, Ben on the couch, him on the side chair, when the shot came through the window. Al says, 'Believe me, Joe, I was afraid I was gonna get killed.'"

Joe insists the stories that have been written in any number of books and portrayed in movies such as *Bugsy* and *Lansky*—that the Siegel killing was a Mob hit OK'd by Meyer Lansky at a sit-down in Havana with the exiled Luciano—are fictional gangland lore gleaned almost entirely from second- and thirdhand information. "We were as close to it as you could get. Whoever did it had to be a marksman that shot through the window from outside, someone that knew how to handle a rifle. The police found casings from a military-type rifle. What we found was that the one that killed Ben Siegel was Virginia Hill's brother. He hated Ben, and Ben hated him."

Joe learned Hill's brother was a sharpshooter in the marines. He had a rifle he kept in the gas station down the street. "The day after the killing, Barney Wozinski went to the gas station looking for the rifle; they called the brother. He disappeared, and the rifle disappeared."

"So the story that Ben owed all the bosses a lot of money in cost overruns for construction of the Flamingo is not true?"

"That's bullshit. Ben owed nobody money, and if he did, he was honorable, he would pay it. As far as the Flamingo, every partner in there knew they were going to make their money back many times over. Nobody was worried. We knew Vegas was going to be big."

Joe shakes his head, sighs. So many wars, so many killings, so many hits: Who can keep them all straight? But the Siegel killing, that one he remembers. "The real story came from me; I told Abe and Meyer it was the brother, and everybody accepted it. If it was a hit, that's not how it would have been done."

He imparts the methodology of a Mob hit. To kill a man like Ben Siegel, Joe says, they would send a friend, someone he would never suspect, who could get in close and shoot him in the head with a revolver. "Never walk away from a body without making sure you put one or more in the head and the party is dead." The way Sam Giancana was killed. Or in a public place, usually an Italian restaurant, send in a couple of torpedoes and blast away. Like the Carmine Galante still life, blood and pasta; or Joey Gallo staggering out of Umberto's Clam House and dying on the side-walk on Mulberry Street. Big Paul Castellano gunned down in front of Sparks Steak House. Classic Mob hits befitting a boss. But snipers? Too risky. If you're going to kill a tough guy like Ben Siegel, you are going to make sure he's dead.

"Always empty a gun before you toss it. Someone finds an empty gun, they're likely to keep it or sell it. If they find a partially empty gun, they'll turn it in to the cops for fear of being connected with whoever got shot," Joe advises, warming to his subject, the fine art of murder. I see the other Joe Stassi, the wily killer, lurking behind the old man's kind, artistic visage.

After a moment, I ask, "How old were you when you first put a gun in your hand?"

Joe turns to look at me. "My ambition was always to be a gangster, a gunman, whatever you want to call it," he says. "What started me was school. When I went into the first grade, I stuttered. The teacher got disgusted with me. She put me in a corner and put a dunce cap on me. The kids in the class all start calling me dummy and stupid and laughing at me. With the result that I started to hate school. I hated that teacher for what she done to me. I start being a truant, playing hooky."

He licks his dry lips a few times. "I was arrested for robbing a bakery shop. After letting me off a few times, the judge had enough of me. He sentenced me to two months in the Catholic protectory." Those two months became the foundation of Joe's education as a professional criminal. "From young lads you had youth up to 16, and we were put into different yards according to age. I was in the small yard with the youngest group. I used to see the older kids, and all I wanted was to be like them."

When Joe was 14, an older boy he met in jail gave Joe his gun to carry. "He had a problem with some people that were looking to kill him. They came around the neighborhood every night around midnight. They used to come down Stanton Street and on Chrystie Street turn left, and we were waiting for them. We shot at them, and believe me, windows were cracking upstairs. Who the hell knew about a gun? You just pulled the trigger. And to make it even worse, the ones that we shot at happened to be good friends of mine."

"Did you kill them?"

"No. Thank God, we missed, both our shots. But I'm saying I wanted to be a part of it. It was all through my environment as a kid. Now," he says, sitting in the driveway and preparing for the ordeal of moving his nearly one-hundred-year-old body into the house, "I regret my life. Oh, there were some great times. It was a glamorous life. When nobody else had anything, I always had money. But looking back at it and what I been through, where I wound up—prison—it's not worth it. What have I got to show for it all?"

When he got out in 1995 after the parole violation, everyone he knew was either dead or locked up. He wound up in one room with his three dogs, trapped in the prison of his infirmities and his memories. "That's why I want to tell my story," he insists. It has become his reason for living, to unburden himself of his past. "When I went back inside, I seen these young kids, from good homes, good families, in there for murder. They wanna be wiseguys. They wanna put a gun in their hand and go out and kill somebody and impress some fuckin' boss so they can become— what? A made member." His voice rises, becomes a strained invocation. "Do they know they're gonna have to kill their best friends? They should kill the fuckin' bosses!"

"Joe," I say, "how do you feel about what you did?"

We start the trek to the front door; I remember how, inside the pen, Joe would walk for miles every day. "It was the life I chose," he says, holding my arm. "I'm not looking to be forgiven. I'm just trying to tell other young fellas what I learned."

The next day, we sit in the garden behind the house, the denture burial ground, with Joe's dogs, Grandma Rose, Lucky, and Penny, at his feet and his birds, a pair of beautiful pale yellow parrots, sitting on his shoulders or his head. It's a tropical oasis in the middle of the hood. From time to time, some of the local kids drop by, all black or Latino, a few of them aspiring gangbangers. They have no idea they've got a real live original gangster in their midst. Joe gives them candy or a couple of dollars and tells them to beat it.

He wants to talk about Cuba. When he was just 22, in 1928, Joe took his first trip to Havana. He loved the place. "It was wide-open. Beautiful young whores everywhere, every street corner, every bar. In one club, there were twenty-five girls. You picked the ones you wanted to be in a live sex show." He remembers there was no crime, no robberies. Maybe an occasional knife fight. Stassi made it his business to become well-acquainted with all the top Cuban officials.

After the gold rush of Prohibition, Zwillman urged Joe to go into that other enduring vice, gambling. Stassi took over the numbers for Zwillman and began opening dog- and horse-racing tracks in New Jersey and Florida. During the Depression, when everyone else went bust, Joe continued to rake in millions in cash, socking it away in a half-dozen safe-deposit boxes in the vaults of the Manhattan Trust and other banks. "I just kept stuffing it in there," he says. "I never even had time to count it." He lived in the best hotels under assumed names, married the lovely Frances Paxton of Charlotte, North Carolina, and was out every night in the most popular restaurants and clubs—El Morocco, Copacabana, the Stork Club. In the late thirties and forties, he took over the Hollywood Restaurant and Nightclub on Broadway between 48th and 49th, which became one of the hottest spots in town. He went to every major heavyweight fight. He hobnobbed with movie stars and celebrities: Jack Dempsey, who was a close friend; Jean Harlow, who had a long, torrid affair with Longy Zwillman; Joe DiMaggio, who took to hanging out in Newark with Richie the Boot; Frank Sinatra, whom Joe first met at Willie Moretti's club in New Jersey; Toots Shor and any number of other savvy denizens of New York nightlife. Joe remembers being unimpressed by the young crooner when he first heard Sinatra sing. "To me, he was nothing compared to Bing Crosby."

But it was Havana that kept drawing him back.

"I used to go there practically every New Year's Eve," he says. "People would come from all over the world to celebrate at El Floridita in Havana." Joe remembers drinking with Ernest Hemingway, whoring with Ben Siegel and other gangsters who came to the island to visit him. By the fifties, Stassi was in partnership with Tampa boss Santo Trafficante Jr. in the Sans Souci casino and with Philadelphia godfather Angelo Bruno in the Plaza Hotel and Casino. "Meyer told me Santo was looking to open up the Sans Souci. Meyer was waiting on the license to open the Nacional, and he asked if I'd be interested in going in on the Sans Souci with Trafficante. I said, 'Yes, lemme meet him.'" It was around this time that the FBI began keeping close track of Stassi's movements. Some of the earliest FBI reports on Stassi, sent to FBI director J. Edgar Hoover from the FBI's legal attaché in Havana, note that Stassi's son, Joseph junior, married the daughter of a Cuban senator, Miguel Suarez Fernandez, who was a close friend of Fulgencio Batista's.

Stassi, Lansky, and the boys underestimated Fidel Castro; they lost millions when Castro's men came down from the mountains and drove the gangsters off the island. "The Plaza was one of the first places they wrecked," Joe says, and shakes his head wistfully. The FBI reports I received say Stassi's casino was singled out because of his close ties to Senator Fernandez, who was one of the first people Castro executed. Joe put his wife and young daughter on a boat to Florida. He and Joe junior, Trafficante and a few others lingered on the island to see if Castro might want to play ball. "One night I went to the movies," says Joe. "The people that were with me went back to the Capri Hotel [the scene of Hyman Roth's rooftop birthday party in *The Godfather II*]. That was when they raided."

Castro's men arrested Jake Lansky (Meyer's brother), Santo Trafficante and a few others. And they were looking for Stassi. "I called the Capri, and they told me, 'Joe, don't come here. They just pinched everybody.'" Before that, Joe says, he got arrested every week, but they never held him. The fact that they had arrested Jake Lansky and Trafficante—Joe knew this time it was serious. He lay low for a while, then fled the island in April. "There had been revolutions before. I thought Castro would last only a year or two," says Joe. "My son stayed on another year. But in the end, I lost everything I had invested there. I had bought a lot of real estate for little money. I had bought a copper mine. I heard the mine became very productive—for the Russians."

In 1961 Jack and Bobby Kennedy came into power. Prior to the Kennedy administration, J. Edgar Hoover adamantly refused to acknowledge the existence of an organized-crime cartel. Ignoring Tom Dewey's racketeering prosecution of Luciano in 1936; the Murder, Inc., trials in the forties, when Abe "Kid Twist" Reles first revealed the existence of the national crime syndicate; and the revelations of the Kefauver Committee Hearings in the fifties, Hoover dismissed the notion of the Mafia. Only after the Apalachin debacle, when dozens of gangsters from all over the country were caught meeting in upstate New York, would Hoover reluctantly admit the possibility that there were criminal groups operating in concert to control nationwide illegal enterprises. The G-men went from pursuing Reds and bank robbers to stalking racketeers. From then on, FBI would stand for Forever Bothering Italians.

When I ask Joe about Hoover, he tells another Swifty Morgan story. Swifty used to run into Hoover while out walking his dog. Joe remembers Swifty as a comedian who would pull stunts like pretending to wipe his dog's ass with a $100 bill, switching it to a one at the last moment. He used to carry one or two items in his pockets that he would offer to sell Hoover. When Hoover said he'd pay $50 for a pair of cufflinks, Swifty replied, "Fifty dollars! The fucking reward is more than that."

Joe says he knew, they all knew, that Hoover was gay, that his lover was his right-hand man, Clyde Tolson, and that he was a gambler. "I used to see them at the track together," he says. And he heard there might have been photos, but he never saw them, so he won't confirm whether the Mob was blackmailing Hoover. Joe says it was a matter of priorities. In the forties and fifties, the priority was Nazis or Communists; in the sixties it was organized crime. What he will confirm is that it was Zwillman who met with Hoover to negotiate a deal for the surrender of notorious Murder, Inc., boss Louis "Lepke" Buchalter. Walter Winchell became the Mob's middleman and went along for the scoop on the night Lepke got into Hoover's car on a New York street after two years in hiding. Hoover promised he would keep Buchalter in federal custody and give him ten years on a tax charge. Joe says Hoover told Zwillman he would see Buchalter was not turned over to Dewey and New York prosecutors, who wanted to give him the electric chair. Hoover didn't keep his end of the deal. Buchalter became the first and only Mob boss to be executed for his crimes.

Nothing had prepared Stassi and the other mobsters for the zeal and power of young Bobby Kennedy. Bobby's drive on organized crime had the tenor of a vendetta with Irish Catholic overtones. Many believe the beef went all the way back to the days of the patriarch, Joseph P. Kennedy Sr., who made his stake as a rum-runner and held on to the distribution rights for Haig & Haig whiskey from England after repeal. He would later be named ambassador to Great Britain. Joe says Kennedy senior was known as a double-crossing, vindictive son of a bitch. He remembers his early brush with the man whose son would be murdered in Dallas.

Stassi was living at the Warwick Hotel at 54th and Sixth, where Joe Kennedy also happened to reside. Stassi tells of a cocktail lounge at the Warwick where he would sometimes meet a woman whose last name was Rogers, coincidentally the same name as Stassi's alias. Joe Kennedy also knew Miss Rogers; indeed, she was his mistress at the time. One time, Kennedy came into the cocktail lounge and found Joe Rogers sitting tête-à-tête with Miss Rogers. "Are you two related?" Kennedy asked with a wry smile.

Joe smiles faintly at the memory. "A fella I knew well tells me, 'I was speaking to the law and was told to advise you to move out. The management doesn't want you. You're gonna get put out, maybe arrested to get you out.' " Joe heard later that Kennedy might have had something to do with Stassi's wearing out his welcome at the hotel. "Joe Kennedy was law in the Warwick Hotel. If he made a suggestion . . ." Joe gestures, cocks his head. "I moved out. Later I'm told Kennedy said I was one of five people in his life he hated."

"Because of Miss Rogers? Seems kind of extreme."

Joe says he doesn't know if it's true any more than he knows why Bobby's office saw fit to frame him on narcotics charges. The nexus between the boys and the Kennedys was long-standing and byzantine, and then it morphed into an unholy covenant. At Kennedy senior's behest, the Mob helped get Jack elected in 1960 by swinging the vote in the West Virginia primary. The CIA and at least two high-ranking mafiosi, Johnny Roselli and Joe's partner Santo Trafficante, with the connivance of the White House, were plotting to hit Fidel Castro. And to make it personal, Jack Kennedy and Chicago boss Sam Giancana were sleeping with the same woman, Judith Campbell Exner. Joe Kennedy's dictatorial influence, his habit of turning on former partners who had helped him along the way and his self-professed bigotry were channeled through the loyal scions.

Stassi was one of the first to fall. After he decamped Havana, Joe was approached by the FBI. He agreed to speak to them with the proviso that he would not discuss anything to do with his personal business or that of his friends; he would talk only about what he knew of the political situation in postrevolutionary Cuba. "They asked me, 'Are you a good American?' " I said, 'Yes, I'm a good American.' " According to the FBI report, Stassi gave them very little information. He said he was returning to Cuba to visit his son and would talk to them again on his return. He never did. In 1962 Stassi was named by Joe Valachi during testimony before a Senate committee as a member of La Cosa Nostra. By then the FBI had already classified him as a Top Hoodlum and opened an extensive investigation. Soon after, he was indicted on a heroin-importation case out of Corpus Christi, Texas. He went on the lam and lived for three years as a fugitive sought around the world in one of the most extensive FBI manhunts of the time. Finally brought to ground at the Canada Club in Pompano Beach, Florida, Joe would spend the next thirty years insisting he was framed on the narcotics charges and fighting to regain his freedom.

In November 1962, almost a year to the day before the Kennedy assassination, Joe met in New York with Santo Trafficante and Carlos Marcello, the New Orleans Mafia boss who was hounded out of the country by Bobby Kennedy. Among conspiracy theorists, Marcello and Trafficante are the prime suspects in alleged Mob plots to return fire on the Kennedys. "What did you talk about?" I ask him, scanning the FBI report of the meeting.

"Nothing. We had breakfast."

"C'mon, Joe. You never met with anyone without discussing something."

He holds up his hand. "I don't remember."

"The Kennedys?"

"We might have talked about all the heat."

"Do you believe Trafficante was involved in the assassination?"

"Please. Santo wouldn't have the balls," Joe says. He is obfuscating.

"I'm not saying him personally."

He shrugs. "Santo was a piece of shit." Joe has nothing good to say about Santo. Cheapest man he ever met. Whenever there was money owed, Trafficante was nowhere to be found. His own people told Joe that Santo screwed them out of money all the time. FBI reports bear out there was rancor among the partners.

"What about Marcello?"

"Knowing Carlos and Santo, no. Unless they had some fool to do it for them."

"Or some patsy."

"Anything is possible," Joe allows. He believes money would have been all the motive they needed, and he admits the Kennedy Justice Department's offensive against organized crime was putting a serious crimp in the bosses' lifestyle. The Mob had never known such heat.

Arnold Stone, a trial attorney with the Organized Crime and Racketeering Section of the Criminal Division, whose bailiwick included Texas and New Jersey and who oversaw the Stassi investigation and prosecution, remembers he was in a meeting with Robert Kennedy at the Justice Department to discuss their Mob offensive on November 22, 1963, the day President Kennedy was assassinated. When I ask Stone about Joe's case, he says the Trafficante connection is off-limits. He'll talk about Joe on the record but not Trafficante, because talking about him could compromise ongoing investigations. I press the issue: "Investigations of whom? Santos is dead." Stone says he simply does not know enough about Trafficante to talk about him intelligently.

According to Stone, the atmosphere in the Kennedy Justice Department was one of professionalism and dedication to honest and just law enforcement. He doubts anything like a vendetta motivated Robert Kennedy, whom Stone remembers as a brilliant and hardworking man with a strong sense of fair play. Stone, who is now in private practice in North Carolina, denies Stassi was the target of a malicious prosecution solely intended to get at Trafficante. Stassi was a target in his own right. "Of course we wanted Stassi, but for the crimes he was committing. Would we have liked to talk to him about Santo Trafficante? Of course we would." Then he adds, "And Vito Genovese. And Lucien Rivard and Paul Mondolini"—two of the original architects of the French Connection. Stone believes it is Stassi's guilt that prevents him from admitting his involvement in heroin trafficking. "Better he should be remembered as a killer of five or six gangsters than a contributor to the miseries and slow deaths of thousands of heroin users, otherwise innocent children and adults."

After the Kennedy assassination, Stone went to Florida while Joe was in the wind and made overtures, through Joe's son, for him to come in and talk to them. No matter how much he may have despised Santo, Joe held true to his vows and refused to cooperate. The feds responded by turning up the heat. The files are rife with reports on the manhunt. Stassi is described as "armed and dangerous" and a "vicious killer." There is almost no mention of Stassi in connection with narcotics.

I'm in New York when the call comes. Joe is in the hospital complaining of severe chest pains. "You better get down here," he orders.

I find him in the Cedars-Sinai Medical Center, sitting on the edge of the bed trying to put on his pants. "Get me out of here," he tells me when I walk in. It turns out the pains were caused by bruised ribs sustained when he took a fall; his heart is still going strong. I talk to the nurse, commandeer a guy with a wheelchair, and we're out. Something in my Karma has me liberating this man from large institutions.

Joe isn't ready to die yet. He's not prepared for the final liberation; he wants to go to the International House of Pancakes first. Afterward, I take him home.

"Dutch Schultz," Joe says when I have him settled on his bed.

The murder of Dutch Schultz on October 23, 1935, like the Siegel killing, is one that has long captured the popular imagination. Just 33 when he died, the Dutchman was one of the most celebrated and feared gangsters of all time. *Kill the Dutchman! The Story of Dutch Schultz*, by Paul Sann; E. L. Doctorow's *Billy Bathgate*, made into a movie starring Dustin Hoffman as Schultz; and any number of other portrayals of the infamous bootlegger and racketeer whose real name was Arthur Flegenheimer—the son of a German Jewish saloonkeeper—carry us inevitably to that

October night in the Palace Chophouse and Tavern in Newark when Schultz was gunned down. Mortally wounded, Schultz lingered for twenty hours in a Newark hospital surrounded by cops, a stenographer recording his dying words. No less a literary outlaw than William Burroughs, the godfather of the Beats, wrote a film script based on Schultz's rhapsodic deathbed dithyramb.

"Who shot you?" a cop asked Dutch.

"Please crack down on the Chinaman's friends and Hitler's commander," Schultz raved. "I am sore, and I am going up, and I am going to give you honey if I can. Mother is the best bet, and don't let Satan draw you too fast." He died without naming his killers.

One of my favorite Schultz stories has him in a meeting with leaders of the Syndicate, Luciano presiding, when a vote was taken on some important piece of business. Dutch, who was suffering from a bad case of the flu, had been sitting off in the corner so as not to infect the others. Everyone voiced his opinion except Joe Adonis, who stood at the mirror combing his hair. Adonis, whose real name was Giuseppe Antonio Doto, had assumed the alias in deference to his conceit that he was the handsomest of criminals. With the other mobsters waiting for him to weigh in, Adonis finally turned away from the mirror and announced, "The star says yes." At which point Schultz leaped up, rushed over to Adonis and grabbed him in a headlock. He slobbered mucus all over Adonis's face and said, "Now, you fuckin' star, you have my *joims!*" Adonis was laid up for a week with Schultz's flu.

Joe hated Adonis, and for good reason. Adonis once called a sit-down that, had it not gone Stassi's way, would have ended in his death sentence. Adonis resented Stassi ever after. There was also an issue over a girlfriend. To Joe, Adonis epitomized the power-crazed boss who orders his soldiers to kill on a whim.

"You killed Dutch Schultz?"

"I got the contract," he says.

At the time, Joe used to meet secretly with Abe Zwillman and Meyer Lansky in out-of-the-way spots so no one would put them together. Prohibition had ended; the underworld was in transition. Luciano, Lansky, and Zwillman were intent on establishing a new order and putting an end to the unbridled murder and mayhem of the 20s. The Dutchman was a throwback to the violent era of the celebrity criminal.

Schultz was trying to sell his New York brewery to raise cash to pay his lawyers and keep his corrupt police and political allies from jumping ship. Hoover's FBI had named Schultz Public Enemy No. 1 after he beat an IRS case. Schultz's legal woes were far from over, however; he was awaiting trial in Jersey on new charges, and Dewey had vowed to put him and Tammany Hall power broker Jimmy Hines behind bars. Schultz fled New York and took up residence in the same hotel where Zwillman and Richie the Boot kept apartments, the Robert Treat in Newark, around the corner from the Palace Chophouse.

Once Joe had been given the contract, he told Schultz he might have a buyer for the brewery. Joe said he would speak to the party and get back to the Dutchman in a day or two. Schultz was pleased with Joe's help, never suspecting it was all part of an elaborate setup. Joe arranged to meet Schultz at the Chophouse.

Stassi says he was too well-known at the tavern to carry out the hit himself, so he brought in two of Murder, Inc.'s most accomplished triggermen: Charley "the Bug" Workman and Emmanuel "Mendy" Weiss. "Abe was tight with Richie the Boot," Joe says. "They had made peace, and it was decided Richie would provide the other men. We used Gyp DeCarlo and a guy, I can't remember his name, we called him Stretch. I gave them a rifle. 'What's this for?' Gyp asks. I says, 'If you're being chased, use it.' "

Here Joe becomes even more sotto voce. "We wait till after rush hour, around eight o'clock. DeCarlo's partner is behind the wheel. Workman and Mendy walk in, and right away the shooting starts.

Dutch has three or four of his men in there, and they all have guns. They're shooting at each other. Workman doesn't see Dutch, so he ducks into the men's room. Dutch had just finished taking a piss, he was washing his hands when the shooting started. Workman shoots him as he turns from the sink, then he robs him, which he wasn't supposed to do. Workman never followed orders. That's when Gyp comes with the rifle, and they shoot all Dutch's men. Mendy and Gyp run out and get in the car. 'Where's Workman?' Mendy doesn't know, lost him in the confusion."

The next day, Workman showed up. He told Joe he had run out the back door and hopped a bus a few blocks away. Workman was eventually arrested for the Schultz hit on the testimony of Abe Reles, the notorious Murder, Inc., killer who turned informant. Reles testified that Workman had bragged to him about killing Schultz; Joe believes Reles made up his testimony.

Stassi says he fixed Workman's trial in Newark. "There was no chance in the world he could get convicted. It came as a shock to everyone when he pled guilty." Workman served twenty-three years in prison for the killing and died without revealing who had orchestrated the Dutchman's demise. A lifetime later, Stassi's confession clears the books on one of the Mob's most spectacular hits.

"Go on, Joe. Who else did you murder?"

After a long pause, he says, "Max Hassel."

"I thought you were close to Max."

"You don't listen. That's what I'm trying to tell you."

But I have been listening; I want him to say it again.

Max Hassel was one of the first men who befriended Joe when he took up with the New Jersey bootleggers. Hassel trusted Joe implicitly; Joe was considered part of the inner circle and took a suite on the floor below Hassel's headquarters at the Elizabeth Carteret Hotel in Elizabeth. Joe had gone over to meet Max at the hotel one day and ended up staying fourteen years. What Hassel didn't know was that Joe was even closer to Meyer Lansky and Longy Zwillman.

Joe was summoned to a meeting in New York. Adonis was there, Zwillman, Lansky—the bosses. They told Joe that Hassel and his partner, Max Greenberg, must go. They were trying to take over; Max Greenberg was cheating people. Joe was shaken. " 'Kill Max Hassel?' I said. 'Why, Max is no more of a threat to you than a cockroach.' Adonis says, 'Yeah, well, that's all he is, a cockroach. So kill him.' " Joe closes his eyes, fighting back tears.

"Max Hassel had been talking to me," he continues after a few moments. "If there's a war, who do I think would win? he says. I used to tell him, 'Max, as far as you're concerned, nobody's gonna bother you.' And I meant it, because everyone knew Max Hassel never cheated anyone, never hit or beat no one. Greenberg was the one; I could understand Greenberg. I heard him bragging, 'I fucked them with a pencil!' That was one of his famous sayings. Greenberg was taking everything, bullying everybody. They all had reason to kill him. But not Max Hassel."

Hassel had paid all Joe's bills when Joe was just getting established in Jersey. He was one of several Jewish gangsters Joe would work closely with over the years. And now he was going to kill him.

"I loved the guy . . ." Joe says.

But he knew that to refuse the order or even to show weakness in carrying it out would give Adonis the ammunition he needed to have Stassi killed. It took all Joe's will to keep his long-simmering hatred of Adonis from boiling over.

"Abe was telling me the trouble they had. They was scheming for months to kill Max Greenberg. They couldn't get a handle on it; it would have to be done so openly. They knew I was the only one who could arrange it. They were all looking at me. What did I have to say? I started laughing. They said, 'Why are you laughing?' I told them, 'It's the easiest thing in the world.' "

Joe once had a woman in his rooms at the Carteret Hotel who became hysterical. She was convinced her husband had followed her and was outside waiting for her to come out. A room-service waiter showed Joe a rear service entrance, and the lady slipped out unseen. It was the crucial piece of information needed when it came time to plan the hit of the two Maxes. Getting in was not the problem; they had the element of surprise. The escape route is the key to a successful hit.

Waxey Gordon, a well-known bootlegger and Lansky rival, was at the hotel visiting the two Maxes. One popular retelling of the killing has Waxey spared because he was in another room with a woman named Nancy Presser, who would go on to prominence as one of the star witnesses against Luciano in his prostitution rackets trial. Joe says that's not true, the woman is a lying stool pigeon. Waxey was there, but they didn't kill him because the contract didn't call for him to die.

"No one was ever prosecuted."

"Who did it?"

"It's not important. What I'm trying to say, anyone who wants to be a gangster, a wiseguy, a made Mafia soldier or whatever you want to call it is going to have to face what I went through."

He licks his thin lips several times. "I killed my best friend on orders from Abe and Meyer," he says.

"Max Hassel?"

"No. Another party."

"Who?"

"I'll tell you . . ."

But he can't quite bring himself to say the man's name. It was his best friend; that's all we need to know. It was the ultimate test of his loyalty, and his treachery.

His friend loved diamonds. Joe used the pretext that he had some stones to sell to lure him to a rendezvous at a train station. This killing, too, was part of the larger power struggle. Joe, being the independent operator he was, had friends on both sides of the conflict.

"I don't believe in killing for money," he says. "There was

always another reason, cheating or talking to the law, disobeying orders. They had a reason, even if the reason wasn't always right."

He knew why this killing had been ordered, but he didn't agree with it. Joe protested to Zwillman, who said he agreed, but it didn't matter; they were outvoted by the others, who believed Joe's friend was in the wrong. Joe believes it was all part of a power play by Nick Delmore to take over running the Jersey operations for the syndicate. The hit had come from Vincent Alo, who took over for Adonis when the latter was deported to Italy. Alo also inherited Joe's hatred for Adonis and went on to provoke plenty of his own. Joe is ready to fight when his name is mentioned. And Delmore? "I'll say it to the whole world: Nick Delmore was no fucking good."

Delmore was supposed to provide a getaway car but didn't. Fortunately for Joe, his friend drove to the station instead of coming by train. Joe killed him in his car, shot him in the head, then used the car to dispose of the body.

"That's how they came to have such trust in me."

"Abe and Meyer. Because you killed your best friend . . ."

He nods. "If you ask me, 90 percent of killings take place between close friends. Nick Delmore," Joe hisses, full of venom. "Later, they made this no-good rat bastard a boss. One regret I got in life: I should have killed Nick Delmore."

In 1959, at 60, Longy Zwillman went into his basement one night with a bottle of whiskey and some antidepressants. When the drugs and alcohol wouldn't exorcise his demons, Longy hanged himself from the rafters with an electric cord. There have been persistent rumors that the suicide was actually a hit. Joe, who was in Cuba at the time, doubts it. He says Longy had no real enemies, except the U.S. government, which had indicted him for bribing a juror in his trial for tax evasion. He was on the inevitable ride to prison. Besides, Joe says, if it had been a hit, they would have shot him in the head, to his face, a death befitting the high regard in which he was held. And not faked a suicide in his home, with his wife and children upstairs asleep.

"The FBI reports call you a 'vicious killer,'" I tell him. "Is that true?"

"No." He shakes his head. "I killed on orders."

"How many people have you killed, Joe?"

He waves his hands, closes his eyes. "So many . . . I can't remember."

It's as though a weight has been lifted. Joe has unburdened himself of his most cumbersome memories. He has rolled aside the boulder at the mouth to the cave of his past. The effort has left him spent and at peace.

"Tired, Joe?" I ask, and help him lift his swollen legs onto the bed.

"No. I'm fine," he says. But in a moment, he has dozed off and I am left to contemplate his ancient face. I see the shamed stuttering little boy in his dunce cap, the lonely kid who wanted desperately to be like the big boys, the bold young soldier who served his commanders, the honorable old don who kept his vows, went to prison, did his time and lived to tell about it. I wonder what other dark secrets lie within this living relic of the century that gave us organized crime.

In this era of *Sopranos* mania, here is the New Jersey mobster incarnate at the end of his days, and I am at once drawn to him and repelled, fascinated and horrified, like the rest of America watching Tony Soprano blast his friend Big Pussy into oblivion.

Loud hip-hop music from outside invades the stillness of the afternoon. Joe stirs. I think of the young rappers appropriating mobster monikers like Capone, Gallo, Gotti. The gangster persona is omnipresent in our culture. Joe shunned the limelight. He says John Gotti was his own worst enemy, he embodied the ambivalence: Am I a movie star or a mobster?

Joe insists there was no glamour, no glory in that moment when he put the gun to his best friend's head.

NORMAN MAILER ON POT

High Times, November/December 2004

Still High After All These Years

Some people never learn. It would appear I'm a periodical publication junkie. Coming out with a magazine each month satisfies a need I have to feel like I'm accomplishing something concrete with my life. People ask, "What're you doing?" You hand them the latest copy of your magazine. So when Michael Kennedy and I got together again two years ago to talk about High Times, *I let myself be seduced by the vision that I could take the thirty-year-old magazine and make it relevant again.*

I was finishing up production on the last season of Street Time, *so I hired John Buffalo Mailer, Norman's youngest son, and Annie Nocenti, who worked with me on* Prison Life *and was the editor of* Scenario *magazine, to take over as editors and help re-vamp* High Times.

From a public relations standpoint, we succeeded. Before we took over, the usual response High Times *provoked in the press was snickers. No one was willing to take the stoner publication seriously except committed potheads who had very little else on their minds. They were content to stare at centerfolds of gorgeous marijuana buds and drool like teenage boys gazing at* Playboy *centerfolds. It had become a pot porn mag. But the founder, Tom Forçade, and the people who worked on the magazine in the seventies up until and just after Tom's death, had something else in mind. Tom was a revolutionary. He believed that the best way to make effective changes in our society was through the media. He always said* High Times *was never meant to be "just a pot magazine." The first thing we did was to get rid of the phony pot ads. Tom would have shut the magazine down before he would have allowed page after page of garish display ads for fake buds that can only have one use—unscrupulous dealers use it as cut or sell it to kids who don't know any better. Naturally we took a hit in ad revenue. But we felt that the fake pot ads were unethical and other pot-centric ads were scaring away other potential advertisers. We split the magazine, made it two—what I called* classic High Times *for people with a broader cultural and political consciousness, and* High Times Grow America *for the hard-core stoners and growers. We changed the tagline from "Celebrating the Counter-Culture" to "Celebrating Freedom." We published provocative articles, interviews, and opinion columns of a caliber the magazine had not seen for a decade. To me, pot is a metaphor, a symbol for freedom, the freedom to think with an open mind and to question authority. When we came out with our Activist's Guide to the Republican National Convention in July, 2004, the* New York Times, *the* L.A. Times, *radio and TV, even Fox News and* The New York Post, *all did stories on us. Smart people with a libertarian view were paying attention to* High Times *again and taking it seriously. We had critical success and given time, we would have attracted more of the kinds of advertisers we wanted: clothing companies, movies and CDs, entertainment. But the magazine was faltering in a financial quagmire too shaky to sustain rebirth. I had screenwriting jobs I had to concentrate on. So, when faced with the prospect of bringing back the fake pot ads and the pot porn content those advertisers demanded, after we published our 30th anniversary edition in the fall of 2004, Annie, John, and I quit.*

Interviewing Mailer for the 30th anniversary issue seemed especially appropriate since our first interview in Rolling Stone *had come out the same year* High Times *launched, 1974. One of the first essays I read on marijuana was Mailer's "General Marijuana" published in*

Advertisements for Myself. *We did the interview in the same home on the waterfront in Provincetown where Mailer and I met that winter night 35 years ago.*

NORMAN MAILER ON POT

THIRTY YEARS AGO, WHEN *High Times* was in its infancy, I did a long interview with Norman Mailer that was published in two parts in *Rolling Stone* magazine. Mailer and I first met in Provincetown, MA, in the winter of 1970 and have been close friends ever since. At one time we owned property together in Maine, which was put up as collateral for bail when I got busted for smuggling marijuana in the early eighties. The feds were all over the connection between Mailer and me; he testified for the defense at the trial of my partner in Toronto, Rosie Rowbotham, who ended up doing over 20 years for importing hashish. Mailer later testified at my trials in Maine and New York. The government became convinced that he was some sort of hippie godfather to the sprawling marijuana-trafficking organization Rowbotham and I ran, along the lines of Timothy Leary's figurehead status with the Brotherhood of Eternal Love conspiracy out of Laguna Beach, CA.

But Mailer was more a friend of the cause than a coconspirator. He certainly had what to an assistant United States attorney might qualify as "guilty knowledge." He knew what I was up to. I remember standing with him on the balcony of his Brooklyn Heights apartment one night, looking out at the glittering behemoths of the Lower Manhattan financial district, then down at the containers stacked on the Brooklyn docks below like mini-skyscrapers and telling him, "Right down there, Norman, in those containers, there's seven million dollars' worth of Lebanese hash. All I have to do is get it out of there without getting busted." The novelist in him was intrigued, but the criminal in him would always remain subservient to the artist. The government put tremendous pressure on me to give them Mailer, as though he were some trophy I could trade for my own culpability. They were star-fucking: John DeLorean had been busted in a set-up coke case; Mailer's head would have looked good mounted on some government prosecutor's wall.

When I went to prison in 1982, Mailer became—after my mother—my most loyal visitor and correspondent. And when I was released in 1990, I stayed in his Brooklyn Heights apartment while the Mailer family summered in Provincetown. I've known Mailer's youngest son, John Buffalo, since he was born and turned to him when I needed someone to act in my stead here at the magazine while I finished work on the TV show I produced for Showtime. But, as with my criminal enterprise, Mailer has no financial stake in the outcome of the *High Times* mini-media-conglomerate conspiracy. He's an interested observer and adviser.

All this by way of saying there's real history here, so much so that there was never any pretense at making this a typical interview; it's more like a master speaking to an apprentice about what he has learned. I'd read Mailer extensively before I met him. His writing, in essays such as "The White Negro" and "General Marijuana," his nonfiction *The Armies of the Night* and *The Executioner's Song,* and the novels *The Naked and the Dead, An American Dream, Why Are We in Vietnam?* and *Ancient Evenings,* to mention just a few of Mailer's works, have reshaped post–World War II American literature. Mailer's whole notion of the existential hipster living in the crucible of his orgasm probably contributed as much to my fascination with the outlaw life as the cannabis plant itself.

I've smoked pot with Mailer on a number of occasions and have always been impressed with where it took him: to the outermost reaches of the universe and back to the murky depths of the human psyche. But I had never really sat with him and got his thoughts on pot until we met, almost 30 years to the day of that first interview, and I asked him to expound on his views of the plant that became the inspiration for this magazine.

Norman Mailer: Looking back on pot—is it 30 years since I smoked?—by the seventies I began to feel it was costing me too much. We'll get to what I got out of it and what I didn't get out of it—but by the eighties, I just smoked occasionally. And I don't think I've had a toke—and this is neither to brag nor apologize—in 10 years. But I look back on it as one of the profoundest parts of my life. It did me a lot of good and a lot of harm.

What I'd like to do today is talk about these dimensions of pot. People who smoke marijuana all the time are, as far as I'm concerned, fundamentalists. Their one belief is that pot is good, pot takes care of everything—it's their gospel. I think they're about as limited—if you want to get brutal about it—as fundamentalists. Fundamentalists can't think; they can only refer to the Gospels. Pot people can't recognize that something as good as that might have something very bad connected to it—which is not to do with the law, but what it does to you. That's what I'd like to talk about. The plus and minus.

The other thing I'd like to talk about is the cultural phenomenon of pot. That is rarely gone into. Instead, people are always taking sides—pot's good, pot's bad; pot should be outlawed, pot should be decriminalized—there's always this legalistic approach. But I think marijuana had a profound cultural effect upon America, and I wouldn't mind seeing this magazine exploring all that pot did to the American mentality—good and bad.

Richard Stratton: Marijuana is already a huge cultural phenomenon. In the 30 years *High Times* has been around, pot has gone from a marginal anomaly in our society to something that's almost mainstream.

Mailer: Yeah, only not mainstream yet. Too many attitudes have settled in on pot, and there's too much dead-ass in the thinking of pot smokers now. Some 30 years ago when it was all new, we really felt we were adventurers—let's say 40 years ago—we really felt we were on the edge of startling and incredible revelations. You'd have perceptions that I still use to this day—that's part of the good. When I first began smoking, I was a typical liberal, a radical rationalist. I never believed in a Higher Power. I still dislike those two words—Higher Power. I didn't believe that God was there. I couldn't explain anything, because when you're an atheist, you're living without a boat on an island in the Pacific that's surrounded by water: There's nowhere to go.

It's hard enough to believe in God, but to assume there is no God, no prime force—how can you begin to explain anything that way?

I was a socialist, more radical than most liberals, but I was altogether a rationalist. I was also at the point of getting into one or another kind of terminal disease, because my life was wrong. My liver was lousy and I wasn't even drinking a lot. My personal life was not happy and I was congested, constricted. I couldn't have been tighter. Then pot hit.

In the beginning, I remember that pot used to irritate the hell out of me, because nothing would happen when I smoked. I've noticed that intellectuals with highly developed minds usually have trouble turning on. The mental structure is so developed, so ratiocinative. So many minefields have been built up to protect the intellect from pot, which is seen as the disrupter, the enemy. The first few times I smoked, I just got tired, dull, and irritated. I was angry that nothing had happened. It went on like that for perhaps a year. Three, four, five times I smoked, and each occasion was a blank.

Then one night in Mexico I got into a crazy sexual scene with two women. We were smoking an awful lot of pot. Then one of the women went home and the other went to sleep and I felt ill and got up and vomited. I'd never vomited like that in my life. It was exactly as if I was having an orgasm of convulsive vomiting. Spasmodically, I was throwing off a ton of anxiety. I've never had anything like that since and I wouldn't want to. Not again. Pretty powerful convulsive experience.

Afterward, I rinsed my mouth out, went downstairs to where my then wife was sleeping on one couch, and I lay down on the other and stayed there. Then it hit—how that pot hit! I don't know if it ever hit any harder. It was incredible: I was able to change the face of my wife into anyone I wanted. It went on before my eyes. I could play all sorts of games in my mind. Whole scenarios. It went on for hours. When it was over, I knew that I was going to try this again.

A couple of days later, I was out in the car listening to the radio. Some jazz came on. I'd been listening to jazz for years, but it had never meant all that much to me. Now, with the powers pot offered, simple things became complex; complex things clarified themselves. These musicians were offering the inner content of their experience to me. Later, when I wrote about it, I would say that jazz is the music of orgasm. Because that was what it seemed to me. These very talented, charged-up players full of their joys and twists and kinks—God, they had as many as I did—were looking for the musical equivalent of an orgasm. They would take a song, play the melody, then go into variations on it, until they got themselves into a tighter and tighter situation with the take-off on the melody. I can't speak musically, but I can tell what was going on in that odyssey. They were saying: This is very, very hard to get out, it's full of knots—but I'm going to do it. And they'd climb a tower of music looking to reach the gates at the top and break through. It wasn't automatic; very often they failed. They'd go on and on, try more variations, then more. But often they couldn't solve the problem they'd set themselves musically, whatever that problem was. And sometimes, occasionally, they would break through. Then it was incredible, for they would emerge with you into a happy land just listening to music. Other times they'd stop with a little flair, a sign-off, as if to say: That's it, I give up. All that was what I heard while high, and I loved it. I became a jazz buff.

Over the next couple of years, I went often to the Five Spot, the Village Vanguard, the Jazz Gallery. I'd hear the greats: Thelonious Monk, Sonny Rollins, Coltrane, Miles Davis. Those were incredibly heady years, listening to those guys for hours on pot, or without it, because once pot had broken into my metallic mental structure, it had cracked the vise, you might say, that closed me off from music. I had become such a lover of pot that I broke up with a few friends who wouldn't smoke it. At the end of a long road—10 years down that road—I committed a felony while on pot. That didn't stop me, but I did smoke a little less as the years went on.

I'm a writer: The most important single element in my life, other than my family, has been my writing. So as a writer, I always had to ask: Is this good for my writing? And I began to look at pot through that lens. It wasn't all bad for editing—it was crazy. I'd have three or four bad ideas and one good one, but at the same time I was learning a lot about the sounds of language. Before, I'd been someone who wrote for the sense of what I was saying, and now I began to write for the sound of what I was writing.

Stratton: Like a jazz musician.

Mailer: Well, I wouldn't go that far, but to a degree, yes. I'd look for the rhythm of the long sentence rather than the intellectual impact, which often proved to be more powerful when it came out of the rhythm. So occasionally the editing was excellent. But it was impossible to write new stuff on pot. The experience was too intense. On pot, I would have the illusion that you need say no more than "I love you" and all of love would be there. Obviously, that was not enough.

Stratton: Let's talk about the detrimental aspects of pot, how you feel it worked against you.

Mailer: Well, the main thing was that I was mortgaging time, mortgaging my future. Because I'd have brilliant insights while on pot but could hardly remember any of them later. My handwriting would even break down. Then three-quarters of the insights were lost to scribbles. Whenever I had a tremendous take on pot, I was good for very little over the next 48 hours.

But if you're a novelist, you have to work every day. There are no easy stretches. You do the work. Marijuana was terrible for that. So I had longer and longer periods where I wouldn't go near pot— it would get me too far off my novelistic tracks. When it hit, three or four chapters of my next book would come into my head at once. That would often be a disaster. The happiest moment you can have when writing is when a sense of the truth comes in at the point of your pen. It just feels true. As you are writing! Such a moment is most certainly one of the reasons you write. But if I received similar truths via pot, I was no longer stretching my mind by my work as a novelist.

In fact, with the noticeable exception of Hunter Thompson, who has broken—bless him—has broken every fucking rule there is for ingesting alien substances . . . indeed, there's nobody remotely equal to Hunter—I don't know how he does it. I have great admiration for his constitution and the fact that he can be such a good writer with all the crap he takes into himself. Unbelievable, unbelievable—but no other writer I know can do it.

Stratton: So you believe that, if you were to smoke some good pot right now, you'd let your mind go—and you might see the rest of the book in your head, but you might not have the impetus to sit down and write it?

Mailer: That's right. One mustn't talk about one's book. For instance, I'm doing one now where I haven't even told my wife what it's about. She's guessed—she's a very smart lady, so she's guessed—but the thing is, I know that to talk about this book would be so much more stimulating and easy and agreeable than to write it that I'd end up talking to people about what a marvelous book I could have done. I believe pot does that in a far grander way—it's the difference between watching a movie on a dinky little TV set and going to a state-of-the-art cinema.

Stratton: Most the writing I'm doing these days is screenwriting. And because of the nature of the material I'm working on, I usually have a detailed outline. I know where I'm going, I've already seen the movie in my head. So when I write, after having smoked some pot, I find that what it does for me is I can just sit back and watch the scene play out in my mind. And I don't have to worry about getting lost, because I've got the structure of the screenplay holding me in check.

Mailer: I can see that would work for screenplays, but in a novel you've got to do it all.

Stratton: What about sex on pot?

Mailer: Sex on pot was fabulous. That was the big element. I realized I hadn't known anything about sex until I was able to enjoy it on pot. Then again, after a few years, I began to see some of the negative aspects. Once, speaking at Rice High School—I had a friend, a priest named Pete Jacobs, who'd invited me to speak there; it's a Catholic high school run by the Christian Brothers in Manhattan, and it's a school well respected by a lot of Irish working class all around New York, Staten Island, Queens, because they give you a very good, tough education there. The Christian Brothers are tough. But Pete told me, "Say what you want to say. These kids will be right on top of it." They were.

They weren't passive students at all. One of them asked me, "How do you feel about marijuana and sex?" And I gave him this answer: You can be out with a girl, have sex with her for the first time on pot and it might be fabulous—you and the girl go very far out. Then two days later you hear that the girl was killed in an automobile accident and you say, "Too bad. Such a sweet little chick." You hardly feel more than that. The action had exhausted your emotions. On pot, you can have a romance that normally would take three to six months to develop being telescoped into one big fuck. But over one night, there's no loyalty or allegiance to it because you haven't paid the price. About that time, I realized that fucking on pot was crazy because you'd feel things you never felt before, but on the other hand, you really didn't attach that much loyalty to the woman. Your feelings of love were not for the woman, but for the idea of love. It was insufficiently connected to the real woman.

It bounced off her reality rather than drawing you toward it. Other times, you could indeed get into the reality of the woman and even see something hard and cold and cruel in her depths, or something so beautiful you didn't want to go too near it because you knew you were a lousy son of a bitch and you'd ruin it.

One way or another, I found that pot intensified my attitudes toward love, but it also left me detached. It was a peculiar business. So there came a point where I began to think: Who gave us pot? Was it God or the devil? Because by now, I was my own species of a religious man. I believed in an existential God who was doing the best that He or She could do.

God was out there as the Creator, but God was not all powerful or all wise. God was an artistic general, if you will—a very creative and wonderful general—better than any general who ever lived. By far. But even so, generals finally can't take care of all their troops. And the notion of people praying all the time—begging for God to watch over them, take care of them—so conflicted with what I felt. I felt that God cannot be all good and all powerful. Not both. Because if He's all good, He is certainly not all powerful. There's no way to explain the horrors of history, including the mid-century horrors of the last century, if He is all good. Whereas if God is a great creator—not necessarily the lord of all the universe, but let's say the lord of our part of the universe, our Creator—then God, on a grander scale, bears the same relationship to us that a parent does to a child. No parent is all wise, all powerful and all good. The parent is doing the best that he or she can do. And very often it doesn't turn out well. That made sense to me. I could see our relation to God: God needs us as much as we need God. And to me, that was exciting, because now it wasn't a slavish relationship anymore. It made sense.

Stratton: You feel marijuana helped you discover this existential God?

Mailer: No question. That was part of the great trip. But I began to brood on a line that I'd written long before I'd smoked marijuana, a line from *The Deer Park*. The director who was my main character was having all sorts of insights and revelations while dead drunk, but then said to himself, "Why is my mind so alive when I'm too drunk to do anything about it?" That came back to haunt me. Because I thought: Pot is giving me so much, but I'm not doing my work. I don't get near enough to the visions and insights I'm having on pot. So is it a gift of God—pot? Or does it come from the devil? Is this the nearest the devil comes to being godlike? It seemed there were three possibilities there: One could well be that marijuana was a gift of God and, if so, must not be abused. Or was it an instrument of the devil? Or were God and the devil both present when we smoked? Maybe God needed us to become more illumined? After all, one of my favorite notions is that organized religion could well be one of the great creations of the devil. How better to drive people away from God than to give them a notion of the Almighty that doesn't fit the facts? So, I do come back to this notion that maybe God and the devil are obliged willy-nilly to collaborate here. Each thinks that they can benefit from pot: God can give you the insights and the devil will reap the exhaustions and the debilities. Because I think pot debilitates people. I've noticed over and over that people who smoke pot all the time generally do very little with their lives. I've always liked booze because I felt: It's a vice, but I know exactly what I'm paying for. You hurt your head in the beginning and your knees in the end, when you get arthritis. But at least you know how you're paying for the fun. Pot's spookier. Pot gives so much more than booze on the one hand—but on the other, never quite presents the bill.

Stratton: I'm not sure that's true of everyone who smokes pot.

Mailer: I'm sure it's not.

Stratton: A lot of people are motivated by pot. I am, for one.

Mailer: What do you mean, "motivated"?

Stratton: I mean that it doesn't debilitate me. I don't want to sit around and do nothing when I'm high. I get inspired, energized. I don't subscribe to the theory of the anti-motivational syndrome. If anything, when I'm straight, I'm often too hyper and too left-brain-oriented. I go off on tangents and I don't stop to look around and try to find a deeper meaning in what I'm doing. Marijuana will slow me down and allow me to connect with the mood of what's going on around me. And that, in turn, inspires me to go further into what I'm trying to do.

Mailer: I ended a few romances over the years because when I got on pot I couldn't stop talking. And finally I remember one girl who said, "Did you come to fuck or to knit?"

[Laughter]

Stratton: That's one of the interesting things about marijuana—how it affects everyone differently. It seems to enhance and intensify whatever's going on in the person at any given moment. Let's say that we were going to do some stretching right now and we did it straight. We'd be like, "Oh, man, this hurts. This is an ordeal." Now if we smoke a little pot and then stretch, it would feel good and put us more in touch with our bodies and the deeper sensations of the activity.

Mailer: I learned more about my body and reflex and grace, even, such as I have—whatever limited physical grace I have, I got it through pot showing me where my body, or how my body, was feeling at any given moment. Here, I can agree with you. Dancing—I could always dance on pot. Not much of a dancer otherwise, but on pot, I could dance. There's no question it liberated me. All of these good things were there. All the same, when it comes to the legalization of pot, I get dubious. Pot would be taken over by media culture. It would be classified and categorized. It would lose that wonderful little funky edge that once it had—that sensation of being on the edge of the criminal. All the same, the corporate bastards who run most of America will not legalize it in a hurry. Pot is still a great danger to them. Because what they fear is that too many people would no longer give a damn about the corporation—they'd have their minds on other things than working for the Big Empty. To the suits, that makes pot a deadly drug. The corporation has a bad enough conscience buried deep inside to fear, despite their strength, every type of psychic alteration that they haven't developed themselves.

NORMAN MAILER ON THE CORPORATIZATION
OF DEMOCRACY

Stratton: It's interesting how the world has changed in the thirty years since you and I did the *Rolling Stone* interview. There's no Soviet Union anymore, Communism is passé, now Islam is touted as the big enemy threatening America, which doesn't surprise me having spent so much time in the Middle East. While living in Beirut, I saw it coming.

Mailer: Yes, it's one of the few times I really saw it coming too. The pieces I wrote against the war before it took place and then right afterward are as good politically as anything I've written. You know, my definition of an expert is that you are right fifty percent of the time, no better. The average person can also be right fifty percent of the time by flipping a coin. What makes the life of the expert interesting is the way in which they build on their knowledge but they do it because they wish to dominate a situation. No man becomes an expert unless somewhere deep down he wants power, power over others. And so you get in these situations where on the basis of not quite enough material you build a skyscraper, and it falls over, which is, I think, what happened in Iraq: the foundations on which they built the war were hideous. They were going to have America take over the world, they'd been scheming over the last ten years, ever since Russia finally collapsed, and Communism collapsed. Why don't we take over the world? Why are we in such a giveaway program? Why are we putting up with all these other nations? All these little irritations? It's ridiculous. We're the only country that knows how to do anything; we're the only country that knows how to rule the world. We just sort of take up our manifest destiny, our true deep manifest destiny, that's what it's all about, that's what America is: manifest destiny. Let's go out there, let's start with Iraq, because that's a little warm-up, then we have Iran, Saudi Arabia, Al Queda.

Stratton: Syria.

Mailer: Syria. Once we control the Middle East—and we will control it—the rest of the world will fall into line. We don't have to conquer the whole world; it'll fall into line. The Chinese will become the Greeks to us Romans, because they can be marvelous with computers those yellow motherfuckers. I think that was the vision, the unspoken vision. I don't think anyone ever sat down and debated it, but the unspoken vision is that it is time for America to take over the world. And we can do it. Europe is Old Europe, etc, etc, etc. And what they left out of the account entirely was this notion that democracy is a grace. I've said this over and over, but democracy is a grace. A country finds its own democracy. It cannot be given to you from without. It cannot be injected into you. And that's what we're going to do, we're going to go over there and show those people how to live. We're gonna inject democracy into Iraq.

I mean, even if they end up with a system where they're voting, they are going to Allah. Well, if Allah is your man, who is then more interesting to you as an Iraqi, America or Iran? That has to breed future trouble. I remember how things got bad between us and the Filipinos back in 1944–1945. They were very happy that we'd driven the Japanese out, but they were very poor, the country was a mess, and some of them turned into beggars because in some places we were the only people around with a lot of food. The chow line became a horror. You had a bunch of kids there with tin cans looking to us when we finished our meals, hoping we'd dump our food that was left into their cans. They didn't care about the mixture of germs that came from fifty different GIs. They soon became an immense irritation to GIs because there we were, it was hot, we couldn't go home, the campaign was over, what the hell were we doing there? It did bring out the worst in you. I remember walking past some of these kids with their cans out and dumping my food into the garbage can rather than give it to them. You finally got so sick of this petty charity. You gave them your remains for six, seven, eight days with phony smiles back and forth, then finally you'd dump your can right into the main garbage can so they couldn't have it. At that point down the road, one kid went reaching into the garbage can and the mess sergeant came along, grabbed him and dumped him in entirely. Scrubbed the can with him. These ugly things were happening in a relatively nice war, but war, under the best of situations, still makes good men become ugly. I knew it was going to be bad in Iraq. An incredibly touchy people were filled with shame. If you or me had been there for those thirty years under Saddam Hussein, how many values would we have compromised over the years? How many buddies did we not quite go to bat for, because we were worried about our families? The only way out was to fight for our liberation or live with our shame. Democracy is organic, it has to build out of itself. You can't inject it. And those assholes at the top, those high great assholes, just assume it's going to be taking this step, then that step. They never see the depth of the problem. I was shocked. Here was I, very much removed from any kind of immediate cognizance of any of that stuff, knowing more about it than they did. It's shocking.

Stratton: Going back to what we talked about before, in the *Rolling Stone* interview, you said that karma is one of God's greatest creations.

Mailer: Yes.

Stratton: Do you believe that a country has a kind of collective karma?

Mailer: It's beyond my measure. It's easy to say America is into bad karma now. You could make the argument and I wouldn't argue against it because I don't know. I see karma as our heaven and hell. I have never been able to comprehend a godlike heaven and hell. First of all, heaven is very hard to picture because it sounds like some version of Club Med. In Islam they've got the seventy-nine virgins all waiting for the hero. That at least has something concrete about it, although anybody who can make it with seventy-nine virgins has to be a superb hero. Heaven I've never been able to comprehend. What is it, a luxury hotel? And in hell you burn forever. Because you once smoked a cigarette and you're a Baptist. Or you went out dancing without your parent's consent. No, I could see no proportion to it. Catholics go into it much more profoundly because they have purgatory. Even so, heaven and hell are absolutes. It never made sense to me. We are all on an ongoing cruise into something unknown, but no one can say what it is. Karma suggests what will happen to you depending on how you lived this life. You are born again, higher or lower than the last time you came out, and that makes sense. If you did ugly things in your life, say, to use a crude example, if you're Leona Helmsley and you yelled at the servants, maybe in your next life you have to clean toilets. In other words, the soul can get bad and ugly and poisonous but there are cures for it. If you don't do better next time out, you go lower. That makes sense to me. But whether you can carry that over to a nation, I don't know, that's beyond me.

Stratton: Certainly the United States has made itself most unpopular with the rest of the world.

Mailer: I think that the real question is not that we're messing up, I take that for granted, but I do ask myself how conservatives—who, after all, very many of them are serious people, deeply devout, really determined to have orderly, decent good lives—how could such people ever decide that George W. Bush was their champion? Couldn't they realize what he was doing?

Stratton: I shudder at this orgy of patriotism ushered in by 9/11, this wallowing in pride, being proud to be an American. What does that mean? Proud of what? Proud that we have become so arrogant and so despised that people will kill themselves before they will become like us?

Mailer: I call Bush & Company, not conservatives but "flag conservatives." There's that famous remark—I can never figure out if it was Samuel Johnson who made it or H. L. Mencken—that "patriotism is the last refuge of a scoundrel." Look, I think something very simple is going on among the coldest thinkers in the Bush administration. What they are saying is, our real strength is money and the more we reward the top earners in America, given the passive, even larval state of the American voter, we can win anything with advertising. But we may not be able to get away with cutting taxes and enriching the rich unless we have something big going for us. We need a war. So I think there are cold calculators like Cheney who would say, "Well, maybe we'll build an empire and maybe we won't, but the one thing we can sure count on, absolutely count on, is that with a war, America isn't going to get too upset about enriching the rich because there will be something more important on people's minds, our American boys, working for us, working for democracy over there. That's what we need, we need a war. The war will take care of everything else. Then, of course, you have the very unhappy business— which I don't want to really get into—the Jewish element of it— being Jewish myself. To have this great little nation, Israel, which was built of the ashes of the holocaust becoming a country that is in danger of becoming repellent. As a Jew I just can't get into that.

I just find it too difficult to consider the options. Not that I hold any brief for the Palestinians, because I hate terrorism, I think terrorism is the ugliest single thing you can do. On the other hand, what a Palestinian would say is, what other recourse do we have?

Compared to tanks, we only have that. We don't have America behind us. So, terrorism is our only recourse.

Stratton: It worked in Spain. Look how quickly they changed their policy and got out of Iraq after the terrorists struck.

Mailer: The difference is that ninety percent of the Spanish people didn't want to go to Iraq in the first place. Now, in America, the pundits kept saying, we can't believe that Spain was so dastardly. What kind of a democracy are they? Well they are a democracy where ninety percent of the people did not want to go into Iraq.

Stratton: Let's talk about your views on the corporations and advertising. I know that's something that's been on your mind.

Mailer: I think advertising is mendacity and manipulation. Laying lies on the public mind, manipulation of the public mind. I believe in small business. I think that Communism failed because there has to be some kind of belief in God. A wholly rational social system can never work because it comes down finally to who is running the show. So long as there is the idea that God is an element in our existence then there's some visceral need for a little modesty at the top. But the moment you become the most powerful person in a country, you're half crazy. One example: it's always hard for heavyweight champions to keep their sanity. Because they might be the toughest guy in the world and they might not. There might be some guy in some jungle bayou who could beat the shit out of them. They just don't know. It tends to imbalance you. By the same token, if you are the head of a very large country, you've got to go insane after a while. Because either you are perhaps the most powerful man in your own world or you're not. I said I believe in small business, because the small businessman is at least gambling that their intelligence, their wit, their perception of reality will be verified or contraverted. And so they learn as they do it. In business you learn a lot, any small business that is even modestly successful does not have a stupid man at the top and there's something marvelous in that sense about small business.

Adam Smith said: Let the best commodity win. Well, for a long period capitalism built itself on that. The fight among manufacturers was who could make the best product. They committed themselves to that and they had some success. By now there's been a profound shift. Marketing has taken over from production. The emphasis is entirely on marketing. And so the real excitement for the marketer, the advertiser, is not to sell a good product, it's to get away with selling a shitty product. Even outsell someone who's making a better product. That passion to market at all costs has polluted corporations. In production, if the level of income is going down slightly at the end of the quarter, they take three peas out of every can of peas or whatever it is they do. They take it out of the product. Also, the most intense form of advertising is commercials on TV. In consequence, they've achieved the dumbing down of the young American mind. Intelligence depends upon powers of concentration. You cannot develop your knowledge if you cannot concentrate. There's no longer such a thing as an uninterrupted story on TV. Programs are interrupted every seven, ten, or twelve minutes with a commercial. So kids get used to interruption as part of the narrative, which means they don't have a developed sense of connection. It's one of the real wastes of big level advertising on TV.

Stratton: My oldest son, Maxx, will be on his computer, instant messaging his friends, watching TV, constantly flipping channels, listening to music. Multi-tasking. I wonder if it's doing him real harm or preparing him for some future when he'll need these skills.

Mailer: There's no doubt in my mind it's doing young minds real harm toward long-term needs. It may be that multi-tasking makes people very fast and very adept at dealing with immediate situations. The best I'll say for multi-tasking is if you are going to be a psychopath, multi-tasking is what you need. But if you are looking to bring some deeper form of knowledge to the world, if you're interested in culture becoming deeper, rather than meaner, smaller, more niggardly and faster, then concentration is crucial. One thing more I'd like to say about the corporations, which I've never said before in print, is that there's a type who fits the corporation and that type is very interesting. We talk about left wing and right wing, but I have this notion of alpha and omega. We're born out of two principles not one. We're created out of two principles, the male and the female principle—the ovum and the sperm cell—and everything about us is dual really, for the most part: two eyes, two nostrils, two lips, two ears, two limbs.

Stratton: Two balls.

Mailer: Two balls. Only one cock, I grant you. And in fact, gestation takes one cunt and cock, but that makes two. So, we're born out of two separate cells. I think, from the very beginning, two people develop within us. As the embryo and then the child grows there are two ways we receive our experience and not one. An example I could use or give is there's a part of you that's a little more critical, more open or responsive. In love affairs you can feel this all the time. The question is, people can be in love, but are they in love equally with both halves of themselves? I once said to a woman who I'd been married to for a few years, we were breaking up and I said, "You don't even love me with half of yourself, just half a half." Which meant it was time for us to break, and we knew it. The point I want to make is this is not schizophrenia; but we do develop two distinct persons within ourselves. The question is how do they communicate with each other? The example I always use is the congress of the United States. You have democrats and republicans, two parties with different values. Different dream schemes, different aims. But the country works when they can communicate with each other; they don't have to agree but they have to be able to communicate with each other. Schizophrenia is when the two halves do not speak to each other.

Stratton: Are you saying you think that half of each of us may be suited to work within the corporation but the other half will rebel against it?

Mailer: I've got a different take on that. I think certain people can work for the corporation, others can't. Obviously neither of us could. Given that, I do tend to be judgmental of people who work for the corporation, even as they would be judgmental about me. Still, what you need to work in the corporation is that, on the one hand, you have to be selfless, and modest, and be able to feel you are a cog in the machine, and that's OK, that's how it should be. This makes up one half of the person who works for the corporation. The other half is that you are part of a mighty venture and that you have more to do with the promotion and promulgation of power than small businessmen and, of course, all those people out on the street. So, there's a corporate type, I would say. Probably the most profound shock of 9/11 was exactly that the one thing you know when you work for the corporation is it's not the army. You are not prepared to die for the corporation. In fact, that's the one thing you don't do because the corporation's policy is a species of security that you are not going to find anywhere else except in government, yet as one of the corporates you sneer at government people because they do not have the—what can I say?—the aplomb of working for a corporation. So the huge shock of 9/11 hit people who worked for corporations deeper than anyone. That is why the Bushies knew immediately that they had a superhighway into the future. As a corollary of this, most people are, by now, led by the corporation.

One more point. I would go so far as to argue in company with Jane Jacobs, that we are wrecking the cities with big corporate architecture, sixty stories of a new building that's absolutely blank, that doesn't tell you anything about the people who work there. In the middle ages, a poor Parisian stonemason might look at Notre Dame and say to himself, "Oh, the people who make these things are so powerful, they're so great, I can never get there." But when you can see why they're so great, you can learn something by looking at it. No young ethnic kid can look at a corporate building and learn any more by looking at it than that, that is them and we are us. So given this emptiness—the central emptiness of corporate life—you are, at once, a cog in a machine and part of what you think is a glorious venture. Of course, there's no connection between the two. That leaves a certain spaciness in the soul which looks to patriotism to fill it.

BEING SEAN PENN

Details, December 2004

PENNumbra

I was in L.A. having lunch with George Waud, an old friend who is now an executive at New Line Cinema. George told me that some producers had approached him with the rights to a New Yorker article about The Brand, the ruling council of the Aryan Brotherhood, known as the most powerful and murderous prison gang in the country. The entire hierarchy of The Brand had been indicted in a massive RICO case out of L.A. A record number of defendants on a single case were facing the death penalty. I'd read the article, I knew about the case even before it hit the papers. Two of the indicted Brand members had been contributors to Prison Life. Eddie Bunker told me they were all going to be indicted months before it happened.

"I said there was only one person I knew to write the script, and that's you," George told me. I thanked him for the referral but I had my doubts about the subject matter, and I expressed them to one of the producers, Anthony Mastromauro, when we met at the High Times offices in New York a few weeks later. I said I didn't think the movie would ever get made. "Too dark," was a lament I'd heard from so many Hollywood executives, and I didn't know of many stories much darker than this one.

"What if I had Sean Penn attached to direct?" Anthony asked.

That was different. I said I thought Sean Penn has the kind of talent and clout it would take to get a movie like this made. I'd seen him in At Close Range, Dead Man Walking, *and his recent*

Academy Award-winning performance as Jimmy Markum in Clint Eastwood's Mystic River. *I'd seen the films he'd directed,* The Pledge, The Crossing Guard, *and* The Indian Runner. *From what I knew of his work and what I'd heard of his character, I believed he had the artistic courage to make a serious, important and compelling movie with this story, not some puerile Hollywood* Con Air *rip-off. I told Anthony, "You get Sean Penn and I'm on board."*

Soon after that meeting, Anthony called and asked if I could fly out to San Francisco to meet him, then go see Sean at his home in Marin County. I met Anthony and an actor friend of Penn's, Paul Herman, at the airport in San Francisco and we drove up to meet Sean.

Right from the start we knew we wanted to work together. We had lunch with a mutual friend, Peter Coyote, who was presenting Penn with an award the next night. Then we spent a late night in the backroom of a bar in San Francisco drinking, talking politics, the coming election and the war in Iraq, art, movies, prison. Penn read some pitch notes I'd prepared on the Brand movie and the deal was set. I hung with him again at the Toronto Film Festival where The Assassination of Richard Nixon *premiered, and I went to visit him on the set in New Orleans while he was shooting* All The King's Men. *The more I know of him, the more convinced I am that Sean Penn is right man to shine his directorial light on shadowy world of* The Brand.

BEING SEAN PENN

I'M WITH SEAN PENN, and we're riding in a flat-bottom airboat skimming over the swamplands of Bayou Gauche near New Orleans looking for alligators. The engine is so loud we have to wear ear protectors, but still the sound seems to drill into the eardrum. Al, our guide and a native Louisianan, says the water level in the bayou is unusually high from the recent hurricanes, so the bigger gators have headed farther inland. But a few four-and five-footers swim in front of the boat, and a young one, too green to fear man, suns himself on a mud bank.

On the way into Bayou Gauche (pronounced "gash"), at what Al describes as "the last outpost of civilization," Penn buys a pair of wraparound sunglasses, "like welder's goggles," he says when he puts them on. "You know about the kid who got a pair of welder's goggles for his birthday?" No. "Well, he loved those welder's goggles. He loved them so much he wore them everywhere. To school. Out to play with his friends. He even wore them to bed. One day he's walking home from school wearing his welder's goggles when a car stops and the guy driving asks the kid if he wants a lift. The kid hesitates, but the man assures him it's okay, he's seen him around the neighborhood, what with the welder's goggles and all, he's pretty recognizable. So the kid gets in the car and they drive off. 'You ever heard of fellatio?' the guy asks the kid. 'No . . . sorry.' 'What about cunnilingus?' The kid says he hasn't heard of that, either. 'What about a rim job? You know what that is?' The kid turns and looks at the guy and says, 'Mister, I think I should tell you. I'm not a professional welder.'"

With an actor's ease, Penn slips into character to deliver the punch line. He is, actually, a very funny guy. Now 44, Penn has always been portrayed as the ultimate angry young man, taking himself and the troubles of the world too personally and too seriously. "Sean and I can have a good time together, no doubt about that," Penn's close friend and collaborator Jack Nicholson told Richard T. Kelly for a new oral biography, *Sean Penn: His Life and Times.* "I remember when we were scouting for *The Pledge*, I got up the next morning for breakfast and there was Sean asleep under the piano. I thought, 'Here's another reason we get along. Another Irishman who don't wanna get up in the morning.'" Penn's friend Christopher Walken told *Details*, "He's a very down-to-earth man who writes beautiful poetry. But I don't know if he'd want me to say that."

Penn is in New Orleans preparing for the role of Willie Stark in the film adaptation of Robert Penn Warren's classic novel *All the King's Men*. Stark is based on the legendary former Louisiana governor and U.S. senator Huey Long. The alligator hunt is part of Penn's quest to absorb the local atmosphere, visit locations, learn all he can about Long. "With this part, I feel like I'm facing a brand-new challenge, maybe the biggest challenge of my career," he says. "I'm not going to be able to draw from my own experience."

Finally Al cuts the engine and we drift in to dock at what he tells us is Grandpa Simineaux's camp, as if that's supposed to mean something. Al can be a little too informative at times, but as Penn remarks later, "he grows on you." We get out of the boat and wander around an empty, ramshackle cabin built on stilts. Long gray sideburns of Spanish moss hang from the cypress trees. It's quiet, no humans but us for miles. Just the gators and giant catfish. "What do alligators eat?" Penn asks Al. "Just about anything. Even each other. They're cannibalistic. And not just big ones eating little ones. Big ones'll eat big ones." From time to time Penn will pull out a little tape recorder and record Al's answers to his questions, studying his inflections and pronunciations.

Having reached a new apogee of fame and recognition with his Academy Award for *Mystic River*—he's now offered parts that once went straight to the two Toms—Penn is relentlessly curious, and relentlessly unintimidated. As a young man, he sought the company of, and became close friends with, the poet Charles Bukowski and Hollywood rebel Marlon Brando. As Norman Mailer put it, "He's not just a great actor. He has real balls."

Penn put his balls—and his reputation—on the line last Christmas when he flew to Amman, Jordan, and took a 12-hour taxi trip through the Sunni Triangle into Fallujah and Baghdad. (The *New York Post* has labeled him "Baghdad Sean.") "I vacillate between rage and deep sadness," he says of the war. "It did not take great minds to anticipate the impending disaster of what we were doing. I got back just days before the capture of Saddam and it was already heating up again. I remember this kid saying to me, 'Now that you guys are here, if you don't succeed, you are going to create a whole nation of suicide bombers.' And that's what we've done. Since we invaded, Iraq has gone from a repressive regime to the chaotic murder capital of the world, where parents can't let their kids walk to school without worrying about them being killed."

Penn continues to thumb his nose at those who hold that actors shouldn't have opinions. He sent a letter to South Park creators Trey Parker and Matt Stone in October after Stone remarked that we'd be better off if ignorant people didn't vote and self-important celebrities didn't urge them to. "It's all well to joke about me or whomever you choose," Penn wrote. "Not so well, to encourage irresponsibility that will ultimately lead to the disembowelment, mutilation, exploitation, and death of innocent people throughout the world."

But Penn comes by his political sensibility honestly: It's partly genetic. His father, Leo Penn, was blacklisted in the forties, during the McCarthy era. "His spirit survived. He never got bitter," Penn says. "He was a forward-motion guy. He believed it doesn't matter how you fall. What matters is how you get up and keep going. It never scratched his patriotism."

"Sean's the family guy," Walken says, referring not only to Penn's wife, Robin Wright Penn, and their two children, but also to his mother, Eileen Ryan Penn, brothers, Michael and Chris, and his vast extended family of close friends and colleagues. Robin Wright Penn told Richard Kelly, "If I had to pick one [word]— loyalty. It's how I would define Sean. He's loyal. To people, to his words. And he expects that of you."

Penn's latest film, *The Assassination of Richard Nixon*, is a tour de force. "It was the championship of misery," he remembers. "The toughest one I've ever done." The actor is in nearly every frame as Sam Byck, an office-furniture salesman with Tourette's-like social ineptness who lives alone but is still in love with his estranged wife. Byck has concocted a harebrained scheme for a mobile tire-repair service, applying for a small-business loan to buy a school bus and convert it into a tire shop on wheels. The loan officer says that he will be notified by mail, but Byck won't take no for an answer; he's ready to kill the president based on the outcome of that loan application. In the film, there is a shot of Penn in his underwear standing in front of the mailbox in his apartment building. He has a sunken chest, potbelly, and a sad, pathetic demeanor. Penn was somehow able to fashion Byck from the same body that was previously inhabited by the muscled, tattooed Jimmy Markum in Mystic River. It's hard to reconcile the two characters coming from the same actor.

Later, Penn calls me in my hotel room. "Meet me downstairs in the lobby in 20 minutes and we'll see where it takes us." We subsequently go crawling from the swamps of the bayou to the swampy bars of the French Quarter. At one point we're behind a shit-faced couple, the woman so drunk she's hanging on to the guy as they stagger along the sidewalk. Her dress is ripped up the middle to the base of her spine and her ass is wobbling along in full view. "That's the real bayou gash," Penn says.

Much later, in a raucous bar, people stumble up to introduce themselves and compliment Penn on his work. "Love you in 21 Grams, man." "Hey, Sean, Mystic River—you were awesome." He's always very polite, thankful. I remember riding in an elevator with him one time. A woman looked at him and smiled. "Aren't you Sean Penn?" Penn glanced down at the floor. "Yes, I am," he said, almost as though he were ashamed of his fame. In a restaurant the waiter handed him a menu and asked, "Are you who I think you are?"

"That depends on who you think I am," Penn said with a smile.

At the Toronto International Film Festival for the gala screening of

The Assassination of Richard Nixon, Penn was besieged by rabid fans and paparazzi who would lie in wait outside wherever he was and pursue him whenever he appeared. "So much of celebrity is really a cultural disease," he says. "It's like the suicide bombers. They could be praying in a mosque when they meet one of these recruiters, and an hour later they are ready to blow themselves up. It's a hunger for identity. People are reacting to a kind of symbolic stimuli. Ninety percent of it has nothing to do with the person you are."

He goes on to talk of Oliver North, how he became a celebrity by lying to Congress. And how President Bush continues to suck people in with his cocksure attitude even when he's lying. "He gets away with it because of his arrogance. Arrogance is charisma in this culture," Penn says. "We don't always know when we're lied to. But we know when we hear truth."

Truth is what Sean Penn wants to bring to the game. "It's all up and down," he says of the vicissitudes of acclaim. "Like being an athlete, you're only as good as your last game. But finally, what you have to do is try to find what part of this is valuable. What part has real meaning. And you hold on to that. You hold on and you dance your own dance."

ACKNOWLEDGMENTS

THE AUTHOR WISHES TO thank Annie Nocenti, a good, dear friend (and fellow magazine executioner) for her thoughtful help in compiling the pieces collected here, and for her talented editing of the new writing. Ruth Baldwin at Nation Books, who encouraged me to collect these pieces and worked and drank with me patiently through the garlic fumes, deserves gratitude and praise. And thanks also to Alana Biden, who proofread the manuscript, to Chris Cozzone, *Prison Life*'s first executive editor and staff photographer for the generous use of his images, and to Kim Wozencraft. The author also wishes to thank the other photographers for their generous permissions; to Fionn Reilly, who took the classic shot of Dennis McKee as Santa in the slammer, Victor Fisher, Mark Benjamin, Judy Marks, Gottfried Helnwein, and to artist Fred Otnes.

In Memoriam

. Sadly, Edward Bunker passed away on July 17, 2005.

He will be missed by friends, family, and fans.